ALTERNATIVE ASSESSMENT OF PERFORMANCE IN THE LANGUAGE ARTS:

PROCEEDINGS

A National Symposium Cohosted by
PHI DELTA KAPPA and ERIC/RCS

Bloomington, Indiana, 27 August 1990

Edited by Carl B. Smith

Copublished by

ERIC CLEARINGHOUSE ON READING
AND COMMUNICATION SKILLS

PHI
DELTA
KAPPA

Published 1991 by:
ERIC Clearinghouse on Reading and Communication Skills
Carl B. Smith, Director
2805 East 10th Street, Suite 150
Bloomington, Indiana 47408-2698

in cooperation with
Phi Delta Kappa
Bloomington, Indiana

ERIC (an acronym for Educational Resources Information Center) is a national network of 16 clearinghouses, each of which is responsible for building the ERIC database by identifying and abstracting various educational resources, including research reports, curriculum guides, conference papers, journal articles, and government reports. The Clearinghouse on Reading and Communication Skills (ERIC/RCS) collects educational information specifically related to reading, English, journalism, speech, and theater at all levels. ERIC/RCS also covers interdisciplinary areas, such as media studies, reading and writing technology, mass communication, language arts, critical thinking, literature, and many aspects of literacy.

This publication was prepared with funding from the Office of Educational Research and Improvement, U.S. Department of Education, under contract no. RI88062001. Contractors undertaking such projects under government sponsorship are encouraged to express freely their judgment in professional and technical matters. Points of view or opinions, however, do not necessarily represent the official view or opinions of the Office of Educational Research and Improvement.

Cartoonist: Dave Coverly

Library of Congress Cataloging-in-Publication Data
Alternative assessment of performance in the language arts : proceedings :
    a national symposium cohosted by Phi Delta Kappa and ERIC/RCS,
    Bloomington, Indiana, 27 August 1990 / edited by Carl B. Smith
        p.   cm.
    Includes bibliographical references (p.   ).
    ISBN 0-927516-24-1
    1. Language arts—United States—Evaluation—Congresses.
2. Language arts—United States—Examinations, questions, etc.—
Congresses.   3. Language experience approach in education—United
States—Evaluation—Congresses.   I. Phi Delta Kappa.   II. ERIC
Clearinghouse on Reading and communication Skills.   III. Smith, Carl
Bernard.
LBB1576.A615   1991
372.6'044'0973—dc20   91-30919
                                                                CIP

ALTERNATIVE ASSESSMENT IN THE LANGUAGE ARTS

**A National Symposium Cohosted by
PHI DELTA KAPPA and ERIC/RCS**

Bloomington, Indiana, 27 August 1990

TABLE OF CONTENTS

WRITTEN PRESENTATIONS

GROUP SESSIONS

LUNCH SESSION

AFTERNOON SESSION

PUBLISHERS' FORUM: THE FUTURE OF ASSESSMENT

CONCLUDING SESSION

APRÈS SYMPOSIUM:
THOUGHTS ON WHAT HAPPENED AND NEXT STEPS

RESEARCH APPENDICES

MODERATOR'S PREFACE

As with photos taken of famous people in public places, transcribing from a tape what someone has said during informal discourse can be an act either of friendship or assassination. The transcriber can make an intelligent speaker seem like a fool, and a foolish speaker seem intelligent. At the National Symposium on Alternative Assessment, we had only intelligent speakers, and we have tried in our transcription of their informal dialogue not to make anyone sound foolish.

We have, however, edited the tapes. Because Spoken English is a different dialect from Written English, cleaning up the transcriptions was the reader-friendly thing to do. We have relieved the speakers of their pensive anacoluthons, reiterations, and throat-clearings, always attempting to keep the essence of their statements intact. Because what people say, and what they intended to have said, are often quite different matters, we reserve the right to have misunderstood. If we transcribed your statement incorrectly, we apologize.

Warren Lewis
ERIC/RCS Director of Publications

ARE THERE ANY REASONABLE PEOPLE IN EDUCATION?

CARL B. SMITH

You will find considerable disagreement among the writers and speakers in this volume. Disagreement is, of course, to be expected when many voices are speaking, and the subject is fresh. Alternative forms of assessment—something other, and we hope better, than the multiple-choice standardized test—are aborning. Out of this creative chaos, new forms of assessment for reading, writing, and communicating are struggling to come to life.

What direction should they take? Should they look like the old tests, only with longer passages and with more expansive responses by the test taker? (Michigan and Illinois tried some expansion techniques in their statewide tests.)

Should they be samples of daily work put into a folder and called "portfolio assessment?" (New Hampshire mandated statewide portfolio assessment.)

Or is the notion of general assessment completely out of sync with new-wave education in which *process* is all that matters? Perhaps we should abandon all product assessment and check only to see if students are engaging in certain processes.

All the above questions are discussed in this book, sometimes with considerable heat and even with a little light. The symposium that spawned this volume was a collective attempt to unravel these knotty issues with as much reason as our presenters, participants, and their knowledge made possible. They explored ideas with reasonableness, with passion, and with considerable good humor.

Shortly after the symposium, I received a call from a reporter at U.S. News and World Report. After a number of conversations, the reporter asked in disgust: "Are there any reasonable people in education? Are there any scientific minds at work here?" The reporter's question burst from his frustration in trying to find hard evidence that a trade-books curriculum actually works. He had heard that schools all across the country were changing their methodology, taking the approach of using trade books instead of textbooks. When he called some of these schools, they had no hard evidence to show improvement—only their belief that the new idea would make the school better. They suggested that he call me in my capacity as Director of the ERIC Clearinghouse on Reading and Communications Skills: Maybe I had some hard evidence somewhere in the ERIC database.

The database, however, was not very helpful in producing the hard evidence that the reporter wanted. That was the point at which he wondered out loud whether there were any reasonable, scientific people in education. It seemed to him that schools were making major changes based on feelings and intuitions alone.

Though I tried to explain to the reporter that this new curriculum movement represents a shift in beliefs that do not easily lend themselves to verification by traditional hard-evidence measures, he remained disgruntled, and he repeated his question: "Are there no scientific minds in education who insist on evidence in order to make reasonable decisions?"

That's when I mentioned the papers in this volume, attempts by reasonable people to find answers to highly complex educational issues. I think the reporter's cynicsm about evidence and performance in education represents the dilemma we educators face in trying to find alternative forms of assessing language performance. On the one hand, we want a performance to be judged reliably in the ways that most products can be judged, while, on the other, we are simultaneously redefining "performance" to mean—or at least to include—the process of learning as well as the products of learning.

Language learners produce things that reflect the state of their knowledge: statements about their reading, compositions, solutions to problems; and those products can be rated. But one part of our educational mind does not want the demonstration of any one aspect of learning, such as writing a short story or engaging in a logically planned debate, to stand for all of what a learner knows. We also want documentation of how a learner thinks so the teacher can help the learner participate more actively in the thinking process. That sounds like a reasonable approach, but its execution is abstract, and the American public is not accustomed to accepting descriptions of procedures as assessment.

What questions, then, should one ask? What evidence can one use to show that a program or strategy, a product or a process, is effective? How can we educators respond reasonably to reporters or parents or to ourselves when the question is asked: "Is this program any good?"

ARE NUMBERS THE BEGINNING OF SCIENCE?

We do not assume that merely assigning numbers to something gives it scientific validity. No one in this book said that. Yet, numbers seem important to us as a way of reassuring ourselves that we have knowledge about that of which we speak. Measuring something with numbers does appear more scientific; numbers seem like the place where science begins. By contrast, if we don't have numbers, it appears that we are expressing a personal opinion, having a gut-level reaction, rather than describing a verifiable phenomenon. Numbers have indeed become a significant part of our view of what educational assessment means.

Another way of approaching the question of how to assess language-arts behavior, however, is to admit that assessment takes place within a theory. For example, if we assume that human behavior distributes itself mathematically so as to resemble the normal curve, the bell-shaped curve, we then measure specific aspects of behavior in ways that will distribute them to approximate the normal curve distribution.

In a contrary theory, if we assume that human behavior can only be described in terms of a particular functional context, only in terms of its meaning related to a particular set of circumstances, we then must describe those conditions and interactions as important parts of our assessment of meaning. The writing of a composition, for instance, can be asessed only through describing the stimulus for writing, the background of the writer, the environment in which the writing occurred, and the mental state of the writer at the moment of writing.

Please don't assume that anyone in this book is proposing either one of these types of assessment as the only valid means for measuring language-arts proficiencies. But you can see what a shift in theoretical perspective does to one's approach to assessment.

These two examples of assessment are based on two theories: one, the regularity of human behavior; the other, the idiosyncratic nature of human behavior. Both intuitions of human behavior are surely correct in important ways; nevertheless, each group rejects the other's assessment techniques in their dispute with an alien theory. In this book, you will see the evidence of that theoretical struggle having taken place at our symposium, from the major presentations to the quiet conversations going on in the corners. You will also see that publishers and assessment specialists, such as Roger Farr, insisted that the new forms of assessment (alternative forms of assessment)—whatever they shall be—must adhere to standards that maintain scientific reliability.

Are there reasonable people, are there scientific minds in education? You bet! Some of the best of them are right here in this book discussing alternative ways of assessing performance in the language arts.

SOME PEOPLE SEEM TO KNOW

I attended a meeting in Cincinnati, Ohio, where a participant told me about her technique for evaluating the effectiveness of her educational program. She was the education director for a local innercity church—quite poor, almost all African-American. Drugs, burglaries, and violence were a regular part of her neighborhood. The church was running an elementary school for approximately 250 children, and it had Sunday School classes for secondary-school kids.

This education director had kept records for the past fifteen years on all the children of the church, those who attended the parish elementary school and those who did not; those who attended Sunday School regularly and those who did not. Now she was wanting to know how the children of the parish did during their years from 18 to 22, the ages when most young people make decisions about their lives as adults.

These grown-up children were all from the same neighborhood, and were all members of the same church, but they did not all go to the parish's school. She claimed that the total number of students from each category—parish-educated and non-parish educated—was about equal. Her statistics are eye-popping! She claimed that 47% of the parish's children who had not attended the parish school and who had minimal or no attendance at Sunday School, were socially dysfunctional in some way, that is, they were on welfare, in jail, or were alcoholics or drug abusers. By contrast, only 3% of the parish-educated children found themselves in those dysfunctional social conditions.

This education director had found a way of evaluating the effectiveness of their educational program by using data quite different from traditional tests. Ninety-seven percent of the church-educated children were employed or were in college. Only fifty-three percent of the non-church-educated children could be described as responsible citizens.

WHAT CAN WE LEARN FROM THIS?

The education director from that parish in Cincinnati opens up new avenues for the rest of us as we look for alternative means for assessing language education. So, I encouraged her to write-up the results of her study and to submit a paper for publication —something she had not thought of doing.

Even though her example suggests alternative assessment, it does not answer the question that the writers and speakers in this volume faced at our symposium. They were dealing with questions about short-term evaluation. The religious education director was looking at the lives of her students years after they had attended her church schools. The presenters in this volume are concerned with evaluation at the end of a semester or at the end of a school year.

They are also struggling to assess a particular aspect of schooling—the arts of language, that is, reading, writing, communicating. Just as the religious education director looked for ways of reflecting the real-life effects of the church school on the lives of their children, so too these conference presenters were searching for ways to determine the real-life effects of instuction on the language performance of students.

The religious education director chose certain characteristics of responsible citizenship as her criteria for success (being employed, going on to further education, abiding by the law). Our presenters struggled with similar questions: What are appropriate indicators of short-term success in language arts? And since these were reasonable, scientific minds at work, they also asked whether the indicators that they recommended are valid and reliable. Do the assessment results that they envision truly represent success or failure in reading and writing? Are these measures reliable enough to assure us that repeated samples will give us similar results?

Validity and reliability are the technical requirements that have been at the top of the test makers' agenda for decades. We expect reliability of measurement in all forms of our lives, for example, when we measure our blood pressure or when we look at our speedometer to see if we are driving within the speed limit.

At the symposium, test publishers discussed these technical requirements in the terms that test makers use when they invent new tests and apply them to new situations. So, too, did Bert Wiser demand validity and reliability from the point of view of a director of assessment in Columbus, Ohio. Not unlike the education director from the Cincinnati parish, he wanted to be able to give parents reliable assurances that their children are making progress towards becoming effective communicators. To him that means either comparing a child's performance to other children or to benchmark performance samples.

Jerry Harste approached assessment from an entirely different perspective. He was more interested in giving children a meaningful experience than he was in assessing their progress along some standard path that, to him, seemed artificial. Language communication is so complex and so context-specific, he reasoned, that it is futile to try to measure it. Rather, we should ask students whether or not their language experiences are making sense to themselves. If they are, then we continue to offer them opportunities to engage in those kinds of language experiences and others similar; if they are not, then we strive to find ways to adjust the experiences to help the learners have experiences that are comprehensible and meaningful.

THE FUTURE OF ASSESSMENT

The papers in this volume and the interactions of the participants that are recorded here raise the swirling issues about assessing language arts performance. The personal reactions and informal interactions are often as revealing as the formal papers because they show our corporate mind at work trying to resolve important questions:

- What are the purposes of assessment?
- Can language arts be evaluated in any formalized test?
- Who determines our standards for reading and writing performance?
- Should the measures for instructional diagnosis and for public ranking be different?
- What legitimate functions can portfolio assessment serve?

You can sense the frustration of those who represent different theories in this discussion. For those who believe that language meaning can be constructed only in a personal, functional context, the idea of ranking a person on their comprehension of a text that they have read or on their writing, is irrelevant if not impossible. For those who believe that there are public standards for language behavior, for comprehending and writing texts in English, to retreat behind a theory of subjective meaning is to dodge public responsibility, at least, and perhaps to undermine the very purpose of language-arts instruction itself.

ERIC/RCS, as a public servant, and Phi Delta Kappa, as the educator's guild, have the responsibility of producing synthesis statements about important issues in language-arts education. The assessment of language behavior is more than a hot topic. The debate over assessment brings into focus the major issues being raised by a paradigm shift that is currently taking place.

By bringing together representatives of various aspects of the assessment questions, ERIC/RCS and Phi Delta Kappa brought together in one discussion the theories, the alternative devices (both published and personal), and the constituencies served by the various assessment reports. We did not assume that a set of papers and their open discussion would resolve the issues in a single conference; rather, we knew that the experts themselves and everyone else who attends the symposium by way of reading the proceedings, would gain new appreciation for the complexity of alternative forms of assessing the language arts.

The future agenda for language-arts assessment institutionally and profoundly concerns ERIC/RCS and Phi Delta Kappa. As educators, we are indeed eager to be, and to appear to be, reasonable people, not merely to reporters but especially to ourselves. The central question that we raise here is this: In terms of our present knowledge, are the proposed and actual alternative forms of language-arts assessment reasonable, valid, and reliable? Will they withstand the scrutiny of other reasonable minds?

Concerned Reader, let us hear from you! Let us know how we can continue the discussion on alternative forms of assessment so we serve the language-arts profession.

Carl B. Smith
Director, ERIC/RCS

GREETINGS

PHIL HARRIS (Director of the Center for Professional Development at Phi Delta Kappa)
CARL SMITH (Director of ERIC/RCS; Indiana University)

ERIC and "PDK" are co-sponsoring this meeting because we think educational assessment is one of the most important—if not the most important—issues in education today. You have been invited to this symposium because you represent important constituencies in the assessment debate. You are theorists, researchers, developers, publishers, state and local planners. You all represent varied opinions about language-arts assessment—not every opinion that exists, of course, but many of the varied opinions. These opinions represent different theories, the needs of practitioners, public politics, and academic politics. Our purpose today is to make a start towards arriving at some common sense of the direction that language-arts assessment is going.

For approximately seventy-five years now, standardized tests have been the primary vehicle for assessment, and they probably have served our perceived needs in language-arts assessment rather well. As you know, those standardized tests have served the broad community in a variety of ways, for example the civil service exams, which have been used to meet not an academic but a social need. The civil service exams were instituted to screen for minimum abilities and to eliminate racial discrimination that existed in many of our public-service jobs. Are these exams completely fair? You already know the answer to that, but at least they served an important purpose.

We educators are currently expanding the purposes of assessment. We are looking at alternative forms of assessment, especially of language-arts performance. The battle lines in this discussion are not clear-cut, so in terms of the debate we don't have a clearly defined central question or issue. You may, of course, be one of those who feels that the artillery line is pointed at the question: "Test or no test?" A recent issue of the *Kappan* magazine quoted a survey indicating that, by the end of 1990, approximately 35 states will have mandated performance assessment—up about a half-dozen states over the number in 1989. Clearly, performance assessment is of high interest to the general public.

ERIC and "PDK" encourage you to express your opinions freely, and to enter the debate with what we will call "academic rigor." We have to have these issues brought sharply into focus. We need to have definitions clarified.

[Here follow transcriptions of four oral presentations, and after them four formal papers that were prepared before the symposium. Both members of the Wiser and Dorsey team addressed the symposium; Farr and Harste spoke without their seconds; Bloom was outstanding on her own.]

CURRENT ISSUES IN ALTERNATIVE ASSESSMENT

ROGER FARR

The paper that Kaye and I wrote was a joint operation. I've never had a more excruciating experience in writing a paper, nor a more delightful one. I learned a lot from doing a paper with someone I sometimes disagree with. The production of that paper is indeeed a compromise between different ways of looking at assessment.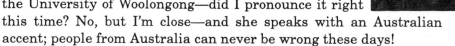

This speech, however, is now my turn, and this is not a compromise. Kaye takes no responsibility for the speech. She said, "Roger, you're up there on your own." I really wanted her to give the talk because she is from the University of Woolongong—did I pronounce it right this time? No, but I'm close—and she speaks with an Australian accent; people from Australia can never be wrong these days!

I'd like to spend a few moments talking about the issues that I think we have to address if we're going to move into alternative forms of assessment. I think those issues are very profound, and, indeed we are often not talking about the same things. I found that Kaye and I sometimes did not communicate at all because we have different, very different, perspectives on what we think assessment ought to do.

The primary issue is that we ought to think about the use to which we're going to put tests. If we could focus on the use of tests, we might have an opportunity to get some place. There are, of course, other issues that are also important: the business of self-reflection, the business of whether a teacher can do a portfolio assessment and use it to understand and help children develop, and have that test serve any gate-keeping function at the same time that it helps the student. How in the world can we do that? This is the test that's going to decide whether I get a salary raise or if my school gets a flag (or whatever else), and yet I want to use the assessment to help children. Those are the kinds of issues we need to talk about.

Reliability is what assessment is all about. If a test or other means of assessment is not reliable, it's no good. You've got to have reliability. If you stand on the bathroom scale and it registers 132 lbs. one morning, but it's 147 the next morning, and 85 the morning after that, you conclude that it's time for a new set of bathroom scales: The old scales' assessment isn't any good because it isn't reliable; it's gotta be fixed.

When you talk to people who have a perspective different from mine about assessment, they say, "Reliability isn't the issue at all." God! Of course it's the issue! How can you have assessment when, in fact, it isn't the same each day?

But these other people come back equally rightly: "I don't care if it's the same each day, but I do want a reliable measure because I want a child to reflect about his own reading. I want him to *think* about his reading. I want that youngster to begin to understand and to begin to share with me what he's thinking about. If he thinks something different tomorrow from what he thought about today, that's OK, because he's going to be reading a different book or writing a different story. Reliability *isn't* the issue, here. The issue is whether I can really get to the heart of what the kid thinks about as a developing literacy learner."

Some of us in assessment have said, "Lookit, you guys are talking about instruction; you're not talking about assessment at all. Go 'way!" I mean, "Go do instruction! We'll do testing."

Then those other people say, "Wait a minute! We tried that. It didn't work because as soon as we went away, you guys built these tests, and all the teachers followed the tests, and now we do have a test-driven curriculum." These critics of traditional assessment are no longer saying, "We're not going to let you get away with those kind of tests. We want new and different kinds of tests." They want in on playing the game because they know that the game is test-driven.

We say, "O.K., come on in our game—but remember reliability!"

"No, no," they say "We're going to play the game, but now we're making the rules. Forget reliability!"

These are the issues that we really have to face in this symposium, and we really have to work our way through. It isn't going to do any good at all to say, "Those tests are no damn good, and you people in assessment never know what you are doing, and the standardized tests have ruined education."

What we really have got to do is start talking together about what these issues are. If you think we're facing problems arguing with each other, wait'll Dr. Cannell comes out of the closet! You know Dr. Cannell, the good dentist, the guy who talks on *Sixty Minutes* about cheating on tests, and everybody in the world is above average (especially in this room!). [Laughter]. That guy and his colleagues talk about teachers sitting down with children and helping them take the test, and they use dictionaries. Oh, yeah, they're doing better in our schools, they're using dictionaries now to take the spelling test!

Well, there are going to be some issues and some problems that the public is going to have to face, and when we start talking about portfolios for school-district and state-wide assessment, we really are going to have problems.

We started with assessment in instruction before 1915—it was something that teachers did in schools, but the kinds of assessment that went on in schools were not very good. As a matter of fact, when kids were tested on how they were coming along as learners, they stood up in front of the class and read orally from their books. They memorized long passages. That's the kind of assessment that went on. It was very low-stakes assessment—not for the kid, who had to memorize all that poetry!—but it was low-stakes for the teacher and the school. There really wasn't much of an issue of school accountability.

Then around 1915, lots of issues came up: not only the business of the First World War and the I.Q. exams and that sort of thing, but people like Horace Mann in Massachusetts and Rice and others wanted to do school surveys. They wanted to find out what kind of student the schools were developing and how they were doing. So school accountability actually started out as an issue from 1915 to 1920.

From 1920 to 1950, we developed standardized tests in one form or another; there was a real growth in assessment in the United States. Even so, assessment was not high-stakes at that time. Mike Beck and I have often talked about those decades as probably a good time for testing. Testing was this little thing off to the side, really not all that major an issue. It was another piece of information to look at. You might want to pay some attention to it, but it didn't drive instruction a great deal.

Moving into the 1950s, testing became more individualized and more high-stakes. As we moved along through this era, there was a constant push to get at the individual. Congress people especially wanted to get at the individual. I talked to a staff member of one Congressman who was just aghast at the idea that we do not have national assessment; he thought that every child in the United States ought to take the test. "How can we do national assessment," he wanted to know, "if we're not testing everybody?" "Maybe we could try matrix sampling," I came back. "I don't know about that," he shot back, "I want to know what every kid does," said the Congressional staffer.

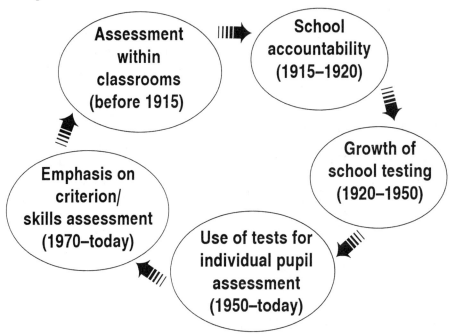

So assessment became more individualized, more diagnostic, trying to do things in process assessment, and also more high-stakes. In the period of the 1950s, a lot of individual tests were developed, and they tended to move in the direction of being high-stakes. When we hit the criterion-assessment era, and the real-school accountability era, boy! things really became high-stakes. The criterion-referenced test—now we'd got something that you could be held responsible for. It was no longer a normed score; it was twenty-three items out of thirty-two that you had to get right or else you didn't graduate.

High-stakes assessment obviously still exists today, and when high-stakes assessment came along, the people who were interested in changing curriculum recognized pretty quickly that if you're going

6

to have high-stakes assessment, it's going to drive curriculum; and if one wants to change curriculum, one had better get involved.

Michigan and Illinois and other states that made changes in the traditional assessment recognized that if you wanted to change curriculum, you had to get involved in high-stakes assessment. You've got to push. Michigan took five, six, seven years—I don't know how long exactly—to produce its tests. But it wasn't the writing of the tests that took so long—they could have done that in a weekend.

What took time was getting the public and the teachers to get behind that high-stakes test, working from school district to school district, from IRA to IRA and from NCTE Council to NCTE Council, and getting them to understand what the test makers were trying to do with assessment, what purpose it would serve, and where we would go with it.

Now, I think, we're moving all the way back into an era in which a lot of people are talking again about assessement that's totally congruent with instruction. People now are talking about individual kinds of assessments—no, not the same kinds of assessment that we were doing after 1915, but, rather, self-assessment. Self-assessment is something that we haven't paid a lot of attention to, yet.

In writing this paper, I became more and more taken up with the idea that the highest level of assessment is personal self-assessment. If you are going to improve at anything, you have to understand your own behaviors, and you have to make a commitment. It's the whole idea of saying, "I'm responsible for my learning, and I'm beginning to think about, and understand, what I do as a learner." That's far more important than whether or not a kid makes some test score.

I think that's true, but I don't know yet how to work self-assessment into the other kind of assessment that serves as gatekeeper assessment.

I'd like to talk about three reasons for testing. For me, this covers the waterfront.

1.   We test so that students—I hope—can reflect on their own literacy development. I think that is the most important reason to assess: to help kids understand. If a kid's going to be a better anything, if he's going to do anything better, if any of us are going to do anything better, we've got to understand how we do that behavior. We've got to understand what it is we want to accomplish.

2. There's no question that teachers need information for planning instruction, and I agree that assessment is all about getting information so teachers can plan instruction.

3. Then, although those who like #1 and #2 areas don't like it at all, #3 area nevertheless exists. External decision makers do exist and have a job to do, and they really want to know about what the schools are doing so that they can make planning decisions.

What we're trying to do is merge these three areas, and I don't know if that's possible. So somebody says, "Oh no, it's not possible. What we need are two tests—one for the external decision makers and one for the teachers."

But that isn't going to work. That's not going to work at all because teachers are going to pay attention to the external decision-maker test, and forget about the rest. They'll say, "Well, those other tests would be nice, but now it's May and I've got to get ready for the high-stakes test." They're going to put the individual portfolios away and get out the ditto masters and start the kids practicing for the big test.

That's the kind of thing we face if we don't get all three assessment areas together, if we don't get product and process together. And if we don't get all three together, I think the whole thing is going to be lost.

Let me talk now about the three objectives in assessment.

1. "Student Reflection." As a teacher, I think that turning the responsibility over to the students to assess themselves is a great idea, and I think it is a good idea to get students to be responsible for their own literacy development. We want to talk to kids about what they know and how they know it, and we really want this talking to be a collaboration, an activity in which the teacher is a coach and a guide helping the kid to reflect on things that count. The new assessments that I've been looking at, that I've worked on myself, are pushing in this direction, trying to help kids do self-reflection.

2. "Teacher Learning" gets us into the whole business of validity. What are we really trying to teach? These issues encompass for me the movements that I see happening in the language-arts curriculum.

This includes an integration of literacy behaviors. I taught high-school English in New York State for about eight years before I did

8

anything else, and I was surprised when I went to the elementary school where they taught reading and writing as separate subjects. I was a high-school teacher who taught reading and writing together. The integration of literacy behaviors is the best way to help a kid become a better writer or reader, by having them read to write better and write to read better.

I think this is awfully important, but we're not going to get reading and writing instruction together unless we get reading and writing assessment together. I think they ought not to be separate. I think they ought to be the same.

Everyone knows that our tests are totally divorced from reality. People don't go around taking multiple-choice tests! Still, people say: "Yeah, but they show us what kids can do in a more realistic context."

Why don't we give students a realistic context as the assessment instrument, instead of giving them something that sort of predicts a realistic context? We want to do that, and we also want to get a student's own insights.

I'm not talking now about a student reflecting on himself; but all of us know that if we've ever sat down with some kids and asked the youngsters why they answered the way they did, we've found out that they give answers for strange and wondrous reasons. Sometimes they give the right answers for the wrong reasons, and sometimes the wrong answers for the right reasons; that's why getting students' insights is so much more valuable than merely having a test score.

We also want to do continuous sampling. Those of you who don't know me would not want to judge me by looking at me today. I don't often wear a tie, and I'm usually swearing more than I am right now, and I'm usually more bombastic; and if they had told me this was a debate, I would have really gotten going.

Here's the point: you need a lot more than just one sample in your assessment. You really need to understand a kid's literacy development over a period of time and through multiple responses. What we do all of the time is dictate to kids, or—as Kaye is fond of telling me—we create boxes for kids, whereas what we ought to do is get kids to respond by having them create their own boxes, by having them respond to open-ended activities. Let the kids build their own boxes.

If we can do all these things, maybe we can give teachers some information for planning. But I think that the present assessments

9

don't do that. They were not intended to. Mike Beck and I worked on the Metropolitan test years ago. We didn't intend to do all of these things with the Metropolitan tests. We thought it was one of those nice 1950s high-stakes tests. That's why Jerry [Harste] said, "That's right, and that's where it belongs!" [Laughter]

3. "External Decision Making" causes us to engage in some other issues. We really have to see that we must get process and product together. I talk about this a lot, but I don't exactly know for sure what that all means. I do know that what we want are "people who learn" rather than "learned people." What we are really interested in are not "right answers," but "people who know how to get right answers." I know what that's all about, but to try to get at it through assessment, and to try to convince those decision makers who are external to the schools— legislators and the public and so on—is a very difficult job.

It's very difficult to get information to them that's comparable across all decision levels. If we collect one kind of information in the school where the teachers are using it to plan instruction, and then we have another kind of information that's used at the high-stakes end of the road, it just isn't going to work well at all.

These charts present the issues in the order in which I believe they are important.

PHILOSOPHICAL ISSUES

✔ **Is assessment congruent with education?**

✔ **Can assessment play a gatekeeping role and a self-awareness role concurrently?**

There are philosophical issues over the role of assessment in education. What do we really want assessment to do? Different ones of us in this room have different views of what role assessment ought to play. If we don't argue about what that role is, we aren't going to get any place.

Some of you want assessment to play a role that is totally different from the role it now plays. You want to do away with traditional assessment altogether, and you want alternative forms.

10

But others are saying, "No, these new alternatives aren't going to work. We've got to have those standard forms for the decision makers, and if we have them, they'll drive instruction." That issue is, for me, the number-one issue.

PUBLIC ISSUES

✔ **Can the public accept more than single test scores?**

✔ **Can the public accept that education's goal is the development of "people who learn" rather than the development of "learned people?"**

A second set of issues grows out of that, namely, the public issues. I worry that we're moving too rapidly in 35 states to develop portfolio assessment or performance assessment; we're going to push it right down the tubes. We're going to screw up another good idea. That really scares me a lot because the public ain't ready for it. We've got to get Dr. Cannell in a meeting to talk about what we're trying to do. We've got a job to do like Michigan did by educating the public about single-test scores: to wit, that they really don't do the job. We haven't convinced the public yet that process is the issue, not product.

Implementation issues, I think, are a third set of problems. In Houston the other day, I was talking to some teachers about portfolios and performance assessment that Gene [Jongsma] and I have been working on, and they said, "It's real interesting." They said, "It's going to take a lot more work isn't it?" I said, "Yeah." They said, "Goodbye!" I said, "We'll have after-school workshops, and you'll learn how to do this"; but it really is an issue of taking a lot more time.

I love teachers; I am one. I think this is the greatest profession in the world, but there are a helluva lot of teachers out there that I don't want to let loose with the kids' responses. That's terrible to say, but I think that some teachers can't deal with such a wide array of information.

This is a part of the third set of issues, though, and not so tough as the first two issues; really, the last issue isn't tough at all, interestingly enough. We've got to hammer 'em and build 'em and shape 'em, and we've got to debate about the kinds of assessment instruments we want, but I think we can do it. So I don't think that the development and implementation issues are really the crucial problem.

I don't think we ought to start with, "How do you build one of these things?" I think we ought to start with, "What do we want this thing to do?" And, "How does it serve these different publics?" Or, "Are we interested at all in having them serve the different publics?"

Larry [Mickulecky] and I were working earlier this summer on a proposal to the U.S. government about job literacy. I reviewed the literature on assessment, and found the literature in that area was summarized very nicely in terms of five points that relate closely to what we're talking about here. All we have to do is translate these five points concerning job literacy into language-arts assessment, and we have an equally nice summary of five of the main points that need to be made.

Work samples are the best predictors of a person's ability to do work. So, if we substitute "reading and writing" for "work samples," then we can say that reading and writing are the best predictors of how a person is going to read and write.

> ## RESEARCH ON ASSESSMENT
> ## AND JOB PERFORMANCE
>
> **1. Work samples are the most valid measures of work performance.**

The second one, I think, is very interesting. Basic skills are valid predictors of job performance only if the assessment determines that the examinees can select and apply information. Our traditional reading and writing tests, however, do not do that. They don't determine whether an examinee, or a kid, can select and apply. In fact, the tests create the boxes for the kids.

> ## RESEARCH ON ASSESSMENT
> ## AND JOB PERFORMANCE
>
> **2. Basic skills are valid predictors of job performance—only if—the assessment determines if examinees can select and apply information.**

Number three says that successful job performers not only do tasks but also know why they are doing them, and they can explain how they complete the tasks. Getting a worker to internalize a task is like getting a kid to internalize and understand.

> ## RESEARCH ON ASSESSMENT
> ## AND JOB PERFORMANCE
>
> **3. Successful job performers not only do tasks but know why (purpose) and can explain how they complete tasks.**

By the way, this research is not just about assembly-line workers, but indeed applies to all levels of occupations. We're not talking about "back to old behavioral objectives" and the assembly-line thing, so don't lambast me for that! We're talking about all kinds of people in all kinds of occupations, from assembly-line to high-level.

The fourth statement is that job performance is more closely related to the metacognitive aspects of information processing than to traditional academic skills. Workplace assessments showed that those who did their jobs better were those who understood and could explain why they were doing their job. This is much the same as the third point.

RESEARCH ON ASSESSMENT
AND JOB PERFORMANCE

4. Job performance is more closely related to the metacognitive aspects of information processing than to traditional academic skills.

The last point is about the future of the workplace, and, I would say, the future of education and the future of our society will depend on people—and not on workers only, but on those of us who just laze around, as well—who have decision-making and communication skills. Our traditional language-arts assessments have not looked at whether or not people can work together, whether they can make decisions together. We haven't even touched that area at all.

RESEARCH ON ASSESSMENT
AND JOB PERFORMANCE

5. The future of the workplace will depend on workers, who have *group, decision-making,* and *communication* skills.

Those are some of the issues, and there are a lot more, and it really is a fun time and an interesting time for assessment; but we ought to keep in mind that our whole goal in getting together here is to figure out how assessment can help boys and girls become better readers and writers. Let's not lose sight of that objective. Thank you.

ANABEL NEWMAN (Indiana University):

Do your comments apply equally to secondary and elementary education?

FARR:

Yes.

ED ROBBINS (Indiana University):

Explain your meaning of "learned people" rather than "people who learn."

FARR:

I think that Hirsch and his issue of cultural literacy sums up "learned people" very well, and the reverse of that is "people who learn." The Indianapolis newspaper this morning said that Indianapolis is the fifth-worst school system in the country, and it's going to hell in a handbasket, all based on the ISTEP scores and "right" answers. But I've already told you that I don't think that there are any "right" answers. If you really want kids to *reflect,* then performance assessment says we ought to be looking at something different.

DIANE STEVENS (Illinois University):

What you're saying comes from an academic perspective; certainly it doesn't come from what teachers are saying. It seems to me that your laying out of the issues suggests that we reorder everything that we call education from the top down. Classroom teachers do not say that what they want is self-assessment. This self-assessment measure will just lay something else on teachers who might not necessarily buy into the philosophy that you're putting forward. I wonder how you are going to change the philosophical base of education?

FARR:

When I was talking about self-assessment, it wasn't teachers I was talking about assessing, it was kids. I think a lot of teachers are very interested in having kids be able to do self-assessment and understand how they're developing as literacy learners. I think that the base doesn't come from on high. The things we're talking about are not what test publishers would probably do of their own accord; they are responding to what teachers in classrooms across the country are asking. So I don't think I'm talking about it from an ivory-tower perspective. I think probably this is another matter about which we're probably not even communicating at all. We're talking about very different issues, and I think that's really important to understand this. I really don't quite understand your question, and you probably don't quite understand my answer. But then, you never did when....no! [Laughter] But I think there's an issue there.

LARRY MIKULECKY (Indiana University):

Roger, I want to ask a question about job performance. My understanding of the sorts of tests you described for job performance is that when workers do work samples, they go to an assessment center and spend maybe a day or a day and a half there, but only if somebody judges that they are worth spending that amount of time on. Usually there is some sort of a much more crude superficial screening measure that would screen out maybe eight out of ten colleagues. Is that the kind of pattern you're talking about?

FARR:

No. Not at all, and I really didn't get into that end of things at all, and really there are some things I don't like at all about the job-performance research literature that I looked at. There's not much in the job world about people doing assessment on the floor or in the office to make a continuous assessment to help people do better in the workplace. That's not there at all, but trying to help people do better is there in education, and the potential for it is very strong.

MARILYN BINKLEY (National Center for Education Statistics, US Department of Education):

Roger, from my perspective, we are dealing with Presidents' and Governors' national goals. I listen to state-by-state NAEP every day. The real push for testing is the public and the really "up high." It's not the universities, it's not the academics, but it's the really "up high." You're talking about the tension between the teacher and the school and self-reflection, and on the other hand you're talking about accountability. Can you please address that tension some way?

FARR:

It exists. [Laughter] And I don't know if there's any easy answer to that. Those in accountability positions have asked for more accountability; it has driven instruction. But those in curriculum positions have said, "Hell with you, I'm getting in this game now because you're driving instruction." It's exactly why the people developed the new test in Michigan. They wanted to drive instruction in a direction different from the one in which they saw it going. They wanted to have tests that were more valid. So because there was more push from the accountability folks, the curriculum folks are now into assessment—a lot of them head-over-heels—because they see now that it really is important, or because it has become so high-stakes.

How to bring those two together, Marilyn, I have no idea at all. I mean, I've got some ideas, of course, and I'd be happy to share them with you, and we spent last weekend in Washington talking; but I think there are things we have at least to explore, and I think we ought to understand that we're maybe not going to solve these problems. Let's not go leaping into something as if we've got the answers and then screw up the performance assessment that maybe can help teachers teach better. On the other hand, if all we've got among the decision makers is high-stakes tests that drive the curriculum, there isn't going to be any chance for teachers to do anything better. I'm glad you're in Washington, Marilyn, and I'm in Indiana. [Laughter]

WHOLE LANGUAGE AND EVALUATION: SOME GROUNDED NEEDS, WANTS, AND DESIRES

JEROME HARSTE

As a *token* Whole Language representative [laughter], I want to start with what many of you think Whole Language people are good at: being arrogant!

Not only is Whole Language "in," but, from what I can tell, the educational agenda is ours. Whole Language has put enough pressure on the system to interest even the establishment in change.

I must admit that I have this fantasy: Roger Farr lying on the couch in his psychiatrist's office saying, "My God, I think they're learning how to assess without standardized tests." [Laughter] I think we Whole Language types have driven basal authors and publishers to see their psychiatrists, and I think many people in the Whole Language movement right now want to see the test makers go next.

Before I get constructive [Laughter], I want to clear the air on just one more thing: Whole Language interest in evaluation is not just about developing a better test; it's about a whole lot more. So, simple solutions and quick fixes are out.

What I want to do today is share with you four basic recommendations for assessment that come out of my understanding of Whole Language. I call them my needs, wants, and desires for evaluation.

Assessment that Is Grounded in Both Theory and Practice

NOSE STORY: A while back I was invited to do a workshop on Whole Language in a school in San Bernardino, California. I flew in early so that I could visit several classrooms in the building and thus adjust what I would do and say in the after-school workshop to make it particularly relevant for these teachers.

18

As many of you know, I have written several children's books. The kindergarten teachers knew this too, and invited me to be a resident author in conjunction with my visit to their wing of the building. When I arrived in the first classroom, the teacher had her class seated in a semicircle around a rocker, the place of honor for authors in this room.

Just as I took my place, a second kindergarten class walked in and took its place behind the first. After them a third kindergarten class came in, and then a fourth. The result was that there was a sea of children in front of me. Despite the noise, everyone seemed well mannered with their seats firmly planted on the carpet.

I said, "Hello." They said, "Hello, Dr. Harste!" With little other pomp and circumstance I began reading *It Didn't Frighten Me!* (Goss & Harste, 1981). Immediately Donald, who was seated in the front row, stood up on his knees. By the time I finished the first set of pages, the remaining sea of children were protesting Donald's behavior, as this meant that they couldn't see the pictures. Under duress, Donald sat down, but as I read the next set of pages, Donald was up again, and so were the protests, more vociferous this time.

Before sitting back down this time, Donald said to me, "I can read that book." I said, "You can? That's just great!" and continued to read the next set of pages.

By the time I finished these pages, Donald was up again—this time standing. "My turn to read," he announced, and grabbed the book out of my hand.

What happened shocked even me. My whole professional life has been a saga of trying to get books in the hands of children. In the midst of cries of "Don't let Donald read!!!" and "We want Dr. Harste to read!!!" I literally had yanked my book out of Donald's hand, the very kind of child for whom I had written the book in the first place!

Thinking very fast, I tried to recover. Calling Donald to me, I whispered, "Here, you can have this book to read whenever you want. Oh look, your teacher would like you to read it to her."

As Donald made his way to the back of the class, I rapidly groped through my duffel bag to find another copy of *It Didn't Frighten Me!* and continued my reading before the class got totally out of hand.

As I continued, I noticed another child. With each succeeding page, he got closer and closer to both me and the book. He seemed totally engrossed. By the end of my reading, he was literally nose-to-nose with me and the book. He, too, was standing on his knees by the end of the reading, but interestingly, no one seemed to mind.

I was delighted. I thought, "What a great demonstration! Any teacher witnessing this scene knows why I think adults should read to children every day. I need to hire this child and take him with me when I do workshops! What a reader!"

To make sure that the moment was not lost on the teachers, I thought I would let the child have the first word. Upon finishing, I paused and looked the child right in the eye.

There was dead silence for a moment. The child read my intent well. He was the first to speak. With due concern he boomed, "Golly, man, what happened to your nose?"

He hadn't been listening to the story at all.[*]

My first recommendation involves setting our theoretical house in order by taking a stand. One of the key principles in Whole Language is using the child as informant. Ken Goodman started the revolution by watching real readers read real texts. Whole Language theory has been built, according to Burke, on the principle of "what's there." This feature distinguishes it from traditional assessment, and it is what has made Whole Language theory, I think, so accessible to teachers. In Whole Language there is no transfer problem, as theory evolves from practice and has immediate instructional implications.

"I only know what I see," someone said to Piaget. Piaget's answer: "No, you only see what you know."

In Whole Language, theory and practice transact.

Not only is Whole Language a call for more authentic assessment—a point that Roger and Kaye develop nicely in their paper—but it's also a call for assessment to reflect what we theoretically now understand. Neither assessors nor assessment instruments are innocent. We can no longer assume that assessment devices are right, and programs that do not make a good showing on

---

[*]Harste's written text included this story and the one on page 21. Time constrained him during the symposium from recounting them, but they are too good to leave out.

these devices are wrong. If our programs reflect what we currently know about language and learning, we have as much right to assume that our curricula are valid and our tests invalid, as the other way around.

Theory divorced from practice is irresponsible, and it constitutes miseducation. She who does not acknowledge a theoretical stand is lost. Eclecticism is a disease curable fortunately by taking a theoretical position.

New assessment procedures must always see the relationship between theory and practice as problematic, and in so doing force assessors and assessment devices to speak. The key to understanding the criterion of grounded theory is dialogue: Said differently, the function of assessment is conversation. New assessment, which understands the dialogical relationship between theory and practice, can play an important part in supporting much-needed conversations in literacy education.

The criterion of grounded theory will not be easy, for tests are currently much better at silencing children, teachers, and theories than at providing them a vehicle by which they might be heard.

> WHO'S TESTING WHOM: Dorothy Menosky, one of the Founding Mothers of Whole Language, has a friend, Lynn, who teaches in Detroit. The Detroit school system uses the old "Draw a Man" test as part of its entrance requirements to kindergarten. (I'm not sure what Detroit does with children who flunk this test. I guess they can't go to kindergarten.)
>
> To make themselves look modern, Detroit has updated the test. It's now called the "Draw a Person" test. (The moral of this part of the story, I guess, is that the long arm of Women's Liberation has hit even Detroit and testing.)
>
> At any rate, Lynn was giving the "Draw a Person Test" to an entering kindergarten student recently. As per the directions, the little girl was told to draw a person and put in as many details as possible. As you know, based on how the subject draws the person—whether it is a tadpole person with arms and legs coming out of the head or a more normal looking creature—the tester supposedly is able to decide the child's current state of emotional and cognitive development.
>
> In this instance, the little girl picked up her pencil and rapidly sketched a head with arms and legs coming out of it. She then added another lump on each side of the head.

"Ears," she said. Pausing a bit she added two dots for eyes, a loop for the nose and a half moon for the mouth, naming each as she added them. Scanning her composition, she added curlicues for hair, and then paused thinking what else she might do.

Assuming the stance of The Thinker, she dramatically put one hand to her brow. With the eraser end of the pencil resting on the corner of her bottom lip, she thought a while and then reflected, "Hmmm, I'm not sure I know where the pancreas goes!"

I like this story because it's a nice instance of "Who's testing whom?"

Assessment that Focuses on the Engagement of Participants in Literacy Events

My second recommendation for how to improve assessment is more easily accomplished. It is to think "engagement" rather than "objectives." This is more than a semantic shift. Experience is the key construct in understanding learning. For Whole Language folks, experience replaces skill sequences and cognitive states.

Can you read Sarah's Mother's Day card? "Once upon a time there was a lovable bunny who picked a rose for his mommy." (Don't you hope she gets a job at Hallmark?) Notice that she writes "once upon a time" as a single conceptual unit. Her "lovable" is written in syllables, and her "bunny" is written using linguistic units that we currently are using. Sarah is simultaneously testing three separate hypotheses on how to script English. [See Sarah's card on page 23.]

Data such as this demonstrates that there is no order in language itself inherent to the way that it's learned—a real blow to a skills model of teaching language. Nor is there any order in the child inherent to what she is learning—unsettling news to those who have used Piaget's developmental stages to lay out curriculum.

Some five-year-olds know as much about stories as do some sixth-graders. The key variable is experience. What children take from a new language event depends on what demonstrations are highlighted as the child transacts with herself and others in the event itself.

Objectives suggest fixed predictable outcomes, and hence they violate what we know.

If experience is key to understanding language learning, engagement offers the wiggle that is needed. Here are some examples:

- As a result of reading a given book, students will be able to relate what they've read to their background experience.

- As a result of reading a given book, students will be able to plan new action.

- When blocked in reading, students will be able to use a variety of strategies, including having conversation over the book with someone involved in the setting.

- When faced with a quandary, students will demonstrate that reading and writing are two of many strategies they use in searching for a solution.

Because this is a testing audience, let me put this differently: Engagement is to demonstration as objective is to fact.

Notice that with engagement there is no one single demonstration of mastery. Notice also that with engagement, a skills model of instruction is not a privileged instructional answer.

Although engagement does not let the assessor set a single criterion, it should be possible to specify a set of literate behaviors that illustrate literacy, leaving assessors always free to add more criteria as new instances occur. This possibility alone should start new conversations, support the development of rounded theory, and do much to propel testing from the mindless state that Whole Language educators charge traditionalists with occupying.

Assessment that Implicates and Holds All Stakeholders Responsible

My third recommendation involves another semantic shift. This shift is to substitute the term "responsibility" for the term "accountability." I think that Whole Language educators will not be happy until this shift occurs.

For Whole Language educators, responsibility and accountability come from quite different paradigms. Three trends in testing serve as example.

- One trend in testing has been "User beware!" It's not the tests that are bad, it's how they are used that's wrong. This is like laying loaded guns on every street corner, and then saying "I told you so" when someone picks up a gun and shoots him- or

24

herself in the foot. The user is held accountable; the test maker is off the hook.

The shift from accountability to responsibility is one of initiative. In accountability, the teacher is assumed to lack initiative, and must be held accountable to standards that lie outside her choosing. There is no sharing of responsibility. She has lost control both of her classroom and of her career.

- A second trend has been to concentrate assessment on the classroom, on students and teachers. The motto has been—and still is, as illustrated in Roger's paper—"If assessment doesn't result in improved instruction, throw it out." Whole Language educators, too, like everyone else, seem to have bought in—hook, line, and sinker.

Teachers are frantic. Even the very best Whole Language teachers are paranoid. They run around collecting everything, from what I can see. It's the old cover-your-behind-just-in-case-someone-asks answer to assessment. This trend has driven some of the very best teachers known to me to look more like unprincipled curators at the Institute of Educational Greed and Avarice than they look like responsible professionals.

Teachers who are responsible for providing high-quality instruction in the language arts, need new assessment devices that will support their own evaluations of how well they did and what else they might do.

But it won't end there. New assessment procedures will help principals decide how effective their current attempts are to help teachers implement what is currently known. It will help school board members decide how effective they have been in supporting teachers and administrators to do what they professionally know needs to be done. It will help parents evaluate the effectiveness of what they are doing to support the literacy development of their children, and it will provide them with ideas as to what more might be done.

The focus of new assessment devices will be self-evaluation, and the range of evaluation will be expanded to include all the stakeholders involved.

- A third trend in assessment has been instructional innocence. Testing has not been seen as an instructional event, but this is sheer nonsense.

The higher the status of the test, the more it instructs by demonstrating to parents, teachers, and children what education really is about. New assessment devices in the language arts will hold test makers responsible for what their tests teach about language as well as about the role of language in learning.

One of the biggest problems we face in assessment is the tendency to use old eyes to evaluate new programs. This is not only reductionistic but also entrapment. Whole Language is about new goals for education; to reduce it to a new method to reach old goals is, quite frankly, to miss the bus.

Assessment that Furthers Inquiry; What Education in this Society Must Be About

My fourth criterion is inquiry.

The function of evaluation, like the function of education, is learning.

Sharon Pugh said it best a couple of years ago: "In the final analysis, our interest in reading and writing is an interest in learning."

Whole Language people have always prided themselves on getting kids in touch with real processes. Instead of talking about reading, children in Whole Language classrooms actually read. Instead of talking about writing, children in Whole Language classrooms actually write.

New assessment procedures in the language arts, if done responsibly, could do much to strengthen this view of education as inquiry. By this, we Whole Language folks mean, however, everybody's inquiry, not that only of some subset of the stakeholders involved.

New assessment procedures in the language arts are not merely about prioritizing a new set of voices. They are about setting in place a structure whereby new voices can be heard, and needed new conversations can begin.

Some Whole Language people, even, don't seem to understand this, either. They develop better sets of criteria to use on their checklist, but the same behavioristic paradigm that has governed assessment remains intact. We will be in only a slightly better mess, it seems to me, if all we do now is let Whole Language people set the new test specifications, but fail to put in place a structure by which we all can continue to grow.

Knowledge, according to Whole Language theory, is socially constituted. By this, Whole Language people mean that facts change.

Ludwick Fleck's *Genesis of a Scientific Fact* is a delightful book that every educator should read; I use it in my doctoral seminars. Fleck traces the human understanding of syphilis from a religious interpretation, the revenge of God, to the discovery that it is caused by a bacterium related, in fact, to athlete's foot. People didn't want to hear this news; hence it took years for this explanation to take hold. Fleck leaves the reader thinking that the final word is not in, and that a new, more powerful explanation is just around the social, political, and historical corner. He also discusses Wasserman's experiences that led him to offer a bacterial explanation of syphilis. These proved not to be replicable. The fact that his conclusions held says something about textbook explanations of the scientific method and its relationship to the real process.

At one level, Whole Language is a reaction against the transmission model of education, in which knowledge is fixed, and the role of the school is to pour knowledge into unsuspecting and often unwilling vessels. That's what Hirsch's *Cultural Literacy* list is all about—5,000 facts every high-school student should know. But whose facts are these? And whose culture? And whose voice is heard when this becomes the educational agenda?

Knowledge both changes and is created through interaction. New assessment procedures can do much to further this view of education, and in so doing they can improve both schooling and the role that schools play in a democracy. That's the hope and the potential of Whole Language.

Currently schools, Whole Language people argue, are better at silencing children than at hearing from them. In some of our big-city school systems, less than 50 percent of the school-aged population graduates from high school. The figures for ethnic minorities are lower, and among Blacks who graduate from high school, 65 percent are females. The males, recent reports suggest, are either dead or in jail. One in four Black males in our major cities will die at the hands of someone with a gun before they reach adulthood.

In Indiana, one-half of one percent of the children in each grade level will be labeled for "special education" each year they are in school.

Whole Language people read these figures less as a commentary on our children than as a commentary on how traditional education has failed.

I won't go into how the schools have failed our Indian and bilingual populations, but I will say that this failure is occurring at the very moment in history in which almost one-half of everything published is in a language other than English. Margaret Meek recently made the argument that anything we do in schools that restricts our diversity will turn out to be a negative.

Whole Language is a promise to hear all voices. To have this promise come true, we need to face anomalies—the children whom we fail to reach—and adjust our theories and practices accordingly.

As test makers in the past have contributed to the problem, so responsible test makers now can and must contribute to the solution.

There are no easy correct answers. We live in a first-draft world, and we, like good writers, will simply have to take our best shots and self-correct as we go along.

Criteria for judging literacy in our attempts to improve instruction must come from our engagement in the event itself. To develop a new set of test specifications in the abstract, and to use these to evaluate the event, is to retreat to an older notion of what education is and how it works.

Learners must learn to ask their own inquiry questions. One cannot grow by testing someone else's hypothesis. Just as without trust, there is no reflexivity, so too without commitment there is no inquiry.

But in testing, just the opposite of what we need is what happens. The test makers decide what our inquiry questions should be; and by framing the question, they have framed the answer as well as what can be known. And I see this same scenario repeating itself in new Whole Language assessments. I've even had my hand in them.

Gloria Kauffman, an absolutely excellent Whole Language teacher from Goshen, Indiana, introduced portfolio assessment into her classroom last year, and she did it right. She brought in an artist who showed the children his portfolio. After he left, the kids talked about creating their own portfolios. They were excited. They conscientiously collected the work that showed their involvement in reading, writing, and other curricular areas. At the end of the grading period, children summarized their progress in various curriculum areas, and they used these summaries to write letters to their parents. These letters were included in the child's report card with an invitation to the parents to write back. Everything went well the first nine weeks. The second nine weeks, some kids were slow in getting their portfolios and letters written. By the end of the year, portfolio assessment had become an "assignment."

Gloria came to realize that *her* questions were not *their* questions. Her students did what she asked, but the difference between her Whole Language classroom and the skills classsroom down the hall in terms of the quality of student-teacher interactions, paled to insignificance.

Everyone has both the right and the responsibility to ask their own inquiry questions. Indeed, it is the plethora of questions and responses that keeps the conversation going.

Some think that Whole Language teachers in the United States, by asking their own questions, are starting a new revolution in assessment, but this is only partially so—in England and Australia, in Canada, in New Zealand, Whole Language teachers have been as feisty. Teachers and school districts here are reclaiming a professional responsibility that teachers in these other countries never lost.

Roger Farr has a right to his own inquiry question; he just doesn't have a right to decide what mine should be.

Mary Douglas reminds us: "Common sense is cultural sense, and so too it is with testing. If we can shift frames, new possibilities open up."

The bottom line is that the role of schooling in a democracy is not to silence children but to hear from them. New assessment procedures, like Whole Language itself, need to be there to remind us and the citizenry of this quest. To reduce education or literacy to mere consumerism is sheer irresponsibility both to our profession and to the society we promised to be.

Conclusion

Whole Language is a philosophy of education; included in it are the following:

- a theory of language
- a theory of learning

29

- a theory of knowledge

- a theory of schooling in a democracy

I hope that I have given you a flavor of how each of these components can contribute to our understanding of literacy and what new assessment procedures must look like. The agenda ahead will not be easy. As some wag once said, "Empires in decline get into some pretty weird stuff." For lack of easy answers, I would like to suggest that we begin by learning how to talk to one another.

[ROGER FARR: Amen. {Laughter}]

I came to IU 20 years ago. Carl Smith and Roger Farr were already here. Under the able leadership of Leo Fay, each of us was permitted to go our separate ways. Even though each of us has proved that what was good for us individually was good for IU, one of our collective disappointments ought to be that we have talked about substantive issues more through graduate students than face-to-face.

This conference, in fact, is a result of a first rather unsuccessful effort to talk together. Last spring we came together to talk about assessment.

Carl, as head of ERIC/RCS, was rightfully feeling pressure to provide a variety of information to the various users of his system. Roger, an author of several standardized tests, was feeling pressure to develop alternatives that Whole Language people and others might find more acceptable. I, as an advocate of Whole Language, felt responsible to be more than just *anti*-tests. I really wanted to use Carl's and Roger's brains to help solve a problem that I see holding Whole Language back.

The problem of how to evaluate in Whole Language is still with us. Fifteen years ago, people said, "Well, fine, Harste, but what does Whole Language instruction look like?" Over the past fifteen years of working with extremely capable teachers, we have worked Whole Language out—though I still don't trust it until I see Whole Language engagements and interactions taking place in the classroom itself.

Now, evaluation in Whole Language is at the same place we were fifteen years ago in instruction. Fortunately, knowing what we don't want is an important first step in knowing what we do want.

I've already started some new conversations. In preparation for these remarks, Bill Bintz and I had several extensive conversations.

I also interviewed Lucy Calkins, Ken Goodman, Pat Shannon, Peter Johnson, Bob Query, Carolyn Burke, and several others. In fact I don't know which ideas were triggered by what conversations. If you quote this talk, give us all credit!

In the process, I've learned to talk about my assessment needs, wants, and desires:

- Assessment that is grounded in theory and practice
- Assessment that focuses on the engagement of participants in literacy events
- Assessment that implicates and holds all stakeholders responsible
- Assessment that furthers inquiry and what education in this society must be about

Whole Language is about knowledgeable teachers who share a developing philosophy of education in which the best scientific knowledge of language, of literacy, of learning and teaching, are brought together with the goal of helping kids to grow in literacy and problem-solving, in knowledge, and in their sense of themselves and their society. That's pretty exciting stuff, and it is an agenda that responsible educators, even if their major role is evaluation, should find hard to resist.

MARILYN BINKLEY (National Center for Education Statistics, U.S. Department of Education):

Your first point was that assessment should be grounded in theory and practice. If I ground assessment in Whole Language theory and practice, how do I compare the results and outputs of other theories and other practices fairly? It's much the same way as your saying that our current set of tests do not fairly and comparably judge the outputs and outcomes of Whole Language.

HARSTE:

Good question! I don't know if the function of a test ought to be a horse race.

BINKLEY:

I don't see it as a horse race either, Jerry, but I sit in a place where I'm constantly barraged with letters that say, "NAEP is aligned to Whole Language," and "It's unfair: Stop NAEP and stop Whole Language!" Now you tell me that NAEP is aligned with other schools of thought in testing. How do I put this competition to rest?

HARSTE:

I'm not willing to assume that one test can serve every purpose. I think the problem is that tests try to serve all theoretical positions. That's what I meant when I said they are eclectic. I think that the problem with eclecticism is that you can't grow. It's the same problem that I found in working with teacher-researchers: Unless you take a position, you don't have a basis from which to reflect and outgrow yourself.

I really think that we're talking different paradigms. That's why when Roger and Carl and I met, and Roger proposed this meeting—he can vouch for this—I wasn't real excited about it, partly because I believe that you don't really convince someone else to take a different paradigm. I believe that you don't settle differences when they're at a paradigm level through a debate. In actual fact, I think that how you win in that case is you produce a lot of doctoral students, and you pollute the world. It's a strategy I've been using. [Laughter]

When people disagree, even, say, people as opposed as behaviorists and developmentalists, but they are working within the same paradigm, then I think they might be able to talk in debates—in that case, they are not really challenging the whole system of beliefs-in-place. I think, however, that traditional tests come out of a view of education about universals, with a particularist view of the world—quite a different paradigm from the one I hold. I'm not at all convinced that one test can serve all functions. I'd love to hear other people's responses to that question. I hope it comes up again.

DIANE STEVENS (University of Illinois):

What you say and what Roger [Farr] says, are not different. Historically my problem with Roger is that we don't necessarily disagree, but we don't have any way of getting at what we agree about. Roger wants kids to self-assess, and you want 'em to self-assess; Roger wants teachers to have information for planning, and so do you.

One thing I've learned by being a Whole Language person at the Center for the Study of Reading, is that we're not all that different, although our language makes it sound like we're a lot different. A test that Dick Anderson writes, and one that Roger Farr writes, and one that Jerry Harste writes, and one that Ken Goodman writes, are going to look a lot different, but the ideas behind them aren't that much different.

Why don't we, then, give the language-arts field a sense of the things on which we do agree? The kids ought to assess themselves. The teachers need good information. The teachers need to know what matters. When you ask: "How can we have one test that reaches one person's goal, and another that reaches another's?"—I think our goals are all the same; I think we just don't have a language, a way of talking, either among ourselves or to other teachers or to legislators or to whoever wants to listen.

HARSTE:

I think that there is something to that. When I was reviewing theories of reading comprehension, despite the fact that we could name different theoretical positions, there seemed to be more and more a tendency to generalize a model of reading, and I think that's somewhat true in the assessment field today, too, about the goals—although I don't want to give in completely.

One of the notes I made in my little journal when I was preparing this speech, says: "I'm not sure educators are in charge of assessment." Recent experiences with the U.S. Steering Committee for the new International Test of Literacy has me thinking that mathematicians call all the major shots. Despite my badgering of Roger, I don't know of any educator who is happy with what tests currently test, and no educator at those International Literacy meetings has ever been happy with tests. In many ways, we never seem able to get any changes because it comes out to be a mathematical decision. The mathematicians, in actual fact, end up deciding which, of all the theoretical arguments that we educators have made, get incorporated into the tests.

WARREN LEWIS (Moderator, ERIC/RCS, Indiana University):

Larry Mikulecky will ask the last question.

LARRY MIKULECKY (Indiana University):

As I listen both to you, Jerry, and to Roger, it occurs to me that your principles have a lot of similarities, as Diane [Stevens] mentioned. Differences become real when one has to decide what to do with limited time and limited resources.

I was in Australia in May, and people there talk the kind of talk you're talking; but when Bert Morris took a look at teachers in classrooms in the United States, he found that only about two out of ten have kids engaged in a lot of literacy activities. In July, I was in Canada, and people there talk the same talk that you're talking; but when you take a look at what they use to do their assessing when time is limited, they use mainly literature when working with adult literates. There's not quite enough time to use other kinds of engagement.

I'd like to get a sense of how you would clarify the problems of limited time and limited resources in terms of the goals you're talking about. When, indeed, stakeholders are involved, we're going to find compromises that satisfy no one, I think.

HARSTE:

I want to respond in two ways. I don't want to give in either to you or to Diane on the idea that we're all really talking the same language. The reason I don't want to give in is because I don't know that I think we are.

I think that underlying these theories of language are very different paradigms of language. Mine is an open meaning system; theirs is a closed. There are different theories of knowledge. The traditional one has been that knowledge is fixed, and testing has been: "Here are the standards; they get applied to evaluate the setting." Whole Language people, [by contrast] are talking about knowledge being created....

MIKULECKY:

The real question is about time and resources.

HARSTE:

I don't know how to do that. That's a part of the question I have no idea how to answer. I think it, also, involves a paradigm shift. Part of the answer to time and resources is that people have a tendency to see evaluation—and I think you and Roger would agree with this—as standing outside of something looking in, rather than being an integral part of the educative process. I think when assessment is part of the process, rather than something particular and separate, the time issue goes away because assessment isn't something different from what normally transacts in the process of education.

ROGER FARR:

Warren, I know you said that was the last question, but I demand another question. [Laughter]

LEWIS:

You'll get a chance to offer rebuttal later. Time's up for this segment.

FARR:

I object to people putting words in my mouth, and for someone to get up and say, "We're trying to get together," and say "The agenda is ours, not yours," and "This is what you believe." I think it's all about setting up strawmen to make yourself look like you know what you're talking about, when you don't! I do have a couple of questions. And I want to know why Jerry won't engage in a debate with me so that I can respond to it and not let him call me names from the podium!

LEWIS:

As soon as we've heard the other two speakers, I fully expect that debate to happen.

STATE POLICY AND AUTHENTIC WRITING ASSESSMENT[*]

DIANE BLOOM

It's amazing what you can do with twenty-six characters in the alphabet, isn't it? You can strike a title like "State Policy and Authentic Writing Assessment." To some, the combining of "state policy" and "authentic writing assessment" may be dissonance, heresy, contradictory—an oxymoron. We have learned in New Jersey, and I'm sure people in other states have learned, that state policy leading to carefully constructed assessment can result in authentic writing assessment. In fact, a state assessment policy can lead to the teaching of writing, as we are defining it for the twenty-first century, an improvable curriculum and improved student learning. That has been our experience in New Jersey.

Let me share with you what we have done in New Jersey. Maybe that will help us draw some conclusions. In New Jersey we have concluded that state policy and writing assessment are compatible. When I've asked individuals, "What do we mean when we say 'authenticity' or 'authentic assessment'?" I get lots of different responses. Some people respond, "Well, that's a scoring method; the method has to be really true to the features of good writing, and the assessment must be really accurate." Others will say, "No, no, no; it really has to do with the purpose for which we're assessing." And

---

[*]Throughout her presentation, Bloom referred to *Report of the Writing Committee: Identification of the 8th-grade Skills in Writing and Test Specifications and Sample Items for the 11th-grade High School Proficiency Test and the 8th-grade Early Warning Test* (May 1990), published by the New Jersey State Department of Education, Division of General Academic Education, copies of which she had distributed to the symposium.

others point out that the task itself must have an authentic ring so that students write for "real" purposes and audiences.

I'm not sure whether authenticity can reside in a single definition. There's a lot of components that belong to authentic writing assessment.

What I do know is that in New Jersey we looked at several elements to get a focus on authenticity. We looked at research nationwide. We looked at trends in assessment. We looked at theories of language, learning, and schooling. And we looked at empirical research and other attendent components. What we found was that authenticity is achieved in many arenas. Certainly, one needs to look at the assessment tool and the purpose for which one is assessing. In addition, one needs to look at the reporting of results. At the center of all this is, of course, the learner, the student.

New Jersey has been doing statewide assessments of students' command of skills since the early '70s. We had a minimum-basic-skills test, and in 1986, we began to test for higher-order skills—mathematics, reading, and writing. In 1986 these three tests became a graduation requirement in New Jersey. We would deny students a diploma if they could not pass their graduation test at ninth grade—with multiple opportunities thereafter for those who did not pass their first time as test takers. In the past three years, we have moved along the higher-order-skills continuum from assessing the skills of fourteen-year-old ninth-graders to assessing the skills of sixteen- or seventeen-year-old eleventh-graders.

We are presently looking forward to 1993, the year when the eleventh-grade students will have to pass their graduation test. Prior to 1993, there are three years of due-notice assessment with matrix sampling. The three years of due-notice time is to help both district and state personnel put together an indicator system to improve program and curriculum. Also, an eighth-grade early-warning test is aligned to the eleventh-grade assessment. The test is not a gate-keeper. The test serves to assess student learning and to inform curriculum and instruction.

Before one leaps into the process of state assessment, and looks to develop large-scale assessment as state policy, one needs to ask, "Who wants this test?" The decisions to develop a test are made in response to requests. Those requests come from several sources. They can come from professional associations or from educators or from legislators or from governors. Once the policy decision is made that there will be a statewide assessment, questions need to be asked, the answers to which will establish the parameters of that examination. Those questions are as follows:

- Who will take the test and for what purposes?
- What knowledge and/or abilities are being assessed?
- What is going to be done with those results?
- What purposes are they going to serve?

These are really important questions! The first task—deciding whether statewide testing should be state policy, and who should take the test and for what purposes—took us one year. Why so long? Because we had to put together a research team to investigate the impact of the national experience, for example NAEP. We needed to talk to business and industry leaders and employers.

New Jersey is a very densely populated, urban state. Like many states, it requires an educated, and increasingly technically expert, workforce. A lot of money had been spent by industry reeducating our students. In response to the needs of our workplace, legislation was enacted establishing the assessment, although the exact nature of the response was left to Department of Education staff, and was to be based on research and our own findings. Two reports were developed at the end of the first two years: "New Jersey's Design for Educational Excellence into the Twenty-first Century," and "Preparing to Enter the Twenty-first Century: Revising New Jersey's Statewide Writing Assessment."

The second question, "What knowledge or abilities should be assessed?" was based on the work of a committee who studied the national experience. We found that the trend is away from the drilling of skills out of context, away from the mechanistic approaches of teaching reading, writing, mathematics, computing, and problem-solving, without meaning. We are encouraging our students to read literature. We are encouraging our students to read and write for authentic purposes.

Robert Glaser from the University of Pittsburgh said that if we are to have an assessment that is to be an assessment "of the people, for the people," then we need to involve the people. A really critical component! Robert Glaser in his research had looked at the past—you have to know the past in order to set your future direction. Both Jerry Harste and Roger Farr have spoken of this, and of the importance of looking at where we've been in relation to where we're going and what's happening, and then working together. Robert

Glaser observed that in the decade of the '80s, we increased the proportion of our children who are attending school. We expanded the range of our education to more groups in society, and we expanded the function, and the amount and kinds of education provided to our students. What does that mean for the twenty-first century? For those of us who are looking at assessment, we need to reach *all* the diverse children and groups of youths—*all* of them.

As a result, New Jersey put together a committee representative of our urban and suburban educators and students—both those who had graduated from our high schools and students who are currently in our schools. Representatives from the military served on our committee, as did business and industry—Johnson & Johnson Pharmaceuticals, New Jersey Bell, and Merck. (New Jersey is known for its chemical industry.) The committee was charged by the Commissioner of Education and by the Governor to identify the skills that students will need when they enter the twenty-first century workplace—skills in language arts, reading, writing, and mathematics. To accomplish their charge, the committee had to look at research, theory, foundations of learning, and cognitive/metacognitive development. Two consultants assisted us in this process: Arthur Whimbey, cognitive psychologist, and Charles Cooper, professor of English language-arts studies. Charles Cooper was our consultant on the development of the new eleventh-grade test. Dr. Cooper is the architect of the California assessment program; and, as many of you know, he and Axelrod coauthored *Reading Critically and Writing Well.*

Conceptually, the committee decided to begin with a definition of "literacy." First they looked at historical definitions of literacy. In the fifteenth century, writing and copying were synonymous. In 1850, according to the U.S. census, literacy was acknowledged on the basis of a self-report. In 1900, it was the ability to write one's name. By World War II, it was fourth-grade reading ability. Today, according to *Business Week* and *Time*, we're expecting students to function at a ninth- to twelfth-grade level of ability; and with the turn of the century, probably at eleventh- and twelfth-grade level of ability. In addition, the committee said, "Literacy demands *increase* after high school." The need for literacy doesn't stop. In the 1800s, unskilled workers were 80% of the labor force, but by 1986, they were reduced to 60% because either they had been replaced by automation or the unskilled work was now being performed by workers in less-developed countries. Thus, the committee embraced the definition of literacy from *Learning to Be Literate in America*:

"Using printed and written information to function in society." Many definitions stop here, but literacy is more than that. "Literacy is using printed and written information to achieve one's goals, and to develop one's knowledge and potential." Certainly, we want our students to graduate. We want them to get a job. We want them to be able to get married, raise a family, be able to buy homes. Certainly we want them to be able to realize that they can seek promotions and move on in their career choices.

Once the skills were identified, what did we then have to do? If it's going to be education "by the people and for the people," the committee that developed this list of skills now had to go out and face the people. So, in convocations held around the State, the committee met with their colleagues, and they presented and listened, and rewrote the drafts. And when those drafts were then corrected, we went out yet again, and we took the skills out in survey format to reflect the consensus.

The personnel of our approximately six hundred schools in New Jersey reviewed the results of the committee's work, namely the skills that were identified as requiring assessment. Ninety-seven percent of the surveys were returned, and ninety-five percent strongly agreed with the writing skills identified by the committee. Following this process of seeking a skills consensus, the State Board of Education adopted and endorsed the skills. The test of "by the people, for the people" had been passed and there was considerable acceptance of that assessment.

At this point the "skills-development" committee moved into its next phase as the "test-development" committee. The test-development committee had to look at how to assess the skills that had been agreed on. If we're going to determine how to assess students, we concluded, then, we have to look at the learner. What is it, we asked, that we want the learner to be able to do? When the committee looked at writing, they looked at purpose-driven and authentic tasks, and determined that writing performance should be assessed by looking at knowledge and ability.

The committee adopted Ted Sizer's "performance ability"—we wanted to see whether students can construct meaning by sustaining discourse, by writing an essay. The committee used the word "essay" generically, all-encompassing. The committee thought about "knowledge"—not just "knowledge knowledge" but also the "how-to knowledge." How does one apply? How does one analyze?

The second cluster on the test is "the reconstruction of meaning for the purpose of revising and editing the written text of another writer." Thus, the committee's goal was to focus on higher-level cognitive processing, with emphasis on the role of the writer—the writer who commands written language, but also the writer who responds constructively to the writing of others. The test's emphasis is on a contemporary understanding of the writing process—I'm thinking of Glynda Hull's work, and, of course, Vygotsky's work: the social context. Over time, as educators, we have moved away from looking at writing as a finished product, to a complex cognitive process, to that of a cognitive process embodied in a social context.

In addition, this higher-order test acknowledges that students need to know the four types of knowledge involved when they are asked to compose: knowledge of the content to be written about; knowledge of the discourse—the schemata, the organizational structures; knowledge of the syntactic forms—how words are strung together, the conventions of punctuation and usage; and the procedural knowledge of how to compose and generate ideas that communicate.

Here is what we don't want—according to Richard Lederer, a student wrote the following about William Shakespeare:

> The greatest writer of the Renaissance was William Shakespear. Shakespear never made much money and is famous only because of his plays. He lived at Windsor with his merry wives, writing tragedies, comedies, and errors. In one of Shakespear's famous plays, Hamlet rations out his situation by relieving himself in a long soliloquy. In another, Lady Macbeth tries to convince Macbeth to kill the king by attacking his manhood. Romeo and Juliet are an example of a heroic couplet. Writing at the same time as Shakespeare was Miguel Cervantes. He wrote *Donkey Hote*. The next great author was John Milton, Milton wrote *Paradise Lost*. Then his wife died and he wrote *Paradise Regained*.

What does this text say about writing? First, that writing is an enormously complex cognitive task. Second, that through an activation of several dimensions of thinking, subprocesses are hierarchically formed. Using the recursive writing process, writers go back to look again at that which they have just written. Our committee came to realize that one can read without being able to write, but one cannot write without being able to read.

The committee therefore concluded that the tests would measure two dimensions of writing—Cluster I: Constructing

Meaning by Writing an Essay, and Cluster II: Reconstructing Meaning to Revise and Edit the Written Text of the Writer. With respect to the first cluster, the committee allotted 60 minutes for students to write their essay, with 10 minutes for planning/ prewriting (not scored) and 10 minutes for revising/editing their own written work. The essay as written in the four-page test booklet would be scored.

In order to elicit student writing and establish a writing task, the committee said, "We don't want to narrow instruction. We don't want to narrow the curriculum. We want it to be robust, and also to attend to known writing theories." We looked at Kinneavy's work, we looked at Moffett's work, we looked at Britton's work. We wanted our students to write for specific purposes and specific audiences. Thus we looked at transactional forms of writing, purpose-driven writing, and various audiences.

We worked with test contractors, and we have always had success: We've worked with NES, we've worked with NCS, we've worked with Measurement Incorporated, Beta Incorporated—we have had success because we did our homework. The state must respond to the questions I raised earlier in order to know what is the purpose of the assessment and what are the expectations of the public. Contractors have always been most helpful in helping us to achieve these goals. Thus, this particular test came out different from what we've seen before. It's not a depersonalized test; it's a personalized test.

With respect to the second cluster on the test, dealing with higher-order thinking skills, these are the features of the registered holistic scoring method, features that measure students' command of standard written English inclusive of the following: knowledge of one's topic (content); cogent application of that knowledge (organization); use of the English language according to a recognized standard (usage); structuring of words and sentences to present a complete thought or message (sentence construction); and, application of the conventions of the English language that serve to clarify the author's intended message (mechanics).

The third and fourth aspects of the paper you received are a discussion of reliability—critical components of authenticity! Here's where empirical research findings are very, very important. In our test, writing is to be weighted 60/40: 60% for the sustained discourse and 40% for the ability to revise and edit the text of another writer. Authenticity does not end with students taking a test. We plan further to target developmental instruction areas. Fifty million dollars was provided by the state to encourage the reeducation of teachers. We have an open portfolio process in the special review assessment process for our students when they have become seniors but have yet to pass the test after multiple opportunities. We believe that this helps also to reduce text anxiety for those students. Aiken from Pepperdine University has researched test anxiety.

Continuing in our effort to strive for authenticity, we continued to review and use the best of research findings. According to the research, multiple-choice assessment can be very humane as long as you allow test takers to comment on their test or questions by providing some kind of response outlet; so, therefore, we designed an open-ended response at the end of some of the test sections. These responses would not be scored.

Research by Savitz in 1985 indicated that test placement was important. In fact, if you put some of your easier items up first, you provide students with a positive anticipation of success. Our committee used these findings to develop the format of the tests. Cassels and Johnstone in 1984 suggested that test-item writers ought to pay closer attention to the structural form, knowing that there are some things that work and some things that don't work. In other words, ask a question in a positive way rather than a negative way; and move sentence construction from complex to simple.

Authenticity in state policy and statewide assessment is effective when test developers are prepared to be suspect. Tension is important! We are suspect when we seek to listen and revise, provide internal checks of validity and reliability, and external checks, too. External checks are possible through the employment of outside psychometric and measurement experts! We have used Sue Phillips from the University of Michigan, Michael Beck from Beta Associates, Jason Millman from Cornell, and Jeff Jenkins from New Mexico. And we actually have asked students to take the test experimentally—a really important aspect of authentic assessment! We want to know empirically as well as rationally how kids do, because that tells us whether items assess the skills they purport to measure.

Authenticity, in terms of an instructional paradigm model, is the last part of my paper. The paradigm is linked to a working relationship with our New Jersey Council of Teachers of English and our New Jersey Language Arts Leaders' Association. If you're going to have assessment, you cannot leave out the retraining of teachers. It's wonderful to know that a lot of teachers go back to school, and that they continue their education. But you would be amazed at how many never pick up a professional journal, have not read the writings of Lucy Calkins, Donald Graves, or Nancy Atwell's book, *In the Middle*.

We have also realized that you can't do workshops in one day. I presented an AERA paper stating that maybe five is a good number of days. We have used five days with two years of wrap-around work with the teachers who come to our institutes. We have, at this point, worked with over twenty thousand teachers, and we continue to work with them, bringing them back for additional training. Student success requires all-encompassing involvement at this teacher-education level. I work with six instructional specialists, and we have three institutes, an academy, and networking to attend to teacher in-service training across the State of New Jersey.

Products are very important to program success. If the teachers aren't able to attend institutes, then they have the opportunity to have other material such as handbooks, how-to manuals, resource guides, and recent publications at their disposal.

I saw a cartoon the other day with this caption: "Maybe this life isn't so bad for a first draft." I would say the same for our first effort at statewide assessment. In terms of proficiency and authenticity, we're chipping away at the proverbial tip of the iceberg. Truly authentic testing, within the context of what we know about our learning processes and where the social constructions of our human complexity are taking us, is a much bigger block of ice.

ANABEL NEWMAN (Indiana University):

I'm curious as to what has happened in terms of high-school graduation in your state, thinking particularly about the ethnic percentages, the numbers of people who may or may not be able to handle these tests. What's happening with them? What's the whole social outcome of what's going on?

BLOOM:

The social outcome, from all early indications has been a positive one. The teaching of writing and thinking skills is on the increase in New Jersey. Increasing numbers of teachers are training in the contemporary theories on these issues. Student achievement has been appreciating. All our impact studies indicate no increase in special education classifications, and *NO* increase in drop-out rates, and we have a relatively low one for an urban state—about 16% from high schools. We have had several safety nets— increased funding for remediation, SRA, multiple administrations while in high school, as well as after leaving high school— numerous programs focusing on improving schools, effective schools, and alternative school settings. We have put much money behind our efforts in assessment, accountability, and improved teaching and learning.

WARREN LEWIS (ERIC/RCS, Indiana University):

Someone asks if the results can be formulated in numbers and percents.

BLOOM:

I can give you numbers and percents on the current HSPT, 1986 exam because the first year of due-notice is happening right now for 1991 and the new eleventh grade. Of all the ninth-grade students who took the 1986 test, only 300 as seniors did not graduate and get a state-endorsed diploma. Ninety thousand students are our test population. For an urban, densely populated state, New Jersey has the highest passing grade. Remember that ninth-grade students have seven test opportunities because of twice-a-year testing in grades ten through twelve. In addition, these students receive targeted instruction.

ANABEL NEWMAN (Indiana University):

How much of your success do you attribute to the development of the test, and how much do you attribute to the change in the teaching staff?

BLOOM:

The test results in New Jersey are reported publicly. The reports have helped cause change. In addition, we have had our student support programs, our products, and our training. The training institutes are critically important to testing and student success. If I did assessment only, with the institutes, everything would fall apart, but it works because TEACHING, LEARNING, and ASSESSMENT are integrally tied both to each other and to successful student outcomes.

LARRY MIKULECKY:

Diane, earlier Jerry [Harste] talked about Whole Language setting the agenda. A part of that agenda involves integrating what's known about how language works, and how learning works, and involving stakeholders. Do you see what New Jersey is doing as doing what Jerry is asking for?

BLOOM:

I believe, in many ways, it is. I think that an assessment measure is but one component of an effective Whole Language setting. What is critical are the other parts of the paradigm: the retraining of our educators and the learning outcomes of our students. As I outlined in both my paper and presentation, the paradigm works because the stakeholders are students, parents, educators, and business leaders, and the learning outcomes are based on developmental learning theories and research models of curriculum and instruction.

ALTERNATIVE ASSESSMENT IN COLUMBUS, OHIO: WHAT WE'RE DOING NOW (NOT MUCH). WHAT WE'RE GOING TO BE DOING (A LOT MORE).

BERT WISER AND SHARON DORSEY

BERT WISER: When Roger [Farr] asked me to do this, he said he wanted the perspective of someone who is Director of Assessment & Testing in a major urban area. Coming from New York, I don't know that Columbus qualifies as a major urban area. [Laughter] I found out that my main qualification as a speaker today was that I live within driving range. [Laughter] Another factor that worked towards selecting me, I think, is that I come from the State of Ohio. Our license plate next year is going to read "The Testing State." [Laughter]

I've been asked by Sharon, who's going to share this presentation, to let you know that my views don't necessarily represent hers or the views of anybody else in assessment, including the State Education Department—*that* they know! [Laughter]

Now a few things to confess: I know you know that I'm a director of testing, but I've only been in that role for one year. Previously I worked for the Psychological Corporation. I did the full trip: I was in New York, Cleveland (which was the real test of loyalty, not being someone who likes clouds and rust). Then I was in Texas, and finally I'm back in Ohio, which is almost East. It's within driving distance of Shea Stadium. [Laughter]

Now I have to confess, too, that I'm a little more emotional speaking to you than I would have anticipated being, before I read some, or at least one, of the papers. I spent the last seven years supervising psychometric research on products like the Metropolitan and the Stanford and the Otis-Lennon. I thought that one of our purposes here was to encourage dialogue, but when I read something as one-sided and quasi-religious as to suggest that standardized

47

testing is morally bankrupt, is anachronistic, is biased—I hardly remember what else—I get the feeling that, unbeknownst to me, I was engaged for seven years in a Fascist enterprise. Normally I don't consider myself to be a member of the right wing—even with my proximity now to Cincinnati. In any event, that was the feeling that I had when I read one of these papers.

Now I know this is not the appropriate forum to talk about "The Magic of Item Response Theory and Everything We Can Learn from Objective Tests," so we won't go into that. I do find it necessary to say a few things about what I think is such a basic issue that it comes up in the most basic introductory classes. Roger touched on it, and that's the importance of reliability in measurement, and I don't think we should forget psychometric theory because none of us would want to take measurement out of testing.

Let me tell you a bit about the problems that one faces as a test director in a major city, none of which I knew about before I took the job. First of all, you have to deal with upper-level administration, and they look at test data often as a weapon to club principals. They want that bayonet so that they can fire the guys whose test scores are the lowest. I try to explain to them, then, that it's time for feedback, and that they should give the guy a chance to respond, and not just that he's "a walking dead man" (which is a quote I've heard). [Laughter]

I've heard reference made to the opinion that test developers today should be responsible for the misuse of their product—a "guns don't kill people, people kill people" kind of thing. Auto manufacturers face the problem that people don't know how they build their cars, but at least they know how to drive them. In testing, you have the problem that you're selling the product when people not only don't understand how they are made but also they often don't understand how to use them. I find this applies to many, many administrators, and they see testing as a gun. I expect that would be true whether or not it's an objective test or a norm-referenced test or CRT. Whatever you give them, that's the way they want to use it, so I feel my major responsibility—or one of them—is trying to stand in the way of that type of use of test results in Columbus.

Another problem is having to deal with the media and real estate agents. Real estate agents call and ask, "What building is number one?" and "What district is number one?" I tell them, just look and see who's got the highest income level, and you'll know. It's the mentality of "We're number one!" But that doesn't apply only in public schools. A lot of you people here work for a major university. You know about universities and employing professional sports teams so that the students can hold up their fingers and say, "We're number one!" The alums will send money in if they're #1, but not if they're number two. Granted, you don't do it in football here at IU, but in basketball. [Laughter]

How different is that from Little League fathers out there, yelling for their kids to win at all costs; and it's no different in the school systems. Constantly "buildings" want to know who's #1. What building is better than what other building? And is the district as good as the suburban districts which adjoin us? And what do they mean by "as good as?" They mean, "Are our test scores as high?" and of course they're not. Is the state as high as the state that adjoins us? That "Who's #1?" mentality happens to be the interest of the media and the people out there and the real estate agents that confront us, and that poses another real problem in dealing with the results.

Next problem is the state. The state requires ability and achievement testing, and I get blamed for that because all the teachers resent it; so I get calls: "How can you possibly be testing language with an objective test? Why are you giving us an ability test?" And I have to say, "Look, I wasn't here, I didn't vote for these guys. [Laughter] This is what's required. This is what we have to do." And worse yet, the results go in the newspaper. That's what places these principals totally under the gun, and you're back to the "Who's #1?" problem.

In addition to that, whatever we may implement in terms of portfolio testing, or whatever, if the results of the State ability and achievement testing and their high-school proficiency testing, which they started this year, go into the newspaper—and those are the results that determine the principals' jobs—that's what the teachers are going to teach to. So you face that problem dramatically.

We're finding that teachers don't want to teach grade four, a grade in which state testing is carried out. They're afraid that if their students screw up on the achievement test, their principal's going to be under the gun, and then *they'll* be under the gun.

The next problem I faced with the curriculum people was that I never knew how much they think that we are the devil incarnate. The best I could get was, "For someone from a test company, you're not that bad," or "If you're a test director, we can live with you"—stuff like that. An amazing thing—and this is actual—I overheard them talking about a person who is very famous in reading circles; someone said: "Yea, but I hear he's a behaviorist; he's got behaviorism in his background." As President Bush would say, "He's a card-carrying behaviorist." As an apostate Skinnerian, I thought that was rather amusing, that that would be considered a skeleton in somebody's closet. [Laughter]

But the most shocking thing to me is about the issue of reliability. I knew from before I left Psych Corp, from working with Roger [Farr] on a pilot of a product that he and Gene Jongsma were doing, that there are people out there who are trying to inject reliability into this performance assessment. I never realized that there were some people who regard reliabilty as the enemy!

I've looked at a writing assessment they were doing in Columbus, and they had an eight-point scale, only four of which were defined at all, and the four definitions were ambiguous. I said, "It can't be reliable." And when we looked at the data, the reliability was under that fourth point. And nobody thought it mattered! They said, "Well, it's good when people disagree." [Laughter] I said, "What do you do about a teacher who is scoring a paper that doesn't agree with anyone?" And they actually said, "Well, you can't throw them out; their ego is fragile." [Laughter] I said, "Well, then, send them to a therapist, but [Laughter] we can't have this score, and we can't have you scoring these papers."

I thought that it was an established issue that if a measurement is inconsistent with itself, it can't correlate with anything else. Little did I know, but I did find out, that not only do some of the curriculum people think that reliability is unnecessary but also they don't even see it as desirable. Mike [Beck] has been quoted many times today, and he's come up with a term that I like, "emerging reliability." Hopefully reliability will emerge down the road. [Laughter]

Now I have a new use for the Spearman-Brown. If you have an objective test with a .9 reliability, how many authentic items do you have to add to bring it down to .6? [Laughter] And, if you have a problem with high inter-rater reliability on objective tests, then we'll build randomized answer keys. Mike tells me he's already working on simulation studies in that area to see how we could diminish reliability in that way. In any event, this Christmas I'm sending our curriculum people rulers and licorice sticks, and we'll see how they react.

We do have a competency-based education program, and that's where assessment comes in. We're doing formative and summative assessments. Basically, in the formative, we have an objective test, but it ties into literary pieces in our literature-based text. (Not "reading passages." I learned that's like "cinema" compared to "movies.") [Laughter] Furthermore, we're going to have writing portfolios, and we do have a summative writing assessment.

I'll let Sharon talk to you about where we are and where we're going to go in assessment; and again let me repeat that my views should not in any way reflect on her.

SHARON DORSEY: Bert is a hard act to follow—which I always have to do! [Laughter]

First of all, I should tell you that I am a teacher—not a real, practicing teacher—but a teacher. I've been a teacher in the Columbus Public Schools for twenty-two years. I was a classroom teacher for nine years. I was a resource teacher in reading and language arts, and I developed, piloted, and implemented new curriculum in those areas. For the last six months, I've been working under Bert.

I was in curriculum to begin with, and when I realized they were going to dismantle totally the reading department that I was in, I felt that if I moved into assessment under Bert, I could have more impact on curriculum than any place else in the district—which is something of a statement. [Laughter]

In the next two-to-three years in Columbus, we're hoping to expand our alternative assessment in the area that Bert indicated in the competency-based education, with formative and summative assessments, because that's the area in which we can have alternative assessment that's guided by the state.

We hope in this area to expand the portfolios that I have outlined in my paper. We hope—as Roger Farr indicated earlier—that by expanding the portfolios, collecting information about students on a range of tasks and in a variety of contexts, and using several assessment tools continuously throughout the school year, that we're going to be providing teachers, administrators, and the community with a better picture of the growth in reading and writing.

Bert's told you that we already have a portfolio in writing that we will be implementing this year K-12. We would like in the next two-to-three years to expand that portfolio so that rather than containing the three components that it now does, it would contain five components. As outlined in the paper, the three components that the writing portfolio now contains are, first of all, writing samples, or what we call "work samples," that are gathered throughout the year.

Secondly, we have a self-evaluation, or self-assessment by the student of those writing samples.

Thirdly, we have a formative assessment that the teacher does. Teacher and student select two of those writing samples and do a district assessment on them, a district-developed rubric, the one Bert spoke of, that we are in the process of revising so that it gets better reliability. The teachers implement this assessment in the classroom, and the result becomes part of the students' portfolios. Those are the three components of the writing portfolio at present.

We would like to expand those three components and add two more components to develop a broader, better picture of the students' writing growth. The reading portfolio that we are now initiating will have these same three areas that are represented in the writing folder along with two new ones that we would like to add to both portfolios.

The two new areas we would like to add are a "teacher observation and assessment component" and an "outside-the-classroom component." We're getting at some of the same issues that have been covered here this morning with these two new components.

First of all, with the teacher observation and assessment, we are already providing for the teachers to add their judgment, their observation, and a variety of assessment tools to the district-developed assessment tool. I think most of us would agree, and from my perspective as a teacher I would argue, that teacher judgment is going to be there. It's inevitable, so I think we have to take teacher judgment and use it to help enlighten, along with the district evaluations and the state evaluations, to provide the best picture. So I think we need to provide for that in the portfolio.

The second component that we are planning to add is called "outside the classroom," and that brings in the social aspect that has been discussed this morning, namely, the parents and the community. The parents and the community need to be informed about what we're doing. We are looking at several different techniques to bring the parents into the portfolio process. We have looked at what's being done in Wisconsin in several school districts, and we like the idea of the student's reading to the parent at home, and the parent's recording that information, perhaps using a checklist provided by the school, so that there is some dialogue going on between the classroom teacher, the student, and the parent about the reading.

As a teacher and as a curriculum person, one of the questions that I have about the portfolios is this: Should there be two separate portfolios? We've talked about an integration of reading and writing, and it's a big question. We have State requirements in regards to reading and writing, so should we have two separate portfolios, or can we combine them?

Our philosophy for the Columbus school district includes an integrated curriculum, so the question of integrating the reading and the writing portfolios is a big question, and I can't answer it now. It will probably be answered over the course of the next two years by committees with teachers; then it will be implemented and piloted, and then decisions will be made.

A component already present in the writing portfolio that we would like to expand, is the self-evaluation. Everyone has said today how important it is that students self-evaluate. We do have a self-evaluation component in the writing portfolio, but I think that it is not at all adequate. If we want to accomplish one of the goals that Roger [Farr] pointed out at the beginning, that the students become monitors of their own reading and writing, then we need to expand this component much further.

There are about six considerations that I, as a teacher and as a curriculum person, deal with continually, and I will probably continue to ponder them over the next three years even more than I have in the past. First of all, what's the relationship of assessment to grading? For a teacher, that's a big question.

In our district we have an agreement in the regulations of the Board of Education, that during the grading period, which are formative assessments, district development is given in reading, writing, and mathematics—the three areas that we call our "compentency areas" in the State. By regulation, that assessement must count for at least 20% of the students' grade during that grading period. This decision was made after a lot of discussion, and there are a lot of people who have strong feelings pro or con about that decision, but it had to be made.

Next, we ponder the philosophy of reading/language-arts curriculum in the district. If we do indeed want assessment to be integrated with instruction, the curriculum is constantly changing. In the past ten years, we have been developing a portfolio that we will be putting in place this year. Yet we will institute a new curriculum and a new course of study this year. That suddenly throws some of the things that we have recently been developing out of line, and it's a constant chasing with each other to keep up.

All of you know that the same situation exists everywhere. There's research, there's instruction, there's assessment, and then there's all the rest, and they're all pulling at each other, and they are all at different points of advancement. So that is a problem.

The third consideration is the teacher's input. This summer I've spent six fast weeks developing a test which I know is not state-of-the-art, but because of the teachers' agreement with the Board of Education made last year, I've had very strict guidelines that I had to follow for unit-objective tests in reading. As someone said earlier, this was a result of teachers' feeling that perhaps if they didn't have control of assessment or some say in it, it might get out of control. If the teachers' union, which I think will have a larger part in the development of curriculum in our distict, continues to play a role, then teachers will have a way to feel comfortable with the type of assessment that is going into place—and that's another pull.

The district is committed, but it takes a long time—as I said, ten years—to develop some of these portfolios and the process orientation in writing. You have to have a superintendent or a curriculum person who is going to hang in there during that whole development. We've had three different curriculum people in reading/language arts, and this turnover has had an impact on what we've developed. We've had at least three different superintendents, too, and that keeps changing things.

I have already mentioned the importance of communication with parents and communities. State and national curriculum models will have a tremendous impact on what we're doing.

I spent the last year with the state committee developing a model curriculum that will be applied to every district in the State of Ohio, and districts will have to be "compared to it." We're not sure, and I think that the state is not yet quite sure, what the legislation means when it says we have to be "compared to it." Depending on how that comparison works, it may have a tremendous impact.

One of the components of that state curriculum is an assessment component. It has been greatly debated in the reading and language-arts areas. I cannot tell you the anxiety, the frustration, and the arguments on a major state scale that have been going on in quiet ways over the last nine months, and will continue to go on, to develop that model assessment component.

Those are my concerns as a teacher, as an assessment person, as a curriculum person.

MARILYN BINKLEY (National Center for Education Statistics, U.S. Department of Education):

Assuming that you can meet Bert's requirement for reliability from time to time within the individual, and across individuals, and across raters—we'll assume that it's all there—you now have a portfolio, which in fact reflects what you believe curriculum and instruction should be about. Could you please describe to me how you will report on that to the public or to the state people in a way that I can use the information?

DORSEY:

I'll use Jerry's [Harste] answer: "That's a good question." I have not gotten an answer for that yet. I have mulled it over in my mind a great deal. I don't want to reduce it to one score or one digit. I don't think one can do that, and I think that's where the education of parents has to come in. I think we have to draw them in and have them work with us as we're working on the portfolio. I think there might have to be a rubric for the portfolio that would be used as well as a rubric for individual components of the portfolio.

BINKLEY:

I think you can communicate easily with the parents because you were talking about one person, a child that you share. But now I'm also talking about communicating to the State House. A lot of people who sit in the State House don't care about one little Johnny: they care about *all* the Johnnies. Tell me, how are you going to do that? And I don't mean just you. I mean more globally.

DORSEY:

"The State House" means many things to me. In Ohio, we have an Ohio Department of Education, to which we have to report our ability and achievement tests and our CBE summative testing, and where intervention has to be done. We have certain guidelines that the state has given us under their legislation according to which we must report. That would be one component of the portfolio. That's the only component the state

55

is asking for at this time, along with some other data. Is that what you're asking?

BINKLEY:

It seems to me that if you put in your rubric as one component along with the standardized tests, then, of course, you've aggregated a single score at that point. Now you have wiped out the purpose of the portfolios in some way.

DORSEY:

That's true.

BINKLEY:

What I'm looking for is some way that we can take to the State House in meaningful ways the richness of the portfolio, or the richness of the case study, the writing sample that Jerry [Harste] put up on the screen. Psychometrics and the notion of anchoring scaled scores to behaviors that are understood, those are attempts to describe the kinds of behaviors that we want to represent. What exists may not be the best mode. I'd like to explore how we can get portfolios communicated better.

DORSEY:

I think you have an excellent point. When I was talking about different components at the State House, or the state level, I was thinking of the legislators as one of those components because they enacted the legislation that asked for just certain information to be reported. As you said, that's just one narrow part of that total picture that we're trying to draw of the students' growth in reading and writing.

I think we have an obligation to educate the legislators who write these laws. We have been working in the past two years since the legislation was enacted. We are trying to do something similar to what Michigan did. Three or four literacy groups have been organized in the state, made up of the top researchers in the universities in the State of Ohio, to do just that: start talking to legislators about what we believe is good instruction and good assessment. That may, we hope, have an impact, but it's just a beginning; and it's not a total answer to your question.

There's also another component at the state level that I have learned about tremendously in the last year while I have been working on the state curriculum, and that is the State Board of Education. The State Board of Education is very powerful. They are the ones who appoint a superintendent of the State of Ohio schools. We are working to develop a dialogue with the State Board so that they too can begin to understand some of the research and some of the literacy beliefs in the state.

MARTHA NYIKOS (Indiana University):

I'm very glad that you brought up the question of teacher judgment. I have two issues that I'd like to bring up in connection with that. Number one being this: Most teachers will probably get most of their direction for teaching through looking at tests and what they are trying to assess.

In relation to that, the other question is this: What role do teachers have—and how do we promote their ability to do it—to teach metacognitive judgments to their students? This is especially critical because many teachers themselves have not taken that kind of reflective position. Many teachers have not yet figured out that they should also think metacognitively about their teaching, being able to step back and notice what's going on in terms of judging the classroom behaviors as well as what their students are doing. In trying to promote the idea of teaching learner strategies in the classroom, many times teachers are not able to make the conceptual switch or shift to being able themselves to promote learner strategies.

DORSEY:

That's another good question. I'd say the key is in-service [training]. It has to be in-service. Diane [Bloom] talked about in-service with a five-day model. When we did the first reading/writing models in the middle-school language-arts classroom, we started out with a five-day model. It wasn't nearly enough. The two-year wrap-around that you were talking about is a minimum because we have such turnover. We have 4,500 teachers in the district, and there's a tremendous turnover. Once we've trained a group of teachers, sometimes half of those people are gone the next year, so that we have to keep training continually through in-service, through modeling. We're setting up what we call a "consulting teacher" plan in the district. We have to have teachers in the classroom to model for other teachers. We have to have teachers supporting other teachers. But it doesn't happen overnight. Two years is a short time.

ROUNDTABLE DISCUSSION

WARREN LEWIS:

I exercise the prerogative of the chair to ask the first question. Professor Farr, in what way do you conceive Professor Harste to misunderstand your position? And following that, Professor Harste, in what way do you conceive Professor Farr to misunderstand your position?

ROGER FARR:

The ideas that we're talking about both in assessment and language instruction are not new. I wrote a book[*] in 1967, calling for a wide variety of samples of assessment and arguing that we needed to be gathering other kinds of information—and so had a heck of a lot of other people before I did. These kinds of changes would have been going on if we had never invented the word "Whole Language."

I don't believe that Whole Language has "set the agenda." I think that the real problem is not what Jerry [Harste] has said (although I don't understand all of what he is saying—I admit that; I just *don't* understand all of what he's saying). He started out by saying that "we have set the agenda." Now, those of you with special name cards, you're Whole Language, and the rest of us aren't—it's a "we" and a "they" issue. [Laughter. People in the

---

[*]Roger Farr, *Reading: What Can Be Measured?* (Newark, Delaware: IRA and ERIC/CRIER, Indiana University, 1969).

audience check to see if their name cards are special.] Naw, I'm only makin' that up! [Laughter]

But it becomes a "we" and "they" issue, and it becomes a straw-man, it becomes an attack, rather than trying to have a dialogue to improve things. I don't think Jerry wants to have a dialogue. I think he wants to have a debate, and I'd love to have a debate, but he won't do that with me. I don't think it's a misunderstanding of the position, although I think he doesn't understand some things about the politics of assessment. I think it really is this whole business of setting up a dog fight—and that'd be OK, if that's what we want to do, but I don't think that's going to help at all, and I don't think it's new.

JEROME HARSTE:

That's the difference that I have with Roger, in that he *doesn't* think it's new. We know from schema theory, even, that we tend to assimilate new things in terms of our old schemas without really addressing the new issues. I think there are some fundamentally different asumptions underlying his position and mine, and I think we need to learn how to talk about those. But I think that it's a really dangerous stance for a learner to take the position that there's nothing new.

JERRY JOHNS (Northern Illinois University):

Kaye and Bill, you're co-authors on these papers with Jerry and Roger. I would be very interested in your perceptions relative to the different positions that seem to be taken here. Is there a way out of the woods? [Laughter]

[Bill Bintz genteelly indicates a "ladies first" stance; Kaye Lowe says, "*Thanks*, Bill!" (Laughter)]

KAYE LOWE:

I sort of feel that I was stuck in the middle between Roger and Harste, and at times that has caused me great stress. It *is* a matter of conversation; whereas we don't sit down and talk about where we're going, we do sit down and have the fight—we're never going to go anywhere. I came to a lot of understandings in having my conversations with Roger, so I think that I don't need to agree with everything he says, but that I need to listen to what he is saying. I think this is an opportunity for us to go somewhere, if we'll only take the time listen to one another.

BILL BINTZ:

I'm not so sure what "out of the woods" you're speaking about, Jerry, and in some respects I'm not so sure I want to be out of the woods. I think when Roger says that we're somewhat unaware of, or naive about, the political situations, that's precisely the thing that got me started into assessment. I realized that what I believe is a political issue and must be seen in a political perspective. The political aspect is a concern I have.

As I believe in what Jerry [Harste] was saying earlier from a Whole Language perspective, in the "child as informant," then I also want to say that teachers are informants. Yet, much of what I hear in conferences pays only token attention to teachers as informants. The "way out of the woods" may be to establish the kinds of relationships with others that we try to create with students in classrooms: namely, we need to privilege teachers and principals and state legislators and national leaders as informants, so that we build a community of informants. The way out of the woods is through conversations wherein we break down the hierarchical, and engage instead in a dialogic process. But I don't see a lot of that going on now.

GENE MAEROFF (Carnegie Foundation for the Advancement of Teaching):

On the issue of portfolios, let's talk about assessment in terms of its serving a monitoring need—accountability or, if you want, use the word "responsibility." Take portfolios beyond the individual level, let's say, for monitoring schools, school districts, and states. How can portfolios be used as an alternative method of assessment beyond the individual level?

SHARON DORSEY:

I'm not sure. I'm really not sure. I think the question is about how to use portfolios to report to the state. The state has only asked for certain things. I think we have to communicate what we feel is the broader picture in the classroom before people are going to understand what a true portfolio means. There are only a few parents now that understand what portfolios mean, and there are a limited number of teachers that understand what a portfolio means. We have to broaden the communication, broaden the knowledge about portfolios to begin with.

KAYE LOWE:

I agree with what you're saying. In Australia last year, the government decided to mandate testing for grades three and six. The parents had the right to withdraw their children, which became a really active way of showing the government that they weren't in favor of standardized testing. In the same way, the Catholic school system refused to administer the test. I think it *is* a matter of getting out there and educating the public, and getting them really to ask questions to be informed rather than just to get what we happen to be giving them.

DIANE BLOOM:

I began my presentation by saying that state policies inform assessment, and assessment can inform state policy. I'm not so sure that the legislators tell you what it is specifically that they want in terms of reporting. In New Jersey, my experience has been that we had to find the best ways to inform the legislators when what they wanted to know was how well our children were doing; and to do that task, if we chose to use a portfolio measure, then—as you've all indicated—we had to educate the individuals who would be using that information.

I think that you cannot exclude portfolio; I just think you need to think about when it should be used. For example, the open portfolio method is used in New Jersey in the senior year, that is, after the student has had multiple opportunities to take the graduation exam, and multiple observations have been given of a student's ability to sustain written discourse as well as to apply knowledge and work an analysis in a given task as a critical reader. By looking at the portfolio in the student's senior year, we counter the effects of test anxiety. Students do not necessarily perform well when they're having to write an exam, so when we look at the portfolio, it opens up a large range of information collected across the subject areas. At that point in time, the decision to endorse a student for graduation is made on the basis of collective decisions in addition to the observations—a ninth-grader could have had as many as nine observations of his or her writing on demand.

GENE MAEROFF:

That's still individual, though. Using the "takeover of Jersey City" as an example, was there anything that looking at portfolios could have done to provide guidelines to enable one to make a statement about the utter failure of education in Princeton and Jersey City?

DIANE BLOOM:

The "utter failure" was not based on an isolated piece of information that might have been found in a portfolio. The takeover at Jersey City, as you know as a Jerseyite, was much more multifaceted.

GENE MAEROFF:

Yes, I know all that. But how could portfolios have figured in that in a monitoring function?

DIANE BLOOM:

It can work in a monitoring function.

GENE MAEROFF:

How?

DIANE BLOOM:

Well, I'll leave that to Roger Farr and Jerome Harste... [Laughter] because they...

GENE MAEROFF:

They'll screw it up for you! [Laughter]

DIANE BLOOM:

...because you're absolutely right in what you're asking: What you are asking is, if we need to quantify information, how do we quantify it?

[Farr and Harste both speak at once.]

JEROME HARSTE:

It seems to me that one of the things that a portfolio yields is a description of the kinds of engagements that the kids are involved in, without setting up an outside standard to the effect that "This is the quality and the variety of engagement a kid should have." By looking into portfolios, people can begin to see the kinds of things that kids can do, and then they can say, "I don't like that; I want them to be more critically involved; this isn't good enough." Then we can begin a dialogue there. I see portfolios not as a means of prioritizing standards for everybody else, but as a vehicle for starting the kinds of conversations with parents, the community, state legislators, and educators, about what education might be. Use them as a vehicle for dialogue.

ROGER FARR:

You gotta have *some* stuff in which you have standards, and you have a task for a kid to do. There are things we're going to have to do in life: We're going to have to read a driver's manual and the editorial in the newspaper, and write a letter to an editor. So I think having some criteria is good. I also think that having kids do free-writing and free-response and "construct their own boxes" is very important. I think putting those things together in a manila folder, we now call "portfolios," and taking a look at them will help instruction, will inform instruction. I also think they will inform administrators.

I think you can do some summary tasks with them, but when you do that, what happens to them will depend on how high you make the stakes, how important the decision is. If portfolios are used as a basis for evaluating the school, they'll cheat. They'll stuff them full of crap, er, stuff, and they'll have all kinds of things going on. There's no question that those portfolios will become an absurdity. At Miami University of Ohio, they now have you submit a portfolio, but they require you to submit a letter from one of your English teachers verifying that all of the things in there were really done by you under certain conditions. What nonsense is that?

GENE MAEROFF:

That's a good point. In Great Britain, where portfolios are widely used, it's not high-stakes, so the student can go from secondary school to an employer and say, "Here's my portfolio." An American looking at that would think, "Well, why wouldn't the kid be putting all this-and-that in there?" The answer is because it's not high-stakes, and they don't regard it that way.

ROGER FARR:

If it's a school-leaving test?

GENE MAEROFF:

I would suggest to people interested in the tyranny of norm-referenced standardized tests and driving curriculum in adverse ways, that they have to start thinking in more substantial ways about how some of the alternatives can be used in a monitoring sense because monitoring isn't going to go away, and maybe it shouldn't go away. There have to be other measures that can be presented to policy-makers in ways similar to the way we use traditional tests.

DIANE BLOOM:

They currently are doing that in New Jersey. The whole monitoring process that I described looks at a full, composite picture of the program that the students have performed, whether it be reading, mathematics, or writing across the subject/ discipline areas.

GENE MAEROFF:

I think the commentary on the monitoring aspect of testing in New Jersey is pretty much taken care of with the fact that only three hundred people failed out of about sixty thousand in districts like Jersey City, Camden, Newark, Patterson, and the rest. So something isn't quite going on there that ought to be.

DIANE BLOOM:

But that's why they're monitoring.

BERT WISER:

I agree with Roger's point of bringing in John Cannell to sober up portfolio assessment. I sat shocked at meetings in Ohio, hearing test directors from large districts bragging about xeroxing copies of standardized tests and giving them to the curriculum people to teach from. Well, what's going to happen if you put those same people in a situation where portfolios will become the high-stakes measurement? They're clever enough to dummy those up, too. So switching from objective tests to portfolios will not in any way take away from the problem of cheating or people trying to magnify the results of their district. I'm sure that when Cannell learns of these techniques, he'll make some comment on that.

JERRY JOHNS:

As a pre-perspective on portfolios, I brought along to this conference a survey among professionals. [See Addendum.] At least in the United States, portfolios seem to be a fairly new device. I surveyed over one hundred professionals attending a summer reading conference. While they agree with some of the philosophical underpinnings of the uses of portfolio in assessment, their knowledge is woefully inadequate, and they sense quite a number of problems in the potential use of portfolios. So, when we talk about communication and portfolios, we must probably first begin by communicating within our profession, then the public, then the legislative bodies and far beyond.

It's a fairly new thing. "Portfolio" is a term that we're tossing around here with a fair amount of assumptiveness, that is, that we think we know what portfolios are. Before the day is over, I'd like to get a clarification on what we mean by "portfolios" and "performance assessment."

LARRY MIKULECKY:

It seems to me that an awful lot of the testing that engendered this conference and is engendering others in almost every state that I've been in, has to do with the fact that education has more stakeholders than ever before. I do a lot of work with the Department of Labor; they're interested. More than parents, more than teachers, more than State Houses, there are lots and lots of people who are now interested in education.

At the last Department of Labor meeting I attended, I suggested that teacher judgment probably serves as well as most other indicators of how somebody performs, and it's a lot cheaper. The response was, "Sure! I'm going to trust the judgment of a teacher in Chicago that a kid can perform well in a job?" There was similar distrust for Jersey and the school districts that Boston University is taking over.

I think the reason that testing and assessment in the United States is receiving so much pressure is that there is a lack of trust that there's anybody responsibly monitoring and making judgments about who can and cannot do things. Until an assessment conference, or until Education, deals with the fact that there is a lot of performance that's not very good, there will be good reason for the lack of trust.

Three hundred out of ninety thousand isn't a good way to monitor it, although it's a start. Saying that teacher judgment works, when in many cases it seems clear to stakeholders that it doesn't—until those issues of trust about judgment are dealt with, I think that these in-house issues are not going to communicate to the audiences.

To send it back in as a question, how does assessment deal with the fact that the range of stakeholders is broader than ever before, and that by and large they don't *trust* the people who are providing the education?

DIANE BLOOM:

Could you go back to your point about the three hundred?

LARRY MIKULECKY:

I thought that there were three hundred students out of a potential ninety thousand who were monitored as not having performed. That was my understanding from your presentation.

DIANE BLOOM:

Ninety thousand students took the test in 1986; in 1986, fifteen thousand failed. Over the four-year time period during which they took multiple reassessments, many of them passed, and of those that passed we were left with three hundred at the end who were not awarded their diploma, whether because of the reading test, the math test, or the writing test. Other local requirements factored in included attendance, course requirements, and so on.

LARRY MIKULECKY:

A lot of the stakeholders would suspect that more than one percent, though, are having difficulty. They don't trust monitoring systems or judgments that tell them things that don't match their own experiences.

Because the range of stakeholders is broader than ever before, the issue of how Education and educators are to communicate at the state level or the school-district level or at the policy level with the federal government, is critical. This question has come up today at least a half-dozen times in one guise or another, but it hasn't been really addressed.

DIANE BLOOM:

I think it's a shame that we don't feel more positive about the successes after four years. I think it's a shame that educators are quick to point their fingers and say, "Aha, you're not really doing a good job because three *hundred* kids out of ninety thousand did not graduate. There surely were more than that!"

We do ourselves a disservice. If there is a monitoring, if there is a check and balance, if you communicate, if those checks and balances are in place, those things do happen. We ourselves are suspect at the state level, so we research, and we go back, and we ask again, and we check again. At some point, you have to accept the data and continue to follow the data and continue to work toward success. But I think sometimes we are our own worst enemies.

ROGER FARR:

Nurturing and gatekeeping don't go together very well. University faculties have the same problem: You help the faculty member, you work with them, and all of a sudden you've got to decide whether they get promoted and tenure. Same thing in the high school—and we're happier if more people fail, and yet we're in a nurturing profession. It just doesn't work very well. I think that's the real problem.

DIANE BLOOM:

That's right.

BILL BINTZ:

Larry, to try and get to your question about trust, I think as long as assessment continues to be a process of verification of predetermined skills *versus* any meaningful engagement, any instance of inquiry for people, I don't think any trust is possible because the stakes are too high. Much along the same lines, until teachers as researchers can feel that they are researchers themselves, enquirers into their own classrooms instead of verifying somebody else's knowledge, teacher-as-researcher won't work, just as alternative assessment won't work. The pressure that teachers feel to be accountable with assessment is in many ways passed on through lots of different messages, subtle and nonsubtle, to kids who also feel that the stakes are high with portfolios. That, in turn, engenders putting stuff in portfolios that verifies what somebody else wants to see.

When assessment is addressed exclusively as a methological issue, as is often the case, instead of broadening the issue out to philosophical and epistemological issues, we cannot use assessment as a means to knowing more than what we currently, already know. That's the challenge for teachers—to use assessment as a way of knowing, but they are not given that opportunity in the classrooms to outgrow their present selves. Until that happens, what you describe in terms of trust will never come about. Teachers will never feel that they can trust their own judgments in their own classrooms until they can use their own professional hunches, their intuitive judgments, to make decisions about kids and about themselves.

FRED FINCH (Riverside Publishing Company):

My concern was reflected by the last speaker, who felt that this is a methodological issue that we should broaden into a philosophical issue, and I almost heard you saying "religious" issue. The danger with portfolios is that we may get to the point of discussing how many angels can dance on the head of this pin. A portfolio is something you put things into. We shouldn't get too complex with it.

I'm not trying to peddle anything, but [he holds up a special folder] we have here an example of a portfolio that has been developed with instructions for using the portfolio, with places for the kids' reading logs, and so forth. This is what a portfolio looks like in our definition. If you think it's great, fine; if you think it's awful, then suggest how we can change it. This portfolio was developed for a portfolio program with a description of how teachers should use it. There's a copy on the display table, and I invite you to look at it. If you're intrigued, then you can pick up this marketing piece which we also have, [Laughter] which only *looks* like a portfolio.

WARREN LEWIS:

Any response to this crass commercialism? [Laughter]

DIANE BLOOM:

In America we call it "portfolio"; in England, Dixon and Strata call it an "exemplar folder," so maybe that's what you have.

ROGER FARR:

In Buffalo, New York, we called them "manila folders." [Laughter]

ALTERNATIVE ASSESSMENT IN LANGUAGE ARTS

ROGER FARR, Indiana University, USA
KAYE LOWE, University of Wollongong, Australia

THE CONTEXT FOR CHANGE

As we consider the development of alternative forms of language-arts assessment, we need to understand the context from which these new developments have emerged, and we need to be aware of the national context in which new assessments must survive. This litany is not new to anyone who has been involved with educational assessment; however, if we are to see alternative forms of assessment flourish—and we have no doubts that alternative forms of assessment are an essential part of the movement to improve language arts instruction—then we need to consider the setting in which assessment takes place.

The national situation is one in which concern over assessment is debated in professional publications, public newspapers, and legislative halls. The apprehension over testing is ideologically based and results in disagreements about issues such as the interpretation and misinterpretation of test scores, the format and content of tests, the focus of literacy assessment, and whether traditional assessment serves any useful purpose.

The mass testing movement has been accelerated in the United States by the basic assumptions that teachers, schools, and school systems need to be held accountable; that learning is finite and can be measured; and that public school education is inefficient. Displeasure with education, particularly literacy education, is growing in the general public.

This is not a new concern. Indeed, when broad-scale testing was first established in the United States in the early 20th century, tests were used to evaluate the effectiveness of schools. As they are today, test results were often used as the sole criterion by which to judge the worth of the schools. The beginning of the widespread use of tests in schools in the decade from 1910 to 1920 was related to the so-called "scientific movement" in education. The scientific movement was an attempt to apply the techniques of the hard sciences for the benefit of education.

As demands for accountability in education have grown "high-stakes," so has the administration of tests. Accountability is often used in decision-making in education. High-stakes decision-making refers to decisions that carry significant consequences, including the determination of teachers' salaries, student graduation or promotion, and college admission. Testing takes on greater importance as the importance of the decisions based on the tests increases. If tests were of little consequence, they would not draw much attention. Test results are deemed to be significant indicators of school quality, teacher competence, and student achievement. Moreover, the curriculum is bound by test preparation. Tests tend to define what is taught, how it is taught, and what is judged to be important.

As accountability has grown, so also have the fears of curriculum specialists in language arts grown that the tests are driving instruction to an ever narrower focus. The development of the concept of test-driven instruction is well documented in the literature.

A sorry state of affairs exists in language-arts assessment. Legislators and the public demand literacy test scores against which they can measure the return on their education tax dollars, while teachers and curriculum leaders cry that present tests do not reflect the true goals of literacy development—that the tests measure only the students' ability to "do" the test. At the same time, school administrators worry that their schools are judged inadequate by narrowly defined assessments. More importantly, the confusion over what should be assessed seems to obscure the most important reason we ought to be using any form of literacy assessment. *That reason is that the information we collect ought to help us improve literacy instruction for students in our schools, not narrow the curriculum to what can be measured.* The chaos regarding reading and writing assessment has resulted in simultaneous demands for more testing, a ban on all testing, the development of new tests, and both major and minor revisions of present assessments.

Another impetus in the drive to modify literacy assessment is the view of the leaders in whole language/integrated language arts curriculum development. They contend that significant changes in education are being hampered by the continued use of invalid language-arts tests. They argue that present testing is not only based on out-of-date concepts of literacy but also that it is based on outmoded concepts of education. Many language-arts curriculum leaders, school administrators, and teachers who have examined the use of traditional language-arts tests have concluded that these traditional modes of assessment are unable to meet the contradictory demands placed on them. Changes are needed in how literacy is assessed, but the changes must be based on careful consideration of the purpose that literacy assessment ought to serve. The quality of literacy learning in our schools will not improve if we merely critique existing tests—and then set out quickly modifying, extending, refining, or replacing the tests that are currently in use. We need first to consider the purpose of testing.

PURPOSES FOR ASSESSING LANGUAGE ARTS

Why test? Until we can satisfactorily answer this question, we will only continue to develop inappropriate assessment instruments. The focus on the purpose of assessment provides us with the opportunity to consider the goals of literacy education. We believe that three primary assessment objectives ought to guide our assessment efforts:

- Language-arts assessment must inform both teachers and administrators about literacy learning by integrating both process and product information.

- Language-arts assessment must inform instruction.

- Language-arts assessment must support students as active participants in self-evaluation.

Objective 1: Language-Arts Assessments Must Inform Both Teachers and Administrators about Literacy Learning by Integrating Both Process and Product Information.

Traditional language-arts tests have focused only on the *products* of learning and have provided almost no information about language *processes*—about how students go about their literacy tasks. Furthermore, because a test only tests for what is included on the test, teachers tend to focus on teaching test content rather than attempting to determine what students know and understand about language, and what they want to know. Traditional tests have separated product and process.

71

Separating process and product does not provide a meaningful description of literacy development; neither is it useful in providing teachers with information to plan instruction. This separation causes teachers to be concerned that the processes they are teaching are not reflected in the products that are being assessed. The result is informal, classroom assessment that looks very different from the formal tests.

Some educators have suggested that this is as it should be: that process and product should be treated as separate, and that we should use different tests—or at least different assessment strategies—to learn about each. This disjointed approach will fail for the following reasons:

Teachers and administrators will continue to emphasize the content of the formal tests, if those are the test scores that determine accountability; process will be forgotten.

Process can only inform instructional decisions if it is related to the products that are the result of those processes. It is through the construction of products that a student demonstrates the necessary processes to construct the product. Product and process assessment must be integrated.

Language-arts assessment must bring product and process assessment together. What we honor as evidence of learning must also provide the information for classroom teachers to plan instruction. Process assessment and product assessment must be based on the same activities.

Administrators will continue to expect test information that will inform them about how well the school system is doing in producing literate citizens, whereas teachers will seek information that will help them plan effective instruction. It is our contention that both administrators and teachers should be concerned with what students know and understand about literacy, how they apply their knowledge—and how well they learn. Thus, it makes sense to develop a single assessment focus that unites product and process.

Traditional assessments of literacy have never been totally satisfactory measures of students' literacy achievements. The tests have provided little information about students' attitudes about reading and writing, literacy habits, reading and writing strategies, or their development as independent learners. In addition, test results have generally been based on the administration of a single assessment, at a single moment in time, and under a single specific set of conditions. The traditional tests have informed us about too little and in too circumscribed a manner. Indeed, the focus on achieving higher scores on tests has caused teachers to focus on teaching the content of the tests, with little attention to the assessment of how students are developing as literate individuals. In addition, traditional tests are totally inadequate when it comes to assessing process.

If we are to plan instruction effectively, assessment must be integral to classroom instruction. It should not be seen only as an end product, that is, something administered at the end of content units to see how effectively content has been learned. A meaningful assessment program is ongoing and enables the teacher to make informed curriculum decisions for each student. Making teachers accountable means giving them back responsibility for assessment, a responsibility that has over the years moved away from teacher control and into the hands of administrators armed with machine-scored tests. Significant change in language-arts education is dependent on returning the responsibility for assessment to classroom teachers.

We conclude that language-arts assessment needs to combine both product assessment and process assessment in one because product and process ought not to be separated. Teachers and administrators alike must look to the same information source to determine the literacy development and needs of students.

Objective 2: Language-Arts Assessments Must Inform Instruction.

Over the decades, the assessment of literacy has not kept pace with our understanding of reading and writing. Our concepts of assessment continue to be based on a deductive approach to assessment in which the products of education are seen primarily as single test scores with pre-determined right and wrong answers. Moreover, it has been assumed that respectable assessment must be conducted under timed conditions, forbidding examinees to use the resources that are a normal part of literacy activities.

Traditional tests have been based on an approach to learning that makes only limited connection between assessment and instruction. If we are to provide teachers and administrators with relevant and meaningful information about their students' competencies, five major validity issues must be of concern:

1. Language arts must be integrated.

Reading and writing are not alternative language behaviors, nor are they opposite sides of the same coin. The thinking strategies involved in reading are the same as those involved in writing. The key behavior underlying both reading and writing is the construction of meaning. We know that both reading and writing necessitate the use of background information, the ability to make predictions, the revision of developing concepts, and a clear focus on purpose. As long as we continue to assess reading and writing as separate behaviors, they will be taught separately, and students will not make the connections that are so vital to both aspects of literate achievement.

2. Assessment must be conducted in the context of real reading and real writing.

Traditional language-arts tests are decontextualized, artificial, and fragmented. The test tasks are often separated into meaningless sub-skills; the use of references is prohibited; revision is usually not possible; and we ask students merely to identify pre-determined correct answers. We need to develop assessments that assess what students know about language and how they apply their knowledge. The use of resources, the opportunity to revise, the delivery of meaningful texts, and the development of alternative answers are important ingredients of instruction. They ought also, therefore, to be essential aspects of assessment.

The means of assessment that we develop must center on realistic reading and writing tasks. The tests must also present students with tasks that have both face and content validity resembling the real-world literacy tasks that students are expected to accomplish. The tasks must be total activities—not fragmented sets of behaviors, and they must provide students with an opportunity to be self-selective. Assessment must consider a student's ability to solve problems inventively and make decisions for which no specific guidelines are given, as well as responding to tasks for which there are pre-determined requirements.

3. Assessment must be ongoing, so that multiple forms and many stages of assessment are possible.

Literacy is a complex behavior. Various elements influence how well a student reads and writes. Why a certain task is being done, how the student feels about the topic, the materials available to complete the task, the student's general mental and physical health at the time, and how the student views himself or herself as a reader and writer—all these factors influence literacy performance. The variety of genres that are read and written is great, and various tasks necessitate bringing those genres together in different combinations. For these reasons, assessments need to be ongoing, include a variety of activities, and be conducted under diverse conditions, if we are to learn anything useful about a student's literacy development.

4. Assessment must be based on a student's own insights about his or her own literacy development.

With traditional tests, if we want to learn about literacy strategies, we are forced to make inferences from the test products. Alternative assessments need to be developed so that the student is seen as a reliable informant about his or her own literacy development. The explanations that students provide are a valuable source of information that are totally ignored by traditional tests.

5. Assessment must provide students with opportunities to respond in a variety of ways.

Traditional tests demand right answers. Yet, our logic and our teaching alike tell us that alternative ways of responding may be equally valid, and that these alternatives are more important in education than mere "right answers." We want to foster conditions in which students make their own decisions, construct alternative means of responding, rather than seeking right answers.

Traditional multiple-choice tests seldom ask for personal reactions and feelings, and yet one of the major goals of literacy education is to help students develop their own reactions and thoughts about what they read and write. The challenge before us is to construct assessment instruments that honor both the "public" responses to information in a text upon which one might expect ordinary agreement among readers, and "private" responses, those reader-based, emotive reactions that tend to be more individualistic.

These five validity issues demand that we examine the ways in which language-arts assessment is currently defined. Language-arts assessment must become an integral, continuing part of instruction, that focuses on what we actually intend to teach.

Objective 3: Language-Arts Assessment Must Support Students as Active Participants in Self-Evaluation

Traditional evaluation has enabled us to make decisions about a student's competencies but only from our external perspective. In the past, we have distanced ourselves from the learner, and focused on what was to be learned. Opportunities for establishing what the learner knows and understands about him/herself as a learner were minimal. To remedy this situation, alternative assessment must be redefined as an opportunity for the learner to be heard and respected. This approach encourages learners to be reflective about their own efforts. When assessment acknowledges what a learner knows, the learner is more inclined to assume responsibility for improvement. Together, students and teachers can become informed decision makers about future instruction.

In order to promote self-reflection, teachers must appreciate the importance of both teacher/student and peer conferencing. Ample opportunities must be provided for students to articulate and discuss their beliefs, understandings, and interests in reading and writing activities.

If students are to be active participants, they must be made to feel that their opinions are valued and respected. The role of teacher is that of co-learner. The teacher should not be viewed as the font of all knowledge but rather as a collaborator whose mission it is to promote high-quality literacy-learning for all students.

Self-evaluation encourages students to be informed and active decision makers in their own literacy development. It provides an opportunity for students to reflect on their learning in progress.

DEVELOPING ALTERNATIVE ASSESSMENTS

Merely identifying the issues that demand reform does not alleviate the present testing dilemma. Our next step must be to identify alternative assessment strategies that overcome or replace what we find to be disturbing and unsatisfactory. These alternative assessments must respond to the three major objectives for language-arts assessment that we identified earlier in this paper. That is, assessment measures must inform teachers and administrators by integrating process and product information, they must inform teachers and administrators about relevant and meaningful literacy performance, and they must involve students themselves in defining the assessment so that students become reflective about their own literacy development.

Traditional assessment has neither met those goals, nor was it developed in order to meet those goals. In general, traditional language-arts assessment has been narrowly defined, product-oriented, and based on a behaviorist model of learning. Language-arts assessment must be broadly re-defined as the collection, review, and interpretation of information for the purpose of making decisions. This definition and the issues already outlined means that the methods of assessment we propose must be radically different from those currently associated with standardized testing.

High-quality assessment can result from a collaboration between the student and the teacher. Product, performance, and process are isolated and meaningless factors of assessment, unless the student is given ample opportunities to discuss, clarify, explain, and reflect on the effort involved. Collaboration enables a teacher to understand better the knowledge and insights of students, to extend students' knowledge and understanding of the reading and writing processes, and to set instructional priorities.

Portfolios provide one means to meet the objectives of language arts assessment.

Portfolios are too often touted as the panacea to our assessment woes—the means by which teachers and students can cooperatively plan to improve instruction. We support the use of portfolios, too, but we register a caveat. If portfolios are simply defined as nothing more than collections of work stored in folders over a period of time, then they are of little value either to students or teachers. To be of use to both, careful consideration needs to be given to what goes into a portfolio, the process of selection, and how the information is to be used. If this is not done, then the portfolio becomes unmanageable; it may be little more than a resource file.

A portfolio is a collection of artifacts purposefully selected from a variety of reading and writing contexts. The literacy artifacts are representative of the developing knowledge and underlying competencies of the student/learner being examined. A portfolio consists of components that demonstrate the changing and emerging role of the learner. Each piece of information is relevant and meaningful, and it helps to present a picture of how an individual student operates as a reader and writer.

The portfolio is a record of the student's strengths—the skills and strategies the student has used. A student's portfolio is an opportunity and basis for the teacher's or a peer's constructive feedback. Assessment of a portfolio yields information on the basis of which individual needs can be identified.

When portfolios are developed over an extended time period as an integral part of classroom instruction, they are valuable for planning both within the classroom and on a school-wide basis. When information is gathered consistently, the teacher is able to construct an organized, ongoing, and descriptive picture of the learning that is taking place. The portfolio draws on the everyday experiences of the students and reflects the reading and writing that a student has done in a variety of reading and writing contexts.

There is no recipe as to how a portfolio ought to be constructed, nor are there any restrictions as to who selects work for inclusion. What is important is that the students understand explicitly the purpose of the portfolio, and that the teachers are fully committed to using portfolios actively both to assess students and to inform classroom instruction. The information contained in a portfolio needs to be organized and manageable. Information could include student texts of all kinds, conferencing notes, checklists, observations and anecdotal records, reading and writing prompts and response sheets.

The best guides for selecting work for a portfolio are these: What does this piece of information tell me about this student as a reader and a writer? Will this information add to what is already known? How does this information demonstrate change?

The portfolio collections form the basis for conferences. Conferencing is a vital component of portfolio assessment. A conference is an interaction between the teacher and the student, and it is through teacher/student conferences that the students gain insights into how they operate as readers and writers. Conferencing is a way of acknowledging that assessment is a shared venture. Conferences support learners in taking risks with, and responsibility for, their learning. Through conferencing, students are encouraged to share what they know and understand about the processes of reading and writing better. It is also a time for them to reflect on their participation in literacy tasks. Portfolio assessment is an appropriate means of recognizing the connection between reading and writing. An absolute distinction between reading and writing ought not to be made. The two must be integrated to form a coherent picture of a literacy learner.

Students, through conferencing and keeping a portfolio, experience making real-life decisions, as well as decisions about schoolwork. Learning to make decisions about something that they regard as important puts students in an improved position to make sound judgments about their own reading and writing and other learning performances. In other words, they learn to self-evaluate. In order for students to take responsibility for their learning and their lives, ownership of their own choices and actions is an all-important consideration. Traditional testing methods emphasize the role of the teacher as an instiller of knowledge, whereas the students need make very few decisions about their own performance. In the traditional approach, ownership of work and learning is looked upon more as the responsibility of the teacher than of the learner. When, however, students actively participate in the selection and discussion of their work, they gain a true sense of ownership, which results in personal satisfaction and feelings of self-worth.

For portfolios to meet the goals of literacy assessment set forth in this paper, they must be developed as follows:

- Teachers and students both add materials to the portfolio.
- Students are viewed as the owners of the portfolios.
- Conferencing between students and the teacher is an inherent activity in portfolio assessment.
- Conference notes and reflections of both the teacher and the student are kept in the portfolio.
- Portfolios need to reflect a wide range of student work and not only that which the teacher or student decides is the best.
- Samples of the student's reading and writing activities are collected in the portfolios—including unfinished projects.

Information collected in a portfolio, when collated and organized, provides a thorough, continuous description of a student's literacy development and attitudes and interests in reading and writing tasks. Portfolios provide a sound basis on which to document individual student progress because they incorporate a range of assessment strategies over an extended period of time.

At periodic intervals, teachers can review what is in a student's portfolio, and they can complete a summary report regarding that student's literacy development. Such summary statements gathered across students in a class provide an administrator with a good grasp of the literacy development of the students in that class.

Summary statements for individual students, as well as those collected for an entire class, can be effectively used as the basis on which to develop instructional plans. The teacher will be able to demonstrate the direct connections between portfolio assessment and classroom instruction. In addition, portfolio summaries provide adequate and relevant information so that parents and administrators can not only gain a descriptive account of a student's competencies but also, and more importantly, see and appreciate how these competencies have developed over time.

ISSUES TO BE STUDIED

The development of alternative forms of assessment in language arts is not a new idea. All sorts of alternative tests have been proposed, developed, and tried out for decades. Most have failed to gain any widespread support. The major reason for this failure has been that tests are developed and administered with little thought given to the objectives for the assessment. The most important issue for those who would develop alternative assessments—and those who want to use alternative assessments—is to consider the objectives of assessment. What information do we need? Why do we need it? What are the aspects of instruction for which we need information?

We need to consider the use we will make of assessment instruments before developing new tests. If we would think first of the most useful and most complete information we could provide a teacher regarding a student's literacy development, we would have a the broad outline for the assessment instruments we need to develop.

If alternative assessments in language arts are to become practical alternatives, and not merely passing fads, there are a number of problems that need to be faced.

These problems can be organized into four major categories; we present them in the order in which we think they need to be addressed. By emphasizing this order, we mean to say that some of the problems are more rudimentary than others. The *philosophical problems* of the role of assessment are fundamental and need to be considered before any assessment can gain popular support; the *public issues* are intertwined with the politics of accountability and need to be addressed so the public will understand and accept alternative assessments; the *implementation issues* need to be addressed so that schools and teachers are prepared to deal with alternative assessments; and finally, the *development issues* as to how such alternative assessments are to be built, must be considered.

Philosophical Issues

1. The role of assessment in language education needs to be considered. Can assessment simultaneously support both student self-assessment and determine the quality of an educational program? Are these two goals compatible?

2. Can assessment be integrated into the fabric of instruction? At present, much of the assessment in language arts is separate from instruction. If assessment is to play a major role in improving literacy instruction, it must be inexorably intertwined with everyday instruction.

Public Issues

1. How to educate the public to accept the notion that accountability cannot be reduced to single test scores?

2. Can the public come to understand that process is product, that the goal of literacy development is students who use effective reading and writing strategies to continue to learn? Will the public accept the concept that the primary goal of education is to produce students who can learn—rather than merely producing students who get "right answers?"

Implementation Issues

1. Can teachers take on the new roles required by this alternative view of assessment? Will they be able to see their roles in assessment as collaborators who help students to understand themselves as readers and writers, rather than, as they generally now function, as judges of literacy products? Moreover, how do we educate teachers into the role of inquirer, when they have more often seen themselves as implementers of programs?

2. How do we provide the time in an already crowded school day for teacher-student conferences? How will teachers find the time to review thoughtfully the contents of each student's portfolio?

3. How do we support the students to become self-evaluative? What is involved in promoting instruction based on inquiry, decision-making, and self-selection?

4. Can procedures be developed to communicate to the public the results of ongoing assessment over a wide range of activities?

Development Issues

1. How can we develop assessment activities that combine process and product so that we can make decisions about the quality of a student's participation in tasks, rather than merely examining the results of the activity?

2. How do we apply what we presently understand about literacy performance so that we are informed observers, and can support students to understand their own literacy development?

Reform must involve the combined efforts of all those in the literacy field. It is only through a process of sharing ideas and understandings that we can begin to learn from one another and develop alternative assessments.

Alternative assessment is possible if we can keep a focus on the purpose of assessment. Kaplan put that point quite cogently in a masterful book that was published over twenty-five years ago:

> Too often, we ask how to measure something without raising the question of what we would do with the measurement if we had it. We want to know *how* without thinking of *why*. I hope I may say without impiety, seek ye first for what is right for your needs, and all these things shall be added to you as well. (Abraham Kaplan, *The Conduct of Inquiry*, 1964, p. 214)

ASSESSING WHOLE LANGUAGE: ISSUES AND CONCERNS

WILLIAM P. BINTZ, Indiana University, Bloomington, Indiana
JEROME C. HARSTE, Indiana University, Bloomington, Indiana

Assessment people assume that Whole Language educators dislike standardized testing. In so far as we are concerned, they are right. We do. In fact, we reject standardized testing, and see it as an anachronistic socio-cultural practice that is theoretically bankrupt.

Many of these same assessment people assume that Whole Language educators don't believe in assessment. They are wrong. We do. What we offer, however, is not an alternative form, but an alternative vision.

In this paper we situate this vision in terms of where we have been, where we currently are, and where we want to be heading.

WHERE WE HAVE BEEN

Standardized testing, as we know it today, is not particularly rich in tradition; in fact, it is less than a century old (Guba and Lincoln, 1981). And yet, in that relatively short period of time, it has rapidly become endemic to American society. Over the years, standardized testing has achieved a privileged status in education, valued for its efficiency, sophistication, and objectivity, as well as for its utility and accountability (Harmon, 1989/90). Today, it continues to enjoy much popularity, prestige, and power. Recent trends indicate that in the years ahead, standardized testing will not only increase but it will also expand.

In 1986-87, for example, United States public schools spent on average at least one month of every nine-month school year administering a total of 105 million standardized tests to 39.8 million students, an average of more than 2.5 standardized tests per student, per year (Harste, 1989). Today, according to Valencia, *et al.* (1989), 46 of our 50 States now require state-regulated testing, and of these, all 46 require testing in reading. Recently, the United States Congress allocated $8 million to the NAEP to conduct voluntary state-by-state comparisons in mathematics at the 8th-grade level in 1990, and in mathematics and reading at the 4th-grade level in 1992 (see Farstrup, 1990). By all accounts, these commitments to norm-referenced tests at the national level, coupled with growing numbers of criterion-referenced tests at the statewide level and teacher-made tests at the classroom level, are symptomatic of an educational system well on its way to being obsessed with, and consumed by, standardized testing.

Moreover, the future of standardized testing will not be limited to education. In fact, a wide range of standardized tests has already been developed for use with different populations. For instance, we now have standardized tests for use not only with students but also with teachers, supervisors, soldiers, and police officers. Indeed, if the testing industry has its way, we will shortly become what Gardner (1988) calls a "complete testing society...one that is driven by a rationale that says if something is important, it is worth testing; if it cannot be tested, it probably ought not to be valued."

In our view, this projection for the future of assessment is unacceptable. Instead, we join increasing numbers of educators who are attempting to develop alternatives that better reflect recent advances in literacy and literacy learning. In the following section, we discuss several of these alternatives with particular emphasis on describing recent attempts to reform reading-comprehension assessment.

WHERE WE CURRENTLY ARE

Many educators are responding to calls for reforms in assessment by proposing a variety of alternatives to standardized testing. These proposals are diverse and controversial, and they include attempts to improve what standardized tests test, develop literacy portfolio approaches, combine informal literacy portfolio data with formal standardized test data, and develop holistic, classroom-based data-collection procedures.

Improving What Standardized Tests Test

Over the past two decades, reading assessment has lagged behind recent advances in reading theory. As a result, a significant gap has developed between our current understanding of reading, and the standardized tests we use to assess reading comprehension. Many educators believe that the most expeditious and efficacious way to close this gap is to improve what standardized tests test.

Recently, reading educators in the United States and abroad have been doing just that.

In Australia, educators have developed TORCH, a test of reading comprehension. This test includes a wide variety of reading materials representing multiple genres; it assesses reading comprehension through analysis of written retellings based on a modified cloze procedure. In Great Britain, educators have developed the Effective Reading Tests, a series of tests designed purposely not to look like tests at all. Reading passages in these tests are high-interest stories, and appear in an attractively illustrated book. Students read these passages, and record their answers to specific questions in a separate booklet (see Pikulski, 1990).

At the statewide level, collaborative attempts are currently underway to reconceptualize reading tests in the State of Michigan (Wixson, Peters, Weber, and Roeber, 1987; Valencia, Pearson, Peters, and Wixson, 1989). These attempts are explicitly designed to make statewide testing more consistent with recent reading theory and research. Today, reading is defined throughout the State not as a series of sequential and hierarchical skills, but more as an interactive process wherein readers actively construct meaning from text.

This reconceptualization has subsequently influenced the development of "prototypical" standardized reading tests. They are prototypical in the sense that these tests include passages and test items designed to reflect influences on reading such as topic familiarity, readability, text variability, metacognitive knowledge and strategies, and attitude and self-perception.

Attempts to reform statewide reading assessment is also currently underway in the State of Illinois (Valencia, Pearson, Peters, and Wixson, 1989). These attempts are directed towards developing statewide standardized reading tests that are based on interactive, rather than skills-based, models of reading. To that end, tests developed so far now include multiple texts, advanced organizers such as text maps and preliminary test questions, and questions designed to activate prior knowledge and access metacognitive strategies.

Developing Literacy Portfolio Approaches

Instead of improving what standardized tests test, an increasing number of educators are developing literacy-portfolio approaches as alternatives to standardized testing. They argue that these approaches better reflect recent reading theory, in that they function as tools for teachers and students to document and monitor learning over time.

A literacy portfolio is a "living document of change" (Krest, 1990). It consists of a chronologically sequenced collection of work that records and traces the long-term evolution of student thinking. This collection is open-ended, purposely diverse, and often includes writing samples, observational notes, audio and video tapes, literature logs, ideas, half-formed thoughts, sketches, photographs, questions, issues, rough drafts, peer feedback, descriptions of reading and writing strategies, personal reactions, self-evaluations, and works-in-progress (see Wolf, 1987/88; 1989).

Research on literacy-portfolio approaches has been directed at exploring the extent to which they can be used in assessing writing proficiency. For instance, at the post-secondary level, portfolio approaches are being used as an alternative to traditional proficiency exams for assessing writing (Elbow and Belanoff, 1986). At the secondary level, teachers in process-writing classrooms are using portfolio approaches as a means to make paper loads more manageable, to encourage and support students in producing their best writing, and to use alternative criteria such as risk-taking, reflexivity, peer-conferencing, and experimentation with different writing modes as alternative criteria in writing assessment (Krest, 1990).

Combining Portfolio Data and Standardized Test Data as Assessment

Recently, much research is being focused on the use of portfolios for large-scale assessment in writing. This work attempts to develop a method of writing assessment based on a combination of literacy portfolios of students' best written work combined with standardized, timed writing samples that permit broader and more accurate profiles of student learning (Simmons, 1990).

Increasing numbers of educators are starting to explore the potential of using portfolios not only to assess writing but also to assess reading. To this end, researchers have developed integrated language-arts portfolio systems for classroom use that combine reading and writing in a single assessment. One system in particular has been designed by Farr and Farr (1990) to allow parents, teachers, and students to include multiple sources of assessment data. Parents include biographical data, as well as information about student reading and writing activities outside of school;

86

teachers include classroom data such as observational notes, anecdotal records, vignettes, impressions, interview data, test records, and audio/video tapes; and students include autobiographical data in the form of journal and diary writing, learning logs, reflection booklets, and so forth. It is predicted that these data will provide insights into such things as student instructional histories, current interests, and future aspirations, so that teachers can then make more informed judgments about student work.

This system is designed to function as an organizational and analytical device for specifically evaluating student proficiency based on a set of prompted reading and writing activities. There are three sets of these activities, and these may be administered throughout the year. The prompts include multiple opportunities for students to use various prewriting strategies, read and write over extended periods of time, and revise their work through ongoing teacher-, peer-, and self-assessment activities.

Overall, this portfolio approach is designed to consist of personal, self-selected instances of reading and writing, as well as three pieces of writing based on teacher-selected, prompted activities. All personal writing in the portfolio is periodically and collaboratively reviewed by teachers and students; it is graded on such things as the amount of reading and writing completed across genres and topics, and the degree to which students engaged in risk-taking, particularly with respect to reading more complicated materials, experimenting with different discourse styles, and writing longer, more complex pieces.

To satisfy the monitoring role that these educators see tests as needing to play, all prompted writing in the portfolio is reviewed by the teacher, and numerically scored from 1-to-4 across three major categories: "response to reading" addresses the amount and accuracy of information comprehended from text; "management of content" assesses student ability to organize, focus, and develop information; and "command of language" evaluates surface features such as sentence structure, word choice, grammar, and mechanics.

Literacy-portfolio approaches, like the one described above, which include assessments on spontaneous as well as prompted activities, have the potential to provide a highly contextualized, informative, and accurate profile of student reading and writing abilities. By combining data from informal and formal measures, these approaches provide a valuable tool not only for students, teachers, and parents to use at the local level but also as a large-scale assessment instrument for administrators, curriculum coordinators, and policy-makers to use at the national level.

Developing Holistic Assessment Procedures

Lastly, an increasing number of reading educators are working to develop a holistic measure of literacy assessment, one that is based on standardized miscue analysis and "kidwatching strategies" popular among Whole Language researchers and theorists for some time now. These educators are convinced that reform in reading assessment can occur only if the criteria for assessing reading significantly changes. Therefore, their efforts are directed towards extending our current understandings of reading by exploring new criteria for reading comprehension, and by developing a classroom-based, learner-driven data-collection procedure for documenting and assessing reading growth.

Recently, we have been involved in a collaborative research project designed to explore alternatives to traditional forms of reading-comprehension assessment (Harste, 1989). In this project we attempted to use recent advances in evaluating writing as a metaphor for what might be possible in assessing reading comprehension. Specifically, we set out to develop a viable, classroom-based, learner-driven data-collection procedure by holistically scoring three different types of comprehension data (in-process think-alouds, retellings, freewrites) collected from 20 proficient readers as they read and reacted to the reading of an intact professional article. We believe analysis of this comprehension data has provided new insights into the reading process and has resulted in the development of several taxonomies that permit assessment far beyond standardized testing. This approach incorporates much of what is known about the dual processes of reading comprehension and writing, given psycholinguistic, schema, and socio-psycholinguistic theory.

The taxonomy constructed from analysis of student freewrites is a case in point (see Beverstock, Bintz, Copenhaver, and Farley, 1989). Traditionally, freewriting has been used as a prewriting strategy for helping students generate ideas for writing. We believe, however, that freewriting also represents unique potential for assessing reading comprehension since it encourages and supports unedited personal responses to text. We decided to use students' responses to text as a window through which we could view not only what readers comprehended from text but also how they went about comprehending through text.

This freewrite taxonomy reflects four major patterns characteristic of the "mental trip" students took as they went about reading. These patterns indicate that students engaged in 1) developing a sense of voice; 2) going beyond the text by making intertextual ties and personal links, as well as by speculating, synthesizing, extending, and analyzing; 3) taking risks by questioning, taking a position, shifting interpretive stances, and rethinking one's current position; and 4) being reflexive by searching out, identifying, and working through anomalies.

From this analysis we have learned that freewriting offers an alternative way of seeing reading, and understanding reading comprehension. We believe freewriting to be a learning potential for identifying, understanding, and appreciating the personal meanings that readers construct from text, as well as the strategic meaning-making processes that readers use while comprehending text. We feel these patterns, when integrated with analytic patterns gleaned from other protocols, i.e. oral and written retellings, think-alouds, miscue analysis, can be used holistically in developing alternative criteria for reading-comprehension assessment.

INTERROGATING ASSUMPTIONS UNDERLYING RECENT REFORM EFFORTS

We believe that recent efforts by reading educators to reform reading-comprehension assessment are positive attempts to close the gap between reading assessment and reading theory; they deserve our continued support. At the same time, we also believe that these efforts are inadequate because, while they have certainly been successful at improving the form of assessment, they have not been successful at changing its function. In other words, while these efforts have certainly changed the surface structure of reading assessment, they have not interrogated the assumptions underlying these surface changes.

For instance, recent attempts to reform reading comprehension, including our own work with holistic assessment, continue to include the assumption that reading is primarily an individual phenomenon, a learning activity that individuals do by themselves, for themselves. Reformers advocate interactive models of reading, and yet they continue to develop assessment instruments and procedures that narrowly define interactions as those instances that occur only between an individual reader and a single, prescribed text. The reformers have ignored, or at best paid only lip service to, the belief that reading is a social engagement, a learning strategy according to which learners not only read for themselves, but also read with others, for others.

This token attention to the social nature of reading is due in part to the fact that skills-based models of reading have historically perpetuated a single-score, single-text, single-reader mentality in reading assessment. To their credit, recent reform efforts have been successful challenges to the single-score mentality by incorporating multiple measures, as well as to the single-text mentality by including multiple texts, in alternative assessment instruments and procedures. Unfortunately, they have neither successfully challenged the single-reader mentality, nor adequately addressed the use of self-selected texts in reading assessment. We believe that these issues can only be solved by developing alternatives for reading-comprehension assessment that invite, encourage, and support transactions between a reader sharing multiple self-selected texts with other readers.

Moreover, each of these reform efforts continues to be rooted in what we believe is a behavioral model of learning. Attempts to improve standardized testing by altering what it tests certainly makes us look modern, up-to-date, on the cutting edge of reading assessment reform, but these modifications are only cosmetic changes, requiring us to take only limited risks.

For example, these efforts temporarily set aside what we all know to be true, namely that assessment is power. It is a tool that is often used to control, rather than reflect, student learning. Our willingness, then, to alter only the form of standardized testing is also indicative of our unwillingness to alter who is in control of learning, reexamine who is in the best position to assess learning, and rethink who decides which learning is to be assessed. In the end, these reform efforts certainly make the assessment deck look different, but it does not alter who is shuffling the cards.

Finally, literacy-portfolio approaches, particularly those that combine portfolio data with standardized test data, are to a large extent also rooted in a behavioral model of learning. On the one hand, by including personal portfolio data, these approaches are attempts to share power and control over learning assessment with learners themselves; this is a significant step in the right direction.

On the other hand, however, those who take these portfolio approaches, while not wanting to privilege standardized test data, nevertheless, still want to privilege standardized test criteria. That is, whether portfolio data or standardized test data (or both) is used to assess learning, in both cases specific assessment criteria have been predetermined and externally defined. These criteria are not individually defined based on purpose and function, but rather are uniformly applied to all students based on convention and control. In the end, literacy portfolio approaches, especially those which use standardized test data, end up amounting to little more than just another form for collecting, representing, and verifying the same outdated criteria used on standardized tests.

In the final analysis, literacy-portfolio approaches and standardized testing represent two different assessment vehicles, each of which is designed to travel a different road to assessing literacy and literacy learning. What is problematic is that in each case, because the assessment criteria remain essentially externally-defined and predetermined, both these roads still end up leading to the same destination. At the finish line, we would argue, a good way to judge whether or not any real change has been made is by watching how interactions change. If nothing changes, if those who were in power are still in power, if those who were silenced are still silent, then the alternative assessment procedure is no streamlined alternative at all, but merely a souped-up old jalopy.

WHERE WE OUGHT TO BE HEADING

We agree with Donald Graves (1990) who recently suggested that now is a very opportune time for experimenting, reflecting on, and getting messy with assessment. We believe a good first step is to recognize what we don't like about standardized testing. On our list is standardized testing's ecological invalidity and its cultural bias; moreover, it ignores the influence of social context on learning; it precludes an understanding of learning processes; it privileges linguistic and logical-mathematical proficiencies over other frames of mind; it focuses on individual weaknesses, not individual strengths; it uses a "single-digit" mentality to represent complex learning processes; and it disempowers learners by preventing them from participating in self-assessment.

With respect to reading, standardized testing has little relationship to real-world reading, that is, to the types of reading that people do in their everyday lives. To date, no data exists that support the belief that what is being tested by standardized testing has anything to do with real-world reading. On the contrary, existing data suggests that standardized testing is based on outdated assumptions about the reading process (Cambourne, 1985).

This, in turn, raises serious questions about what standardized testing really tests. After all, if it doesn't test real-world reading, then what does it test? If you ask those who wish to ban standardized testing, they will most likely answer that it has nothing at all to do with real-world reading. If you ask others, many will answer that they simply don't know. What they suspect is that they do little more than measure students' "test wiseness," that is, students' ability to take tests. We believe that this suspicion is worth exploring.

A second step is to recognize that Whole Language is based on a view of literacy and literacy learning different from the behavioral view which drives standardized testing. Whole Language involves literacy and literacy learning in terms of function, purpose, and social context, whereas standardized testing measures them in terms of convention and control. Furthermore, standardized testing is a focus on externally-defined criteria for cross-evaluation purposes, whereas Whole Language is a focus on internally-defined assessment as verification, inquiry, and "thoughtfulness" (Brown, 1987). Whole Language is a critical process of open-ended questioning to which no one knows the answers, and of presenting problems to which there may be many possible solutions.

A third step is to recognize that Whole Language has not been dragging its feet when it comes to developing alternatives to standardized testing. In the past two decades, advocates of Whole Language have made significant advances in literacy assessment by developing a methodology based on the best we currently know about literacy and literacy learning. This methodology includes the assumptions that assessment is synonymous with instruction, that assessment involves using multiple methods, that assessment focuses on the multiple dimensions of literacy, that assessment is ubiquitous, that assessment is context-specific, and that assessment is sensitive to cultural background (Teale, *et al.*, 1987).

More specifically, Whole Language methodology includes the assumption that assessment is a continuous process of observation, interaction, and analysis. These processes are interrelated, and they can occur formally through systematic record-keeping as well as informally through natural contact between teachers and students.

These processes can also occur incidentally, for instance, when teachers have a "professional hunch" or "intuitive judgment" by which they predict that specific activities may yield important insights about student learning (Goodman, Goodman, and Hood, 1989).

Likewise, Whole Language advocates have been busy developing a variety of observation- and interview-based, "kidwatching" strategies for use in assessing student learning. (Goodman, 1978) These strategies include systematic observation, periodic sampling of student reading and writing, peer conferencing, formal and informal interviews, standardized miscue analysis, retrospective miscue analysis, anecdotal record-keeping, and developing cumulative records such as writing folders, literacy portfolios, and so on.

A fourth and final step is to recognize that assessment is more than a methodological issue. It involves deeper issues that transcend familiar debates over the form and content of standardized testing, as well as the use and misuse of test results. We believe that assessment is a methodological, epistemological, and philosophical issue. We further believe that if Whole Language is to play a major role in shaping the future of assessment, then its advocates need to develop a model of assessment that is firmly based on the best of what we currently know about language, learning, knowledge, and schooling, with conversation presumed to underlie the whole process.

Assessment as a Theory of Language

What is the best that we know about language? We know that language is an open-ended system of symbols. This system functions as a tool for individuals to understand, name, and reflect on their social worlds. Language is both generative and representational in nature. That is, it is a means by which individuals generate meaning in their lives, as well as a way to communicate that meaning to others.

Whole Language is based on a theory of language that sees reading as an instance of language use. In other words, what we believe about language also holds true for what we believe about reading. In fact, what we believe about language also holds true for what we believe about any communication system, whether it be reading, writing, speaking, listening, art, drama, math, etc. Assessment is no exception. We need to start making connections between what we believe about language, what we believe about reading and writing as instances of language use, and what we believe about assessment.

Assessment as a Theory of Knowledge

What do we believe about knowledge? We believe that knowledge is socially constructed, that knowledge is historically and culturally-rooted, that knowledge is deeply embedded in the social context in which it is learned, and that knowledge is connected knowing, conceptualized as a complex web of current understandings influenced by prior knowledge, past experiences, current interests, and future aspirations. We also believe that learners extend these understandings through meaningful conversation with other learners in supportive learning environments.

Assessment as a Theory of Learning

What do we believe about learning? We believe that learning is a process of outgrowing our present selves. Learners can't do that by answering other people's questions; they can only do that by asking their own questions. It is this notion of learning as a question-asking process that makes the difference between educative and miseducative experiences. Educative experiences propel learning forward and outward; miseducative experiences keep learning at rest.

Assessment as a Theory of Schooling

What do we believe about schooling? We believe that schooling is the practice of freedom. Whole Language teachers seek to maintain classroom contexts that are democratic; in which diversity is a value; and in which teachers, students, and parents alike are recognized as stakeholders and collaborators in the learning process. In these contexts we function not to transmit knowledge, but actively to construct and transform social worlds.

SOME CONCLUDING THOUGHTS

Although neither one of us claims to be clairvoyant, we are confident in predicting that, if education in this country is ever to be more than just a practice in mediocrity, then the future of literacy assessment must look significantly different than it does today. We believe this can occur only if the future is constructed on the best we currently know about language, learning, knowledge, and schooling, and if conversation plays a central role.

Whole Language is essentially a theory of voice, and an affirmation that all voices must be heard. All voices includes teachers as well. Indeed, as Carolyn Burke (1990) reminds us, we can't hear other people's voices until we start hearing our own. Conversation is the medium by which all voices are heard.

We do not see conversation in hierarchial terms. On the contrary, we agree with Freire (1973) who reminds us that "At the point of encounter [dialogue], there are neither ignoramuses nor perfect sages; there are only men [and women] who are attempting, together, to learn more than they now know." We see conversation as inquiry, a potential for starting new conversations where none existed before, for hearing new voices where only silence prevailed before, and for democratizing social relationships where only hierarchical ones existed before.

Through conversation, we see assessment not as a matter of teachers verifying student learning, but as a process wherein learners collaborate with other learners in generating and answering their own questions. The process is generative in the sense that through conversation, assessment becomes an occasion for learners to ask themselves "What have I learned?" "How did I learn it?" and "What do I now want to know more about?" It is this ongoing question-asking process that affords learners opportunities to use themselves as research instruments, and to use assessment as a tool for outgrowing their present selves.

We see assessment through conversation as an opportunity for learners not only to engage in learning but also to reflect on that learning. At present, we spend a great deal of time collecting data, but not nearly enough time reflecting on the data we collect. Nevertheless, reflection, more than collection, puts an edge on learning; reflection pushes us to make public what we currently know, so that we can then move to what we don't know.

We do not claim that the Whole Language vision is a panacea to the problems facing literacy assessment today. We do claim, however, that we have some very high standards about what assessment should look like in the future. These standards are based on a set of assumptions about literacy and literacy learning in terms of purpose, function, and social context; about knowledge as a complex web of socially constructed understanding; and about assessment as inquiry, a process of continuous conversation between learners about the meaning of their work. We believe that these assumptions should drive the future of assessment because they not only situate learners at the center, rather than at the periphery, of the assessment process, but also they make possible the conditions in which assessment can be used as a means to hear new voices, start new conversations, and structure new social relationships in the classroom.

REFERENCES

Beverstock, C., Bintz, W., Copenhaver, J., and Farley, T. (1989). "Exploring Freewrites as Assessment: Insights and Patterns." Paper presented at the National Reading Conference, Austin, Texas, December 1, 1989.

Brown, R. (1987). "Who Is Accountable for 'Thoughtfulness'," *Phi Delta Kappan*, September 1987.

Burke, C. (1990). Personal Correspondence.

Cambourne, B. (1985). "Assessment in Reading: The Drunkard's Search." In Unswroth, L. (Ed.), *Reading: An Australian Perspective* (Melbourne: Nelson).

Elbow, P. and Belanoff, P. (1986). "Staffroom Interchange," *College Composition and Communication*, Vol. 37, No. 3, October 1986.

Farr, R. and Farr, B. (1990). (Personal Correspondence).

Farstrup, A. (1989/90). "Point/Counterpoint: State-by-state Comparisons on National Assessments," *Reading Today*, Vol. 7, No. 3, December/January.

Freire, P. (1973). *Education for Critical Consciousness* (New York: Continuum).

Gardner, H. (1988). "Assessment in Context: The Alternative to Standardized Testing." (Cambridge: Harvard Project Zero), Unpublished Paper.

Goodman, Y. (1978). "Kid Watching: An Alternative to Testing," *Journal of National Elementary School Principals, Vol. 57, No. 4, 1978.*

Goodman, K., Goodman, Y., and Hood, W. (1989). *The Whole Language Evaluation Book* (Portsmouth: Heinemann).

Graves, D. (1990). Presentation at the International Reading Association Annual Conference, Atlanta, Georgia, May 1990.

Guba, E. and Lincoln, Y. (1981). *Effective Evaluation* (Beverly Hills: Sage).

Harmon, S. (1989/90). "THE TESTS: Trivial or Toxic?" *The Whole Language Newsletter*, Vol. 9, No. 1.

Harste, J., Beverstock, C., Bintz,, W., Copenhaver, J., Farley, T., Kelleher, C., Chase, M., Tseng, Yueh-Hung, Meng, A., Alwasilah, C., Chandler, P., Poling, N., Ono, N., Mustapha, Z., (1989). "Assessing Reading Comprehension Wholistically," Symposium presented at the National Reading Conference, Austin, Texas, December 1, 1989.

Harste, J. (1989). *New Policy Guidelines for Reading: Connecting Research and Practice* (Urbana: NCTE).

Krest, M. (1990). "Adapting the Portfolio to Meet Student Needs," *English Journal*, February.

Pikulski, J. (1990). "The Role of Tests in a Literacy Assessment Program," *The Reading Teacher*, May.

Simmons, J. (1990). "Portfolios as Large-scale Assessment," *Language Arts*, Vol. 67, No. 3, March.

Teale, W., Hiebert, E., and Chittenden, E. (1987). "Assessing Young Children's Literacy Development," *The Reading Teacher*, April.

Valencia, S., Pearson, P.D., Peters, C., and Wixson, K. (1989). "Theory and Practice in Statewide Reading Assessment: Closing the Gap," *Educational Leadership*.

Wixson, K., Peters, C., Weber, E., and Roeber, E. (1987). "New Directions in Statewide Reading Assessment," *The Reading Teacher*, Vol. 40, No. 8, April.

Wolf, D. (1989). "Portfolio Assessment: Sampling Student Work," *Educational Leadership*, April.

Wolf, D. (1987/88). "Opening Up Assessment," *Educational Leadership*, December/January.

STATE POLICY AND "AUTHENTIC" WRITING ASSESSMENT

DIANE S. BLOOM
Project Director, New Jersey Statewide Writing
Assessment/Instruction
New Jersey State Department of Education

INTRODUCTION: THE NEW JERSEY EXPERIENCE

"Authenticity," an élan term bantered about in social-educational circles, is a word causing educators to reexamine and redesign their existing accountability measures. The American Heritage Dictionary defines "authenticity" as the condition or quality of being authentic, trustworthy, genuine. In New Jersey, where high-stakes statewide assessment affects the award or denial of a high school diploma, authentic, genuine assessment is the state's credo, not its song. In New Jersey, state policy informs assessment, and assessment informs state policy.

CONCEPTION

The decision to assess and develop a statewide assessment measure is generally made in response to requests from educators, professional associations, legislators, and/or the governor. In New Jersey, it took a year for a fact-finding committee and skills-identification committees to research, study, receive public input, and publish their recommendations for the next progression of statewide assessment. The skills-identification committees (reading, writing, and math) comprised representatives among the public and nonpublic sectors (i.e., business, military, industry, students, graduates, professional educators, organizations, and community groups). The committees' findings and the response to the impact of those findings were published in two reports focused on preparing students for the twenty-first century (NJSDE, 1988a & b).

The fact-finding committee responded to the following questions:

- Who will take the test and for what purpose(s)?
- What knowledge areas/skills should be assessed?
- How will the results be used?

In their search for answers, they reviewed the outcomes of prior statewide assessments; other state and national assessment programs; the theories and research on language arts, instruction, cognition, assessment; employment trends; and the critical-thinking, problem-solving skills required for the 21st century. In addition, current ninth-grade graduation test results were reviewed, and it was determined that success was achieved by at least 90% of the students who attended the 600 public school districts. Thus, the statewide fact-finding committee, based upon its study, recommended that the New Jersey High School Proficiency Test (HSPT) move to a grade-11 assessment, effective December 1993 (due notice testing commences in 1991 inclusive of an aligned "Early Warning Test" administered statewide at grade 8).

THE INFORMANT: STATE POLICY

State policy on assessment in New Jersey consists of identifying the skills to be assessed; giving assistance to school districts (training, funding, and innovative programs) to insure the opportunity to learn; the monitoring of district and school for student success; and the public reporting of that success. Policy established by the legislature and the State Board addressed the need for students to have requisite basic skills in order to perform economically, socially, and politically in their adult world. The skills defined are reading, writing, and mathematics. The policy has transitioned basic skills from minimum to increasingly more difficult, higher-order basic skills, including those of critical thinking and problem-solving.

The writing assessment, like the math and reading, has annually moved 90,000 students along, and exposed them to, a skills continuum, beginning in 1979 with a minimum basic-skills focus. Minimum skills were extended to higher-order cognitive skills in 1986, assessed at the ninth-grade level, and revised again in 1990, to be assessed at the eleventh-grade level, in order to prepare our students for an increasingly complex and technological society.

In addition to implementing the test as a graduation requirement, the state board of education further made the policy decision that the test should count toward the receipt of state certification of the effectiveness of the school district as well as the public reporting of the test results for public accountability.

These policy decisions were faced by New Jersey educators, students, parents, board members, representatives of professional associations and industry as they accepted the charge of developing a graduation test at grade 11.

THE INFORMANT: RELATED FACTORS OF ASSESSMENT

The national movement in language arts, similarly enjoined by New Jersey's members of the fact-finding and skills committees, sought to encourage students to read literature and to read *and* write for authentic purposes—the trend was away from drilling students on skills out of context and mastering the mechanics of reading and writing apart from meaning. Thus, the complexion of New Jersey's new assessment program at grade 8 and grade 11 reflected this movement and directed students to read and write for specific purposes.

Although reading and writing are integrally related, they are, in fact, in some ways distinct. This distinction is indicated by separate sections on the test for reading and writing. "One can read without writing, but one cannot write without reading" (Bloom, 1990a). According to Hillocks (1987), "writing is an enormously complex task" that is hierarchically related to its recursive sub-processes and the arousal of several dimensions of thought. When writers write sustained discourse, they must, at different points of time in the construction of the discourse, go back to review (read) that which they have already written. It is when we look to the purpose for which a learner writes or reads, and the authenticity of the task for audience and purpose, that the factors related to learner, task, and purpose become keys to the construction of the assessment tool.

ENGENDERING AUTHENTICITY

Among New Jersey educators, authenticity is not a state-of-the-art, new concept; rather, authenticity is what must be, when one considers responsible, large-scale assessment that is a high-stakes graduation requirement for all its eligible students. Thus, authenticity is engendered in New Jersey by employing the following elements and procedures:

1. Authentic writing assessment encompasses the diversity of the American experience—our cultural melting pot.

Robert Glazer (1985) commented that with each decade in the twentieth century we have "increased the proportion of children attending schools;...expanded the range of social groups; [and expanded] the amount and kinds of education offered." The challenge to the populace of the twenty-first century is "to teach successfully all of the diverse children and youth...of our educational systems." This challenge requires educators to develop new approaches to testing and instruction.

The development of the assessment instrument and infusion of identified skills into the local curriculum and instructional programs includes the following processes:

- The need for assessment is identified by the citizenry, legislators, educators, business and industry representatives, and promulgated by the New Jersey State Board of Education.

- Committees of educators, parents, students, business/ industry community, are identified and convened to ascertain skill requisites in writing for the age, grade and interest of the population to be assessed. Skill specifications, conditions and prototype items are written. Recognized outside consultants and experts assist in this process.

- All educators and professional associations' representatives participate in a formal review and evaluation of the skills. Consensus and endorsement are reached by said groups.

- The state board adopts the skills. The skill specifications, conditions, prototype items are disseminated statewide to each school district's chief administrator, director of curriculum, instructional specialist, and teachers

- The state department publishes a hands-on document to "help educators prepare their students for the new test" (J. S. Bloom, April 1990). A parent and guardian information guide is also distributed.

2. Authentic writing assessment embraces the learner and reflects what the independent, self-sufficient learner needs to know and can command at a given point of time.

This learner-centered assessment is rooted in a social context that is purpose-directed in task and artifact.

- The writing-skills and item-development committees, therefore, focused on the student learner as a writer in particular social contexts. (Hymes, 1972; Vygotsky, 1978; Hull, 1989).

- The committees identified what a writer needs to know and do as a writer (Bloom, 1989; May 1990b). The committees identified the following:

I. Construct Meaning by Writing Sustained Discourse (An Essay)—assesses student's ability to command written language employing a writing situation or task inclusive of audience and purpose

    This is performance ability wherein writers must apply four types of knowledge as they compose sustained discourse: "knowledge of the content to be written about; procedural knowledge that enables the manipulation of content; and knowledge of discourse (inclusive of structure [schemata]), syntactic forms, and conventions of punctuation and usage; and the procedural knowledge that enables production...." (Hillocks, 1986/1987).

II. Reconstruct Meaning as a Critical Reader to Revise and Edit the Written Text of Another Writer—assesses students' knowledge of revising and editing skills employing fictitious writers' error-riddled written text.

    The focus here is on "how" knowledge is applied and analyzed.

- The committee further defined the social context for the assessment measure by including general information and comment sections for student participation in self-assessment; real-life critical readings; real-world writing purposes/audiences; authentically designed tasks/items (Cohen & Riel, 1989); and open-ended response items that not only permit students to address attitudes and self-perceptions but also explain and support their answers (David, 1981; Aiken, 1987).

3. Authentic writing assessment employs a test-development process that ensures validity and reliability through a process of internal and external checks and balances.

    In New Jersey the process to attain content, and construct validity includes the following:

    - all educators giving input and reaching consensus on the identified skills

    - a subset of those educators confirming content validity of the test items constructed to measure those skills

- multifaceted, two-parameter views and weighting of students' writing skills employing multiple-measures (the ability to sustain discourse and the "how to" knowledge to revise/edit)

- affording students multiple assessment and re-assessment opportunities

- developing test formats that are standardized with respect to writing tasks, time, process—planning/prewriting to revising/editing, constraints, and so on

- offering developmental and remedial instruction to all students

- designing/offering a "special review assessment" (SRA) as a one-time opportunity for seniors, inclusive of an "open" portfolio to address the issue of test anxiety

- an appeal process, recognizing that mechanical or human judgment is not error-free (Essays are returned to the teachers/students following the scoring of their essays.)

- working with measurement and psychometric experts both from inside and outside of the test setting to perform independent checks and balances (e.g., internal consistency analysis; equating) on the assessment instrument and system

- seeking out and including empirical findings related to test construction such as attending to an item's structural form (Cassels and Johnstone, 1984); optional student commenting (Nield & Wintre, 1986); and item placement to help students acquire "positive anticipation of success" (Savitz, 1985)

The reliability is established through the following requirements:

- the selection, training (3 days), and qualifying of essay readers

- a minimum of two or three readings of every essay in the scoring process

- the use of a scoring method known for reliability and validity (Bloom-Braungart, 1984). New Jersey uses the Registered Holistic Scoring Method (RHSM). Researched and applied with uniform standards under known conditions, RHSM reflects the features distilled from analyses of composition features referenced by expert readers and three years of summary reports (Bloom & Rabinowitz, 1986). These features are inherent in sustained discourse in which students' first-draft writing is considered along a 1-to-6 descriptive score scale. The scale represents a range from (1) low, an inadequate command, to (6) high, a very strong command of standard written English. RHSM highlights quantitative differences as well as qualitative differences (Bloom, 1988a; 1985b). (Papers on this topic and/or procedures can be obtained by writing to Diane Bloom, NJSDE, CN 500, Trenton, NJ 08625.)

- student-based (field-tested) and committee-reviewed empirical data related to the essay-writing tasks and multiple-choice items. (Embedded items would be part of this process.) This would be the second review of tasks and items by the skill/item-development committee and the minority advisory committee.

4. Authenticity is a requisite of the instruction paradigm: Teaching-Learning-Assessment. This model focuses on the systematic retraining of teachers and their administrators to realign curriculum and address program needs as they relate to the assessed skills.

- In order that students be taught the skills identified by educators and others, and that the on-going assessment of skill attainment be achieved, three components were activated to address the Teaching-Learning variables of the paradigm. All had a significant impact on curriculum and instruction (Bloom, 1987). Based on our statewide graduation test results (high-order assessment of reading, writing and mathematics skills), we have found that student growth was consistent with a statewide effort to retrain educators/administrators—at least a $50 million effort. In other words, in 1986, when the graduation test was first given, 30,000 ninth-grade students failed the test; four years later, 1990, only 388 students failed to pass one or more parts of the secure graduation test (reading, writing, mathematics).

To ensure this success, curriculum, program and instructional needs were, and continue to be, addressed through the following state funded training, products, and innovative programs:

Training (e.g., Whole Language approaches, methods, strategies, processes, knowledge strategies and procedures—heuristics, metacognition)

- 11-day workshops and wrap-around; two-year follow-up workshops offered at grades K-1 and 2-3

- 5-day workshops and wrap-around; two-year follow-up workshops offered at grades 4-6, 7-9 and 9-12
- understanding and applying the RHSM scoring method
- participating in curriculum alignment

Products

- User-friendly products were developed that were state-of-the-art and included how-to manuals, test-analysis and reporting documents, instructional guides, and desk-top resource guides.

Innovative Programs

- Delivery of on-site assistance to schools, particularly urban ones, in order to implement the effective-schools research.
- A state-funded summer school program for students who either are at-risk of not mastering the tested skills or have not passed the test.

CONCLUSIONS

New Jersey's authentic assessment has been developed over a 10-year period. There is much more to be learned and applied in conducting authentic writing assessment. In New Jersey we are moving from a one-parameter model to a multi-parameter model that reflects audience and purpose while maintaining a robust curriculum that is inferential in its framework and built around an understanding of how students learn. We firmly believe that with this change in assessment, and our continuing emphasis on training that is informed by research and sound instructional strategies, New Jersey educators will achieve a high degree of enhanced literacy for New Jersey students. By helping students to achieve the higher-order reasoning skills, educators will enable students to equip themselves with some of the skills they will need to function politically, socially, and economically as adults. It is this emphasis that informs State policymakers and test developers. For educational researchers and classroom teachers, authenticity is the glue that holds writing assessment together with the cognitive process of learning. After all, the purpose of educational assessment is ultimately to contribute to the improvement of teaching and learning for all students.

REFERENCES

Aiken, L. R. (1987). "Testing with Multiple-Choice Items," *Journal of Research and Development in Education, 20* (4), 45-88.

Bloom-Braungart, D. S. (1984). "Measuring Writing Proficiency: A Registered Holistic Scoring Plan." Paper presented at the Annual Meeting of the American Educational Research Association and National Council on Measurement in New Orleans, Louisiana. (ERIC Document Reproduction Service No. ED 270 488)

Bloom, D. S. (1985a) *The Registered Holistic Scoring Method for Scoring Student Essays* (NJSDE Report No. 500.12). Trenton, New Jersey: New Jersey State Department of Education. (ERIC Document Reproduction Service No. ED 273 667)

Bloom, D.S. (1985b). *The Registered Holistic Scoring Method: Scoring Guide for Training* (NJSDE Report No. 500.38). Trenton, New Jersey: New Jersey State Department of Education. (ERIC Document Reproduction Service No. ED 860 515)

Bloom, D. S. and Rabinowitz, S. (1986). "Assessing Holistic Raters' Perceptions of Writing Qualities: An Examination of Hierarchical Framework Following Pre-post Training and Live Readings." Paper presented at 1986 American Educational Research Association Annual Meeting in San Francisco, California. (ERIC Document Reproduction Service No. ED 270 477)

Bloom, D. S. (1987, April). "The Impact of State Testing on Curricular Reform: The New Jersey Experience." Paper presented at the annual meeting of the American Educational Research Association, Washington, D.C.

Bloom, D. S. (1989). *Report of the Eleventh-Grade High School Proficiency Test Writing Skills Development Committee* (NJSDE Report No. 900.40). Trenton, New Jersey: NJSDE.

Bloom, D. S. (1990a). "Conclusions of a Study of a National Sample of Children's Writing." Unpublished raw data. (Available from R. Farr, Smith Research Center, Indiana University). In D.S. Bloom (1990b, May).

Bloom, D. S. (1990b, May). *Report of the Writing Committee: Identification of the 8th-grade Skills in Writing and Test Specifications and Sample Items for the 11th-Grade High School Proficiency Test and the 8th-Grade Early Warning Test* (NJSDE Report No. 1000.46). Trenton, New Jersey: NJSDE.

Bloom, J. S. (1990, April). *Helping Educators Prepare Their Students for the Eleventh-Grade High School Proficiency Test* (NJSDE Report No. 1000.32). Trenton, New Jersey: NJSDE.

Cassels, J. R. & Johnstone, A. H. (1984). "The Effect of Language on Student Performance on Multiple-Choice Tests in Chemistry," *Journal of Chemical Education, 61* (7), 613-615.

Cohen, M. & Riel, M. (1989, Summer). "The Effect of Distant Audiences on Students' Writing," *American Educational Research Journal. 26* (2), 143-159.

David, P. (1981, November). "Multiple-Choice under Fire: United States," *Times Education Supplement*, p. 11.

Glaser, R. (1985). "The Integration of Instruction and Testing," Proceedings of the ETS Invitational Conference on the *Redesign of Testing for the 21st Century*. Princeton, New Jersey: ETS.

Hull, G. A. (1989). "Research on Writing: Building a Cognitive and Social Understanding of Composing." In L. B. Resnick and L. E. Klopfer (Eds.), *Toward the Thinking Curriculum: Current Cognitive Research* (pp. 114-128). Alexandria, Virginia: Association for Supervision and Curriculum Development.

Hillocks, G., Jr. (1986/1987, May). "Synthesis of Research on Teaching Writing," *Educational Leadership*, 71-82.

Hymes, D. H. (1972). "Models of Interaction of Language and Social Setting." In J. J. Gumperz & D. H. Hymes (Eds.), *Directions in Sociolinguistics*. New York: Holt, Rinehart & Winston.

New Jersey State Department of Education (1988a, March). *Preparing to Enter the 21st Century: Revising New Jersey's Statewide Testing Program* (NJSDE Report No. 700.66). Trenton, New Jersey: NJSDE.

New Jersey State Department of Education (1988b, July). *New Jersey's Design for Educational Excellence: Into the 21st Century*. Trenton, New Jersey: NJSDE.

Nield, A. & Wintre, M. (1986). "Multiple-Choice Questions with an Option to Comment: Student Attitudes and Use," *Teaching of Psychology, 13* (4), 196-199.

Savitz, F. R. (1985). "Effects of Essay Examination Questions Placed at the Beginning of Science Multiple-Choice Examinations," *Journal of Instructional Psychology, 12* (1), 6-10.

Vygotsky, L. (1978). *Mind in Society: The Development of Higher Psychological Process*. Cambridge, Massachusetts: Harvard University Press.

ALTERNATIVE ASSESSMENT IN READING AND WRITING: WHAT WE'RE DOING AND WHAT WE'D LIKE TO DO IN COLUMBUS PUBLIC SCHOOLS

BERT WISER, Director of Assessment and Testing
SHARON DORSEY, Teacher on Special Assignment

I. What We're Doing

    A. Reading

        1. Elementary Schools (K-5)

            a) Teacher-developed literature-based assessment that includes multiple-choice items and an open-ended question scored by a primary trait scale

            b) Trade books that are thematically correlated to units in the literature-based reading program, and which have teacher-produced assessment

            c) Teacher-developed intervention packets containing both alternative instructional and assessment suggestions

            d) Pilots of alternative assessment.

        2. Middle Schools (6th-8th grade)

            a) Classroom teachers apply primary-trait scoring to students' written responses to reading selections

            b) Trade books that are thematically correlated to teaching units, and have teacher-produced assessment

            c) Pilots of reading folders

        3. High Schools (9th-12th)

            a) Classroom teachers apply primary trait scoring to students' written responses to reading selections and assist students in building small reading portfolios

b) Teacher-developed packets containing alternative instructional and assessment suggestions

B. Writing: Elementary, Middle, and High School Individual Student Writing Portfolios

    1. Contains summative writing assessment (at grades 4, 7, and 10 the student's writing sample and the computer printout explaining scores).

    2. Contains work samples.

Each nine-week grading period, students select their strongest final draft.

Students complete and attach a self-evaluation form to the back of the selected draft; they place it in the folder.

At the end of the second and the fourth nine-week grading period, a student/teacher conference is conducted. One of the two portfolio papers from that semester is selected and evaluated using the Columbus Rubric for Writing (analytic trait scoring).

The scores are recorded in the appropriate place on the cover of the portfolio.

During the last grading period (when four papers have been placed in the portfolio), the student and teacher jointly determine which of the four portfolio papers best reflects the student's growth in writing. An asterisk is placed on that paper.

The writing portfolio, including all four writing samples and the district-wide summative assessment at grades 4, 7, and 10, is passed on to the student's next-year writing teacher.

II. What We'd Like to Do in Reading and Writing in Elementary, Middle, and High School:

A. Broaden the portfolio approach to assessment

B. Broaden Contents

    1. Required school forms

District-developed formative assessment

District-developed summative assessment

2. Work samples

    a) **Reading**

        List of books read

        Tape or video of oral reading (elementary)

        Student's published books

        Selected entries from reader's response journals

    b) **Writing**

        Different types of writing produced in a variety of contexts and representing students' progress throughout the school year (Selections are made by student and teacher jointly.)

        Descriptions of the assignments for each piece of writing enclosed

3. Student self-assessment

    a) **Writing**

        Self-evaluation questionnaire to guide reflection on the *process* of writing and the *quality* of the product for each piece of writing selected for inclusion in the portfolio

    b) **Reading**

        Attitude/interest inventory

        Self-assessment conferences

4. Teacher observations and assessment

    a) **Reading**

        Running records (elementary)

        Concepts of print test (elementary)

        Strategies, interviews, and observations

    b) **Writing**

        Writing process, strategies, and quality of work interviews

5. Outside the classroom

   Parents' observations of students' reading and writing

   Students' observations of their reading and writing habits outside the classroom

C. Broaden and support teacher- and/or school-initiated pilots on a variety of assessment tools

   1. Running records in elementary schools

   2. Performance-based assessment

   3. "Writing and reading across the curriculum" assessment

III. Considerations

A. Relationship of assessment to grading

B. Philosophy of the reading/language-arts curriculum in the district

C. Support of the teacher's union

D. Commitment of the district

E. Communication to parents and community

F. State and national models for curriculum and assessment

GROUP 1

WHAT ARE THE IMPLICATIONS FOR INSTRUCTIONAL MATERIAL IN ALTERNATIVE ASSESSMENT?

Spontaneous vs. Prompted Writing Samples
MARTHA NYIKOS (Indiana University):

When people were talking about portfolio assessment, it seemed that they were looking for a variety of different engagements and writing samples that were primarily, actually teacher-dictated. In that case, the teacher would need to decide which types of writings would be given as assignments to the students, teach to that, and finally do an assessment accordingly.

Spontaneous written samples should also be included. In terms of instruction, then, the interesting issue to be figured out is at what point to plug in the spontaneous writing, as opposed to the writing that has been solicited in a more structured fashion.

CARL SMITH (Indiana University):
Instructional materials can provide prompts for writing, Martha, especially if we think of writing as a response to reading, whether students are responding directly in a structured way or in an open-ended fashion. Instructional materials can provide for writing in response to reading in other ways, too, whether through live prompts from teachers or printed prompts within the student materials, conversations, or tape-recordings.

"Authentic" = "Real-World"
LARRY MIKULECKY (Indiana University):
The Department of Labor is about to recommend a whole series of ways for teachers to bring authentic tasks into the classroom. They're suggesting especially that these tasks cross the lines of

what adults actually do, such as work together with a group, reading and writing to gather information to implement a plan.

For fourth-graders, for example, this approach might entail collaborating to look up addresses and writing for information to learn how to take care of the gerbil; at the high-school level, the students might be working together to gather information for running a student-run bookstore—everything from which books to order to the economies of how to market them.

Instructional materials and alternative assessment could profit from this approach by moving up in difficulty level, rather than having language-arts assessment be mainly a literature-based response to a piece of writing that somebody has provided. This real-world approach asks us to engage our students in real human activities that are multi-stepped, that may take two or three weeks to complete, that involve different aspects of groups working together as well as individuals working independently, and reading and writing. In this approach, the materials of instruction might well become the means of assessment. The teacher is asking the learners: "Can you take notes for a group that somebody else can understand?" "Can you order something that arrives?" Do that, and you begin to have an authentic kind of assessment in real-world terms.

"Assessments" as Instruction

MARILYN BINKLEY (National Center for Statistics):

What do we do with all these things that we collect? We're collecting all these writing samples, tape-recorded discussions, video tapes—now who's going to review them? Who's going to evaluate them? Along what lines? According to what dimensions? Larry has just proposed that the measure might be some variation on whether or not the students can enact a plan. We already question whether assessment does its job well or not—that is another question. What are we going to do, then, with all these other, different samples?

KAYE LOWE (Indiana University):

The conversation thus far seems to make an assumption that "portfolios are the answer." If we view assessment as being ongoing and integral to the classroom, we wouldn't be so tempted to take this oversimplification as a solution. Because teachers are in a position of constantly conferencing with children, assessment isn't something that they do separate from what's happening in instruction. Assessment and instruction take place in the classroom and happen at the same time.

CARL SMITH:

Disagreements over what we mean by "assessment" are at the heart of this symposium. Gene Maeroff said that his notion of assessment is a monitoring function, which is more typical of traditional or statistical approaches to assessment. Assessment in that tradition has never meant many of the kinds of things that we're talking about today, things we've always labeled "instructional."

Good teachers have always had conversations with kids, and have always collected things from kids and shown them, and teachers and kids have always interacted. Now we're trying to apply the word "assessment" or "testing" to that kind of behavior in a classroom context, and it doesn't seem to correspond with the notion that we've had in the past of "monitoring."

This morning I had breakfast with a group that I meet with once a month, most of whom are not educators. I told them what I was doing today, and I asked them: "What do you want to know from schools when you think of the term 'assessment'?" I didn't use "test"—I deliberately did not use "test."

One fellow answered, and the rest agreed, that the first thing they want to know is just what Bert [Wiser] this morning said they want to know: "How does the school that my child goes to compare with other schools? And that includes the Japanese! And the second thing I want to know is, how is my kid doing compared to somebody who's successful?" Both their questions were comparative.

I said, "One of the things we're trying is a portfolio."

"What does that mean?" they asked

I said, "We put all kinds of stuff in there—samples of work that the kids have done, and things of that nature."

And the guy said: "Oh, you mean like the old work folders that teachers have been showing me when I go to school to see how my kids are doing. Teachers have been doing that with my kids forever. My wife and I go to a conference, and the teacher says, 'Here's a sample of what your kid has done.' We all applaud because the teacher pulls out good things, of course, and we say, 'That's great!' But I still want to know what does it mean?"

I think that's the issue. Everyone in the past has related portfolio-style activities to good instruction, and now we're using the term "assessment," and it doesn't seem to fit.

What Is the Purpose of Assessment?
So the Bureaucrats Can Monitor Something or to Help the Kids Learn?
MARILYN BINKLEY:

Assessment in terms of instruction I see as ongoing in the classroom every day. These are the kinds of judgments that a good teacher constantly makes. But I'm interested in the monitoring function.

The purpose that the standardized tests have served in the past is the monitoring function. This was something outside of instruction. It was a comparison across various instructional environments.

Standardized tests are now being attacked because they do not reflect instruction, but I hear the discussion of performance-based assessment or portfolios or whatever as an opportunity for instruction and curriculum to be reflected not in the instructional daily give-and-take but in the monitoring function of assessment. I'm curious as to how we can get that kind of instruction and curriculum and teacher judgment reflected in the monitoring function in an efficient, usable form. That's what I'd like to push you all to answer for me.

KAYE LOWE:

One of the issues we're failing to address is the purpose of assessment. Why do we assess, and why is this monitoring thing such a big issue? I have trouble comprehending this in the USA. In Australia the pressure isn't there, and the public are not asking for it; there must be some level of trust that exists there that doesn't exist here. Why did that come about? I don't know. But I ask why we need this monitoring function? What purpose does it serve other than to allow someone to say, "Sixty percent of these kids aren't doing well enough," or whatever.

HAL OLSON (The Psychological Corporation):

I spent quite a few years as a teacher and principal before I worked for a publisher. There's lots of good instructional materials available these days. That doesn't mean that we shouldn't be keeping up–to–date applying new techniques, but teachers and school systems can be more successful than ever before in assessing performance by using the measures that are now available.

The Politics of Assessment

JACK HUMPHREY (Evansville, Indiana, Public Schools):

The public knows what our schools can do on scores because we're mandated by the State to publish those scores in our annual budgets and the newspapers. If I were trying to rank the schools to decide where to send my child, I'd pay attention to those scores, and I would send my child to this or that school depending on the test scores.

The tax-paying citizens of Indiana, and of the United States, are putting up a lot of money for education and they want to get their money's worth. So, schools are evaluated, just as judges are evaluated, and everybody else is evaluated. In the United States, everything we do has some kind of evaluation with it. That's just the way we do things.

I'm not so certain that that's all bad. I've seen that, as a result of our state testing, many parents whose kids don't fail, work harder to help their kids make it. There's more homework going on; there's better attendance at school. The threat of the state testing just moves everybody a little bit faster, including teachers. We are driven by the tests, but we've got to be driven by something— maybe.

I'm wondering if there isn't room for portfolio assessment as well as standardized assessment. I think our citizens will continue to want to know how our schools are doing, but I agree that that's not always helpful for the individual children or for the interaction between teachers and children. I think maybe there's a place for both.

Whichever way we go, there'll be criticisms. Anything that adds to a teacher's workload, the teachers will criticize. Anything that does not report to the public, the public will criticize; and if the public loses interest, the schools will lose the money we've been accustomed to. So I'm in-between, here, because I think the public really is interested in knowing; and at the same time we want something that will really be helpful to children.

Standardized Tests Miss the Disadvantaged Kids

KATHY EGAWA (Indiana University):

I would like us to stop assuming that when test scores are not high that it's automatically either the teacher's fault or the child's fault. Curriculum can be at fault, and testing can be at fault.

Moreover, I am very much an advocate for the underadvantaged child. I worked for seventeen years in an urban school district with the kind of students in whose real-estate area you would not want to live, and today I have heard very few people here advocating anything that represents them.

Some of the research done by Jay Simmons and others comparing portfolio assessment to standardized testing has shown that children in the top two-thirds look the same from both perspectives. The picture that one gets of the children in the bottom third, however, is much broader. So, if we want a better perspective on their performance, standardized tests are not enough.

Assessment as Instruction, Again

WALTER HILL (State University of New York-Buffalo, Emeritus):

I'm wondering whether the issue here is, "Should instructional materials be used in alternative assessment?" If it isn't that, then it seems to me that the implications for instructional materials in alternative assessment is the same as for any kind of assessment. You use the rich variety of available materials to teach kids—or whatever you can get your hands on if you're working in a poor school system. But if the point of this discussion is that instructional material *should* be part of the assessment, which seems to me to be the overlapping of portfolios and measurement, then that might be a different issue.

LARRY MIKULECKY:

A technical answer to the instructional-materials-and-assessment question grows out of the NAEP (National Assessment of Educational Progress): It's possible to survey a wide universe of different materials that might not be the same everywhere. By acknowledging the different mental processes that people use to perform a task, it's possible to have different people do different things. Use for assessment of a wide variety of instructional materials would allow us to report out that "students are able to do certain things that are at this difficulty level" such that "x-percent of the population seems to have difficulty with these things."

ETS is designing simulation activities that revolve around samples of real-world reading and documents from different industries as a way of allowing people to build assessments in the workplace. They are using Item Response Theory, which yields a rank-order number on a task, with the result that not everybody is assigned to do the same task.

If we applied this approach to schools, the schools would not have to have somebody coming from outside to administer a test. What one might have to do is take a look at the curriculum, and assess its relative difficulty. Also, there are technical problems with background knowledge. But this is a direction we could move with instructional materials and alternative assessment.

Assessment: What Are We Counting? Why?
CAROLINE BEVERSTOCK (Indiana University):

There are several points to follow through with from what Larry has just said. Simulations are exciting because as another form of assessment, they get closer to having people exercise actual abilities to perform actual tasks represented to them as real—quite unlike school-based tasks.

The next level of task in assessment alternatives that intrigues me is getting the learner, teacher, school principals, school curriculum people—each level—further involved in doing the analysis.

Someone brought up the point that alternative assessment will take more of the teacher's time. That's an important question because we are involving people in doing something that largely has been imposed upon them.

Further, the reporting of results has never gone very far beyond attaching a few meaningless percentage points to what was done this year as compared to what was done last year, but with very little sense of what any of that means for what *my child* can do.

I think that we have an opportunity each time we do an assessment to do an analysis and an inquiry as well. What are the challenges we are facing? Are we doing anything new? Where can we go from there? If we continue to do assessments in response to what curriculum was ten years ago, then we're reporting old news; but if we're doing analyses that are about the curriculum being taught today, then we're getting closer to what we need to be doing.

MARILYN BINKLEY:

If we keep changing the assessment to reflect the curriculum that we are doing today, how do we know that it is better or worse, more or less effective, accomplishing more of our goals or fewer of our goals, than did the curriculum that we had ten years ago?

CAROLINE BEVERSTOCK:

Clearly, we have to come up with some new items to count. A piece of that counting question came up dramatically in response to Diane Bloom's numbers about 90,000 students, and only 300 got stopped by the New Jersey setup.

One way to assess whether or not present curriculums are working is in terms of retention of students in school. For instance, in California, more than half of the Hispanic women are dropping out of school. [Muttered objections from the group.] There are other things that we can count, if you don't like that particular example.

The Schools are Failing: The Demand for Assessment is a Symptom of Public Mistrust
MARILYN BINKLEY:

Considering the lack of success of our schools in producing people who can function in the workplace, the rising rates of dropouts, and a number of other indicators, we need to monitor our schools. In the New Jersey situation, where only 300 failed—that's ludicrous inconsistency; but the test givers are taking over the schools in Jersey City. There's *reason* not to trust. There's *reason* to hold the schools accountable—and it comes out in the workforce, and in our educational "products." What is the function of our faulty educational system? Are we meeting the need? Apparently we're not.

James Smith of California says that there are three ways that the State Department of Education can improve the schools: through the curricular framework, textbook adoption, and assessment— the way to hold everybody accountable. Taking the three together, Smith views them as the biggest policy tool, and he's monitoring that way. That's a way of getting the product out.

CAROLINE BEVERSTOCK:

I've been able to look at the new language-arts framework in California in the context of the three pieces just mentioned— curriculum, textbooks, and assessment. My first question is whether James Smith, or anyone here, would be satisfied that the assessment being used in California has any relationship whatsoever to that framework, and if it doesn't then we have to circle back to how are we going to effect a relationship between framework and assessment.

KAYE LOWE:

What are we actually attempting to monitor? Is it just performance on a test? How are we really tapping into whether the curriculum's appropriate to the kids' needs anyway? What are the real issues that we need to be assessing? Is it just that these kids can't pass the test? How will that relate to the workforce?

MARILYN BINKLEY:

The whole revolution in assessment is not about assessing whether kids can pass some test or not, but about ways of figuring out what we should be assessing in order to reflect what is needed in our society. I see it as a much bigger political issue than what is going on in the schools only.

Assessing the Failures Will Not Produce Success

KAYE LOWE:

Coming in at this level, we're missing out on the overriding issues.

What's the purpose of assessment? Assessment *should* inform instruction—it's not just to have teachers teach to the test, which is what's currently happening. I think that's a bad thing.

Alternative assessment is for more than helping the teacher make decisions; it ought also to involve a collaborative process so that the students get to self-evaluate and become decision makers about themselves and the progress that they can make.

MARTHA NYIKOS:

So we're teaching them metacognitive skills through a test.

KAYE LOWE:

Assessment *should* be self-evaluation so kids can start to see themselves as decision makers.

MARILYN BINKLEY:

But why do they need an assessment instrument to do that?

KAYE LOWE:

I don't think that they do, in a formal sense.

Teachers Are Better Assessors than Are Tests, but Economics Is the Point

LARRY MIKULECKY:

On the question of the purpose for assessment, as a teacher in high school and junior high school for seven years, and studying the question even more since then, this seems to me just to be a joke! I don't know any teachers who make judgments about kids who would trust a test that somebody else made in preference to their own insights. Teachers who would consider using such a test usually do so because they lack the energy to make judgments on the basis of their own observations.

I think that it's just flat-out not true that assessments developed by anybody else but a teacher are useful to inform instruction directly. At best, it's a coercion; it informs instruction because it forces the teacher to say "I'll teach to the test."

I think that tests in the United States exist because people other than teachers and students are major stakeholders, and they want to know, "Is the money being well spent?" They want to know, "Are children doing well here?" as opposed to doing well across town or doing well in another city.

MARILYN BINKLEY:

...or "well enough."

LARRY MIKULECKY:

...or "well enough" or "better than somebody else." I think that to deny that aspect of human nature because "it is not healthy," is senseless. The purpose for tests *really* is to inform people who pay the piper.

This Is Not a Pretty Picture!

KATHY EGAWA:

One of the bigger issues is that tests do drive curriculum. Then, we have labor saying, "Your students are not prepared to come work in our fields." We have students (one-third over all, not including minority students) saying, "Your high schools don't meet my needs." We have a tension here that we need to address in a new way. Testing is one of the forces that drives the parts of the problem apart.

In California, the student population is 51 percent minority. In Chicago, Hispanic children are dropping out of school at an 80-percentile rate. We need to see ourselves invested in those minority children's futures, because, at the moment, 17 of us are supporting each one of us who is on Social Security, whereas when this generation begins to receive Social Security, there will be three people supporting each one, of which one will be a person of color—the very people who are dropping out of school at the greatest rate. Our curricula are not meeting their needs.

Teachers aren't even thinking, teachers are so driven! I was pleased to hear Bert [Wiser's] comments—I really wasn't *pleased,* because they're so cynical!—but at the same time, there's cheating—rampant cheating—going on with tests *all over* school districts. I'm interested in teacher education, and I admit a certain negative attitude towards teachers, at the same time that I realize that a lot of teachers have never *thought,* that they've never been asked to think! The distrust of teachers in this country just makes me sick, especially after all the years I've taught.

I sit in meetings with my colleagues, and I could just cry at the *level* of the discussion! The tension is great, the gap between the many issues is great, and we're certainly losing more kids all the time.

The Purposes of Assessment
JERRY JOHNS (Northern Illinois University):

What are the purposes of assessment?—this is one of the most fundamental questions to which a number of people have spoken this morning. Some of the answers that we're getting are these: (1) accountability (2) to give feedback to the people who are supporting education in the United States (3) to inform instruction (4) to provide opportunity for student and teacher interaction. There may be a host of other purposes, too.

Strange to me about this conference is that there's a search for a single purpose and a search for a single instrument. Larry [Mikulecky] said that people in the United States naturally believe in accountability. That may be true in the United States, but it's not necessarily true in the rest of the world.

I think it a fatal flaw in our approach if we think we can determine one purpose for assessment that everyone would agree upon, and one way to bring that about that everyone

123

would agree upon. Given the high value that we place on freedom in the United States, there will always be differing viewpoints, and we can never ask one assessment device to answer the various purposes which different people have for assessment. My own professional and personal opinion is that the search for a single answer is a search in futility, unless you intend to wield the sword that eliminates all other freethinkers. It's not going to happen in the United States.

ROGER TRENT (Ohio Department of Education):

Jerry, I concur. Forward, full-heartedly! I think you're right.

CAROLINE BEVERSTOCK:

I'm really with you. *De facto* in the schools, teachers are using various kinds of assessment, and yet policy decisions are being made on the basis of the results of wholly other kinds of assessments that, in many cases, the teachers don't believe. The *de facto* situation is multiple assessments, and the issue is one of where the credibility lies, using instruments at the policy level that have some credibility.

JERRY JOHNS:

Were we to move portfolio assessment, so that it would have impact at the policy-making levels, it might completely distort the very basic nature of portfolio assessment. I think there may be some basic incompatibilities between some of the purposes of assessment and the uses to which we put assessment. I venture to say that we will always need multiple levels of measurements, some of which at any given point will have much more political impact than others. By the time you could get a group of assessment professionals to quantify portfolio assessment—which is what Marilyn [Binkley] wants—the professionals in the class- rooms would no longer be interested in the portfolio concept because it had been so distorted.

KAYE LOWE:

If we are going to regulate classroom instruction, and require that portfolios look a certain way, and if assessment has to look "this way," it's really taking away the individuality of the teacher. Teachers teach differently, and they all have to come up with the portfolio approach that suits their respective teaching methods.

124

Standards Are Standards
HAL OLSON:

One of the issues here is, "Should we throw out the standard type of assessment that we now have, and go to something else as a positive replacement?" Even if we do, the students that do well on the performance assessment are the same ones that are doing well now. That seems to happen every time we turn the curriculum. If we improve what is working, that's one way to go; and if we have things that aren't working and continue to do them, they still aren't going to work—even though ofttimes this is what we do.

Whoever said that teachers won't accept somebody else's test scores, hasn't been around. The large suburban high schools all use the same tests, all the students take the same tests at the end of each grading period, and teachers have no choice but to accept one another's test scores.

Are there only two types of assessment? Portfolio or multiple-choice—are those the only two kinds? Those two kinds seem to be the narrow focus of this conference.

The Final Assessment: "Can You Do the Job?"
CARL SMITH:

One of the things that drove the reform in California had nothing at all to do with test scores. It had to do with the dissatisfaction of industry with the graduates of California schools. I happened to be part of a consultant group present when Honig and Deukmajian were fighting that battle, out there. What really started that whole reevaluation of the California curriculum was a group of industrialists who said, "Your kids can't do the jobs that we have to have done." That's a very real form of assessment!

They're not asking what the curriculum is, they're just saying that the kids who graduate from the schools can't perform the reading and writing tasks that they need to do within the industries. The school people's first response was, "Well, our kids are scoring just as well now on standardized tests as they did before. They haven't fallen down." But the industrialists said, "We'll get behind you, put up money, and help you accomplish something different, if you'll find a way of making a change in your graduates."

125

There *are* various ways of getting assessment different from a standardized test, and that's a very harsh example, but it's an example of one way we could go.

GROUP 2

WHAT ARE THE CONNECTIONS BETWEEN THE THEORY AND POLITICS OF ALTERNATIVE ASSESSMENT?

There's More to "Alternative Assessment" than Portfolios
BARBARA CAMBRIDGE (Indiana University/
Purdue University at Indianapolis):

I'm appalled that we have limited our discussion in the general category of alternative assessments to portfolios only; and under "portfolio," we have not looked at a range of possibilities, but in fact we ended up the morning session looking at a *folder,* which is certainly an absolute negation of anything that most people who support portfolios hope that a portfolio will do.

So I'm wondering if we could in this group maybe open up the definition of alternative assessment, perhaps talking about the ways in which portfolios in fact accomplish things different from just sticking a bunch of papers or some other records of learning into a manila folder.

STEVEN OSTERLIND (University of Missouri):

I share your *appallation.* I also think we have been too limited. What we would like to build towards, I think, is the integration of curriculum, instruction, and assessment. The integration of those three requires that we have a common understanding of the purpose of each, a common understanding of the definition of each, and a common language. I think there is near unanimity of opinion on the importance of each of those three, and the integration of them comes as we talk about them. We have been too limited thus far in focusing on portfolio assessment only.

Gatekeeping vs. Nurturing
ROGER FARR (Indiana University):

I agree with that. The discussion this morning did not provide an opportunity to talk about a wide range of things. I believe what you [Steven Osterlind] just said: We find unanimity about integrating instruction and assessment, but as soon as you do that, then it becomes a nurturing/gatekeeping function—and I have a real problem with that.

I just don't understand how we're ever going to break through having assessment inform instruction and be used in a helping way, and then worry—as some people did, even though they may not admit it—*worry* that not enough people failed the New Jersey test. How could that test be nurturing and at the same time serve that gatekeeping function? Yet we want to bring instruction and assessment together. I find it almost impossible to think about bringing those two together, even though I agree that it ought to be done.

STEVEN OSTERLIND:

Phi Delta Kappa published a book by Steven Daily, titled *The Purpose of Education,* and then John Goodlad's later book called *What Schools Are For*—excellent books, really fine! If we were to approach these issues from Daily's and Goodlad's points of view, then we have hope of integrating curriculum instruction.

Philosophical Implications: The Epistemology of Assessment
BARBARA CAMBRIDGE:

I'm a newly appointed member of the Higher Education Commission for the State of Indiana. One of the things I hear at Higher Education Commission meetings is a lot of confusion about what certain terms mean, and I think those terms are not just diction choices. They are terms that reflect epistemological systems. As educational institutions, we have not done a good job of being forthright about where we stand. One of the things I like about Jerry's [Harste] talk this morning, and about his positions that I have read and heard him speak about in other situations, is that he is very forthright about it. To pretend, as the Riverside editor did, that there is no epistemological position stated in the kind of folder that he held up for us as a model, is just false.

One thing we need to do is to start talking about where we really stand when it comes to learning theory and when it comes to education. Be forthright about that, and say that there are certain kinds of instruction and certain kinds of assessment measures that grow out of those kinds of theoretical positions; there are others that don't. We must be willing to take a stand, and not pretend that we can accept any assessment measure for any epistemological system.

JACQUELYN KOMAS (University of Florida):

I'd like to hear what other states are doing to bring about dialogue between educators, legislators, and State Departments of Education. In Florida we realized that we had to begin with a dialogue. Working through the State Reading Association, we hired a state legislative activist who goes to all of the committee meetings held in our state legislative body, and then reports back to the Association, where we have representatives who are supervisory reading personnel in each district for the state. These representatives take that information back to their districts.

Our dialogue allows us to talk together about what things are acceptable at the State Department of Education level, and what things are acceptable in the legislative body. When they seem to be totally oblivious to what we're interested in as a body, then we're able to present position papers and have them listen to us. Now, they are beginning to have public hearings throughout the state when information needs to be disseminated, though people don't attend the public hearings in the numbers that we would like. I'd like to hear what other states are doing to foster dialogue.

SHARON DORSEY (Columbus, Ohio, Public Schools):

You sound like you're more advanced than we are in Ohio. We're just beginning. The past two years we have suddenly realized that we suffered from a lack of information, from legislators to the State Department of Education to school districts to literacy groups throughout the state.

Several different groups popped up, and they have different interests, but we have developed a network among them. One is called LEAF (Literacy Educators & Advocates Forum), and it is made up of the leading researchers at the different universities in the State of Ohio. We come together several times during the year, and we have two goals. One is to share research that is in process, and the other is to talk about how we can deal with legislative issues that are present.

The second group is called OCLA (Ohio Coalition of Literacy Advocates). It is made up of superintendents throughout Ohio, a lot of Whole Language people, and the presidents of most of the literacy organizations in the state.

The Ohio Council of Teachers of English has representatives from the OCIRA (Ohio Council of the International Reading

Association), which is even more active. The two groups together have set their goal as contacting every single person on the State Board of Education, and developing first-name, personal rapport with them, so that we can directly call them when we have an issue at hand. We have also set up contacting all of our legislators. There are two new commissions that were set up at the legislative level, and we deal first-hand with those people now.

The Ohio Council of Teachers of English also took money out of their pockets and hired a liaison with the legislature. They now sit in on all the State Board of Education meetings and important hearings, and they send out information so that all the members across the state can realize when a hearing is coming up. Sometimes, even *that* is news to a lot of people.

We can now pinpoint certain people—legislators and people on the State Board of Education—who take certain philosophical stances, as you [Barbara Cambridge] said, and we know certain key people to work with when we want something accomplished.

We're learning a lot about politics, being very informed by some people from Ohio State University that used to work in the National Education Department in Washington, D.C. They have told us how to meet and greet a legislator, so we're learning to become political, but we're at the beginning of that stage.

What we would like to do is develop a situation like Michigan had, where we have strong communications set up, wherein, as you [Jacquelyn Komas] said, we can present papers and so on. We are planning right now a tea—legislators wouldn't like to hear it called a tea!—we're holding a *reception* for the legislators in a place where legislative receptions are usually held (being led by these political people now) to get to know both the candidates for governor. We're dealing with the candidates' Education people so that we can let them know that when they become governor, we want to have straight lines to the governor's office, too. We're *working* on developing political lines.

Open Communication Is a Better Style of Politics
DIANE BLOOM (New Jersey):

I really hate the word "politics"—it always sounds like such a dirty word. I don't think you have to have so much politics as long as you have a lot of open communication.

It depends upon on where your question is asked: If you're trying to inform legislators on how you want a test to look, and what it should assess, then you want to have key players. You have to know who your major organizations are. When we get the OK to go ahead and develop a test, we put on all the presidents of all the major organizations—ASCD, PSA, NJCTE, NJLA. When you name your organization in your state, you put those presidents on, you put those vice presidents on, because they are the ones who then, in turn—when it comes time for them to do their spring conference or fall conference, their workshops—will invite either you or your committee members to present and to share what's happening. That opens up communication on that avenue.

If the idea has nothing to do with actual legislation but simply to have networking and sharing, then we make use of our academies, doing workshops and retraining teachers. We've used Roger Farr's premises; we've used [Jerry] Harste's premises; but we do jigsawing with a look at all kinds of position papers and theoretical papers.

Then we let those educators make their own decisions jointly about the way they think things should be working in the classroom. In that group setting you network because these people, when they get finished with their training, become turn-key trainers: they go back to their school districts and train others. The more people they involve from their school districts, the larger the body of people who are knowing. Not only are they "up there" with what is happening in the state but also they are causing the things to happen in the state; they are the force behind it.

We try to make sure that we sit on NJCTE committees. If possible, I try to get on the board of directors, as I was for the Reading Association in the state. It's really critical always to keep the lines of communication open, whether with a friendly letter or just a note: "I want you to know this is what we're doing now." This kind of work has to fall on somebody's shoulders, and in my situation, it falls on mine, even as some of my colleagues who serve at a similar level will acknowledge it falls on theirs.

How It Works in Ohio
BARBARA CAMBRIDGE:

Sharon [Dorsey], who constituted those groups that you mentioned, and what was the impetus? How does the State Board of Education relate to those two groups?

SHARON DORSEY:

LEAF (Literacy Educators and Advocate Forms) is mainly made up of research people from the different universities in the State of Ohio. We have also drawn in the president of the English organization in the state, the NCTE affiliate; the president of the Reading Association; and a few school-district people, like myself. There are two emphases: One is political, to help suggest to legislators policy that might support research or be in line with research; the other emphasis is to share the research in process.

The Ohio Coalition of Literacy Advocates is broader based; it has a lot of university people. (Some people sit on both LEAF and OCLA. I'm on both of them.) Among the university people on OCLA are Myra McKinsey, Martha King, a lot of researchers from Ohio State, and people from the English Department at Ohio State. There are people from Public Policy—they're the ones who really know politics in Washington, D.C., and how to deal with politicians. There are superintendents, there are teachers, there are also a lot of presidents of organizations represented on that group. In both OCLA and LEAF, we have invited adult literacy groups, too.

The similarities between the two caused a debate as to whether both of the groups should exist, and that is not settled yet. Right now they have a slightly different purpose, but the link between them is very tight.

As Diane [Bloom] mentioned for New Jersey, so also in Ohio: The State was not always turning to the appropriate groups or to the top research institutions in the state. When they were forming legislation, they were going outside of the state to people from New York or New Jersey who lacked credibility with the different universities in Ohio. We didn't agree with them philosophically and we didn't feel that they had credibility, yet the state legislators were bringing them in and paying them large fees to suggest legislation, and the legislation was enacted. That highly offended various researchers at Ohio universities. We felt we had within the state much more expertise and much more credibility among our teachers. That was the impetus for the beginning of these groups. We're trying now to make the State Board of Education and the legislators know that they have a rich resource within the state that they should rely on.

ED ROBBINS (Indiana University):

I want to shift gears. I've heard what to me are two quite contradictory points of view. Several people have said, "We're all saying the same thing, we're just using different words." Other people have said, "We're epistemologically worlds apart." My question is, which of those is the case? And what kind of evidence do we use to decide which way it is?

BARBARA CAMBRIDGE:

This morning, we heard one speaker talk from a stated epistemological position. Therefore, we could understand the assessment stand. When I don't hear that from someone, then it's hard for me to know what the connection is between the speaker's epistemological basis and the stand on assessment. Given our respective theories of language, the words we use are part of the conception of the idea. So I think that the language we choose is very, very important.

ROGER FARR:

I think that conceptions of language are changing constantly. To expound on a theory, and say, "Assessment is going to be based on this," locks us in. So I tend not to do that a lot. I think you have to have developing theories. If I were asked to, I could expound on the theory of language that I believe in, but it's changing constantly, and really I am looking at lots of evidence.

I'm impressed with Marilyn Adams' new analysis of how kids learn to read. I think her approach has a lot to say, although I don't agree with all of it; and it has changed some of my views, especially the part about parallel distributive processing. They think, perhaps, that we've got an analysis of how the brain might possibly function. Don't think that I'm a phonics advocate or a skills advocate, but she makes some very important statements that ought to be thought about and argued about and discussed.

My work reflects what I think needs to be developed, not just in a theory about language, but what I believe also about keeping school. What one believes about keeping school and language and the politics of the real world, have to be fitted together. The kind of politics that we heard being talked about in putting together groups of constituents, and Larry's [Mikulecky] constant reminder that there are other stake-holder groups in all of this, cause me to think that we have to be very careful about just saying, "Oh, here's my theory, and this is what it is in terms of assessment." I don't think that'll work a lot of the time.

JERRY HARSTE (Indiana University):

My criteria for whether or not there really are theoretical differences is, if your theory doesn't change anything, you don't have much of a theory that's added something. What your theory does, says a lot of about what your theory is. I think we get a lot of people saying that they have new theories, but it doesn't change the interactions they have—who's interacting with whom, and it doesn't change the power structure.

That's why I'm uncomfortable with the sense that this is really a conference about portfolio assessments, as if we somehow agreed that portfolios are the answer. If portfolios don't alter the interaction pattern, and the power structures that are in play, it seems to me that it's not a new theory.

I really thought I had written my speech better in the sense of being clearer about what I believe. I really think that we need a shifting of the power structure. It's not just a matter of establishing new criteria. I think it's OK if Roger and I disagree; I want to have those conversations. It's OK if you look at a portfolio, if you develop some standards for it; I want the opportunity to look at the portfolio and set up a dialogue with that. This is not a matter of which group of stakeholders gets to speak.

What Education has learned from language is that the nature of language and the nature of knowledge is affected by the interactions that take place. In Education what we need to do is set up a structure that provides for multiple conversations. When, indeed, different structures are in place, then the teachers will no longer be at the bottom of the totem pole, and the kids lower than that.

Roger [Farr], too, has to take responsibility for what his tests test, and the model of language, wherein everybody in actual fact becomes interrogated in the process of assessment. Then I'll think we've made a significant change. I won't think so merely by identifying a new object, by portfolio. I want to see the quality of interaction. When your theory changes your action, that's how we know what your theory is.

BARBARA CAMBRIDGE:

I link what was just said to what we've been talking about in working with legislators. Whereas in the past, the State Board of Education has looked elsewhere, outside the state, the groups that have now constituted themselves as having a stake in the need to change policy *are* themselves a change in the power structure. The power struggle takes place both inside the classroom between the students and teachers and also outside the classroom at the state level with legislators and other people who are making policy decisions.

ED ROBBINS:

But I assume that neither you [Barbara Cambridge] nor Jerry [Harste] are saying that the only evidence of something being grounded in theory is that there is some demonstrable change that results from the application of that theory. While a change might happen, it seems to me that a position that is grounded or reflected in the status quo is no less theory-grounded. We can't claim that somebody is not theoretically based or grounded merely because they can't point to the changes they're making in the world. What we are already doing may be an embodiment of the theory that we already hold.

Farr vs. Harste

[Harste responded, talking about "revolution" and "dialogue," but did not come to the microphone, and therefore cannot be heard.]

ROGER FARR:

Jerry [Harste], who sets the standards, or are there none?

[Farr and Harste, failing to make use of the microphone, altercate about standards, state legislatures, and whether or not people in New Jersey think that correct spelling is the most important thing their children can learn.]

ROGER FARR:

...Do you think that people don't think about those things theoretically before they build them? Do you think that they don't invite in a whole range of respondents to debate and discuss what those standards ought to be? Why do you think that those things don't go on, Jerry? Why do you think that people don't work very hard on their theories of language development, and what they want to look at—not necessarily what *you* want to look at—but what they want to look at? They *do* invite in all kinds of constituent groups, and they have those discussions, and they produce from it, and they're willing to have you criticize and comment, and provide an alternative interpretation. But the groups *are* doing that, Jerry, and assessment has changed. For decades, it hasn't remained the same; any student of assessment can show you the remarkable changes over a long period of time.

[Harste's reply cannot be heard. The Farr/Harste altercation continues energetically, but out of microphone range, and is therefore unintelligible.]

How It Works in New Jersey
DIANE BLOOM:

Can itsy-bitsy New Jersey say something? Our skills committee did represent the various constituencies, and before they were finished, Jerry [Harste], they had to go out before their peers and hold open convocations to hear further suggestions for what needed to be changed. And the committee had to defend what they believed in, and many, many drafts were rewritten.

We still thought that the teachers had not had enough input, so we made another effort, and we sent out surveys about skills to all six hundred schools asking for their input. On the basis of the educators' strong agreement, we moved forward with the next phase.

Standard-setting for us opened another question. On the '86 HSPT, we do contrast grouping. First, we show the educators—all the educators in the State—the test, and we ask them to respond on behalf of the students that they have taught all year long. We ask them whether they think each child would be proficient on that exam. Do they think the child would pass—be a master, a non-master, or somewhere in between, borderline?

Then, after the student actually takes the test, we have the teacher's perception, and we have the student's actual performance.

Then, we do another contrast group. We say to the student, "Do you believe, after you have looked at this test and looked at these items, that these are things that you know and you can do well?"

This way, we have two sets of contrast groups. The educator who has worked with the children all year long, and then the perceptions of the students themselves.

[Harste and Farr continue their discussion, but out of microphone range. Bloom and others become involved. Overlapping conversations and laughter.]

ROGER FARR:

I gotta respond! First of all, who ever said that we're all after trying to make people look alike? All of us have really emphasized that the goal of education is to make people look different, not look the same. I know people who have been working on the sort of assessment that provides those kinds of opportunities, and trying to get it going, for a long time.

But I ask you, how *can* someone do what they want to do, when in fact they are hamstrung by not being able to read and write? How much diversity can you develop when the people can't go to the library and read a book, for example? I think that the legislators are saying, "We have to reeducate people when they get on the job because schools haven't done a good job."

We want to put in place at least some minimum standards so that people can go on to great diversity. New Jersey, and a lot of the other states, are saying with their skills tests that at least we can make sure that students have the opportunity to become

diverse. Give them some essential skills that they can build on and develop from! Let's make sure that this kid, who maybe isn't interested in reading or writing at all, at least gets up to some minimal level, and is a positive thinker about himself, so that he can go on and be diverse!

WHAT ARE THE THEORETICAL ISSUES INVOLVED IN ALTERNATIVE ASSESSMENT? WHAT ARE THE PRACTICAL ISSUES INVOLVED? HOW CAN THESE ISSUES BE ADDRESSED TOGETHER?

Assessment vs. No Assessment

BARBARA BACKLER (Harmony School, Bloomington, Indiana):

My school is an alternative school. Bill Bintz will be doing research in my classroom this year. We do no formal grading at our school at all. My daughter has been attending a college that uses only portfolios as assessment. Her whole first year just ended up with a portfolio "that big." She had absolutely no grading. I think it can be done.

In hearing Harste and Farr go back and forth, it strikes me that there is a real, basic difference between the person who believes in a "sacred" curriculum, a "canonical" body of knowledge that must be imparted, and the person interested in what students want to know and how they want to learn it. I think those are two terribly opposed approaches, and I think we need to be clear on what we believe in before we can go any further.

HENRY SHERICK (Measurement Inc.):

Even if there is a dichotomy like that, there still remains the issue of how one assesses.

BARBARA BACKLER:

But it's so different, depending on what you believe. Not believing in the sacred curriculum, I look at assessment as part of instruction. Someone else hears assessment as asking: "How am I doing? Am I accountable? Am I teaching what I'm supposed to be teaching?"

BARBARA LAWRENCE (Research & Training Associates; Chapter 1 Technical Assistance Center):

Another related issue gets at the theoretical underpinnings of both of those positions. One theoretical position asks, "What if students want to learn?" But, what if students don't want to learn?

A lot of students—and especially in big, inner-city schools—don't want to be in school, don't want to learn, don't know enough about learning to know what they want to learn. How does that impact on assessment? How do we make decisions about what to do with those students both in terms of curriculum and instruction, and of assessment? How would these two different theoretical positions address that issue?

HENRY SHERICK:

I agree with that, Barbara. As I listened to the speakers this morning, I thought a lot about the problems of—I don't want to call them all "inner-city" because all problem learners are not necessarily in the inner-city—students taking responsibility for their own education. I also have a problem with understanding how a teacher is going to implement an alternative assessment for either a very diverse classroom or a classroom that is mostly of the disadvantaged "Title One" kinds of students.

It's terribly difficult to get the slower–learning students involved in the conversational type of assessment or the alternative kinds of things in which students take their own responsibility. One can arrive at a theory of learning, but then one has to deal with the practicality of putting it into place. I don't doubt that the less talented student can learn under that method, but they can't learn under that method with thirty of them in a classroom. The teacher can never control it, never handle it.

Barbara, the Realist vs. Barbara, the Idealist

BARBARA BACKLER:

I want to respond first to Barbara Lawrence. Have you ever met a student who doesn't want to learn?

BARBARA LAWRENCE:

I've met students who didn't want to learn what was being taught in the classroom.

BARBARA BACKLER:

OK! That's totally different, though. I have yet to meet a child who doesn't want to learn, who doesn't have some innate curiosity that hasn't been stifled. But what I think stifles learning and curiosity is grading. There's no question in my mind! I refuse to grade, and I get kids that come to our school who were virtually problem students, but I take those grades away and—I'm not saying it's magic—it's pretty dramatic what happens.

BARBARA LAWRENCE:

Which brings us back then to the issue of reporting and monitoring at state and federal levels the progress of students in school. I don't necessarily agree that that should be a fundamental part of education, but in all practicality, one way or another, we're not going to get away from it.

BARBARA BACKLER:

Why not?

BARBARA LAWRENCE:

Because it would involve changing the entire philosophy of education in the country, and although it might be done, I think it would take a hundred years to do it.

BARBARA BACKLER:

I hope not!

BARBARA LAWRENCE:

I'd like to be an idealist in thinking that it's going to come about quickly, but from my realistic experience, I don't think it will. This is so particularly because people at the federal level are making comparisons between students in the United States and students in Japan, making comparisons across all countries in the world about where our students stand; because corporations are interested in those kinds of comparisons; because a lot of people are looking very hard at education and saying, "We're spending all of this money on education! What have we got to show for it?" Those are the forces that dictate that measurement is going to take place.

What we need to do is focus not on "What's the ideal?" but on "What's the best we can do given the constraints that we are under?" and "How can we go about making *some* changes in educational philosophy without entirely changing it?"

How to Measure the Heart

ANABEL NEWMAN (Indiana University; Chair, National Coalition for Literacy):

I work with a job-related adult literacy program in Indianapolis, and I work with students at the Reading Practicum Center who are "problem readers." But what I have found out is that they aren't "problems," and that we can teach them to read.

Over about the last twenty years of my observing in this arena, I have seen that there have to be affective changes that come first, attitudinal changes coming after that, and then we see what we would consider to be success. The success might be that the students read a book for the first time, they begin to want to go to the library, etc.

Now, we are making these measures accessible so that people who are charged with the responsibility of caring for the education of a whole state can monitor. Any five of us can look at those measures of success and say, "Those all make sense to me because they are quantifiable." We have bowed before the aspect of quantification for so long that what we're trying to do now is to add to measures of quantity the quality measures that come closer to being the measures of real educational change. Somebody who studies just to pass a test is not going to measure up to the development of someone else who is a lifelong learner.

If our tests force people to be dishonest, then we're going in the wrong direction. If we're forcing teachers to mistrust their own judgment, then we're going in the wrong direction. At the same time, we've got to have measures that are going to be accessible to people that have to be decision makers. So we're looking at these changes in affect and attitude and then in overall success. We define that overall success differently, depending on the person.

HENRY SHERICK:

How do you communicate the changes in attitude?

ANABEL NEWMAN:

We can apply what we developed in Cedar Rapids, Iowa, where we used what we called a "teacher quality index" (TQI). Three of us would observe the same person over time. We had a list of about twenty-five items to watch for, ranging from choice of resources to the ability to draw out the child. Scores on those items were averaged, and we assigned a TQI rating to each of the teachers.

We can do something similar now: We can say, "Affect has improved," and we can quantify it. "Attitude has changed," and we can quantify it. Then we can give a quantified report of the quality changes that have taken place in behavior, whether the change is high, medium, or low. That gives us a pretty fair shake at being able to communicate to a broad audience what's gone on with these kids and young adults.

141

BERT WISER (Director of Assessment Testing, Columbus, Ohio, Public Schools):

I have a question for Barbara [Backler]. I would agree from an idealistic point of view that extrinsic reinforcement can get in the way, that when kids become more and more turned on to learning for the gold stars and the pats on the head and the smiles of approval, that detracts from their intrinsic motivation. I see it in my own kids, and I know it in myself growing up, reading for the book reports and for the tests, etc. However, do you see this portfolio approach, or any other performance-appraisal type approaches, being viable for large-scale assessment?

BARBARA BACKLER:

What do you mean by "assessment?" Is assessment any different from the kind of instruction that allows for "growing," so that a person can see: "This is what I know right now; this is where I want to go; this is how I'm going to get there." All these interact.

I wish I had brought my daughter's portfolio. It is brilliant! I've read every single page of it, and I know that I can look at it and say, "Hey! That woman learned a lot in one year."

BERT WISER:

I'd bet that your daughter was not a Chapter-1 student or didn't go to an inner-city urban school. Do I win those two bets?

BARBARA BACKLER:

Well, sure! But it would work, it would work, inner-city or otherwise.

ANABEL NEWMAN:

Talk about some of your Harmony School kids.

BERT WISER:

Here's a for-instance: a high school proficiency test. They do multiple-choice testing in reading, in math, and what they call "citizenship," and then there's a writing assessment. To get the three multiple-choice tests scored, is nothing. The expensive, time-consuming, impossible task that they're facing is this writing assessment. Imagine if we were assessing the other subject matter areas that way! How could we ever get it done pragmatically?

Now, you're saying, "Why do we need all of this? The only thing we should care about is the learner looking at himself and saying, 'Am I learning what I want to learn?'"

Well, we have to deal with school superintendents, and they're not putting everything in the learners' hands. They want to know, "Are the students in Columbus mastering our course of study objectives?" And the state wants to know that.

Now, they also want norm-referenced information, and we can debate whether they need that or not, but they certainly want criteria-referenced scores. They want to know with each of our objectives, how the kids are doing. It would be very, very time-consuming and expensive and a real problem if we had to provide that information strictly on the basis of these large portfolios in every subject–matter area, both at the district level and at the state level.

Idealistic Barbara vs. Pragmatic Bert, and Gene, the Learned

BARBARA BACKLER:

[It would be hard] for a teacher to do that? To evaluate? That's all I do with my students. They write, they read, and I read and write with them.

BERT WISER:

If we let each teacher evaluate his or her own students, there'd be a bit of skepticism because it's rather self-serving. When you're making your own judgments about how your students are doing, and then you can pat yourself on the back and say, "They're doing great!" then every teacher will be doing great, and every building will be doing great, and every district will be doing great!

BARBARA BACKLER:

Don't you think every teacher wants every child to improve?

BERT WISER:

Well, sure they do, but the issue is, are they improving? I don't trust a teacher to be her own judge. We don't let basketball coaches ref the games! They've got too much at stake in the outcome.

Whether I like it or not, in Columbus our teachers have a stake in how well their students are doing on their tests. The principals have a stake, too. So, if we said, "Score your own! (Nobody's looking)," who knows what would happen?

I've sat at meetings when the directors of testing were talking about xeroxing the test forms and turning them over to the curriculum people. They were willing to say that in front of state people! What do you think would happen if we gave them those portfolios?

I trust Hank's scores. [Henry Sherick's company conducts school assessments in Columbus]. They have no vested interest in who's going to do well. They don't know the names on the papers. Furthermore, they've been carefully, extensively trained. They are closely monitored on a daily basis, and if they're not cutting it, they're dropped. (Isn't that correct? [Laughter]) I wouldn't trust teachers to do that because they haven't been trained, they're not being monitored, and they do have a vested interest in the scores.

BARBARA BACKLER:
I don't get it. What's our vested interest? That our children grow?

BERT WISER:
No, no!—Seeing that the kids get high scores, vested interest in seeing that the scores are high.

BARBARA BACKLER:
You're talking about a sacred curriculum. You're saying that I want my students to be able to say that they know "all this" by the time they get done. I'm saying, "No. I want my students to know who they are, where they want to go, and how they're going to get there." It has nothing to do with any sacred body of knowledge!

BERT WISER:
What were the three things you wanted them to know?

BARBARA BACKLER:
Who they are, what they need to know, and how they're going to get there.

GENE MAEROFF (Carnegie Foundation for the Advancement of Teaching, Princeton):
And that's all somebody has to know when they finish high school?

BARBARA BACKLER:
Yes!

GENE MAEROFF:

It's all over, if that's it!

BERT WISER:

That's why you go to a therapist!

GENE MAEROFF:

You can't be learned on that basis.

BERT WISER:

You're talking about self-knowledge and self-awareness, and we'll all be Rogerians, and that's all we've got to know.

BARBARA BACKLER:

Do you think that every student comes out of high school with the same body of knowledge? Do you think that they are all *learned,* or whatever that word was?

BERT WISER:

Of course not.

BARBARA BACKLER:

It's so artificial! It's such a big farce!

GENE MAEROFF:

That's not an alternative that *you're* offering.

BARBARA BACKLER:

I think it is. I want life-long learners. I want people excited about learning. I want people who want to grow constantly, but if you start grading them and telling them, "Oh, you don't know anything, you forgot to dot your *i!*"—forget it! They're not going to take risks. They're not going to grow.

And speaking about taking risks, I think we as educators have to take risks. We as educators have to say, "We don't want to report to the state and tell you all what our people know. What's important is what *I* know. What's important is how I know this child because I know this child a heck of a lot better than you do. And if I say that all these kids are making the progress that I think they should, then I think that's all that's necessary.

The Teachers Are Part of the Problem

BARBARA LAWRENCE:

If the majority of teachers had your viewpoint, I think education would be in a lot better circumstance than it is today. Unfortunately, I think that though there is a large percentage of teachers who are very motivated and who have indeed the best interests of students at heart, certainly one can't say that about all teachers.

BARBARA BACKLER:

That's a sad commentary.

BARBARA LAWRENCE:

It is sad; I agree with that, but it's also true. Having worked in approximately fifteen states observing and working with teachers, I can say that, in fact, it is true that there is a large number of teachers who, like in any other job, are there just to put in their time and take home their pay. So we can't turn these issues exclusively over to teachers; we can't put it in the hands of any single group.

There has to be cooperation among all levels of Education, from the state to the local government, to the administrators, teachers, and those outside of the public school system who are still in Education. We all have to work together because no one group among us exclusively has the interests of kids at heart. I think that's the bottom line. Rather than saying, "Turn it all over to the teachers," I think we have to learn to work together to produce the information in the best interests of kids to have them come out of school with the level of education that they need and that they want.

Barbara, Bert, and Gene Have Another Go

BERT WISER:

Barbara [Backler], I think that all you could teach is heuristics and inquiry skills. Would that be enough?

BARBARA BACKLER:

Well, yeah, yeah, teach them that, and they can find out whatever they need to know.

BERT WISER:

Supposing I came to you and said, "I know who I am. I know myself. I'm a functional illiterate. I don't wanna read." What would you say? "I have no interest in reading. Reading is boring."

BARBARA BACKLER:

How are you going to find out things you want to know then?

BERT WISER:

I'll ask.

BARBARA BACKLER:

OK!

BERT WISER:

Would that be OK?

BARBARA BACKLER:

Sure.

GENE MAEROFF:

Well, you certainly don't need assessment for that.

BARBARA BACKLER:

There's more than one way to learn. All of our people don't learn through reading. I went to Sears the other day, and they had this whole video on how to use a machine or whatever. Nobody's going to have to be able to read a manual. I just don't think that a person who doesn't read, good God! that it's the end of life for them. If they don't see the need, they're not going to learn to read anyway. I'm sure that all you people in Title 1 have met children who are not motivated to read, and they're not going to learn. And once you put a grade on them, and you start evaluating them, you kill *all* interest in reading.

Grades Aren't All Bad

ANABEL NEWMAN:

You don't need to. You absolutely do not need to. They can look at their own performance. They can look at their performance with their peers. And your students can agree on these things.

I have to turn in grades each semester in my college classes. I'm not keen on grades, but I've found that when I didn't give them, I lost a qualitative measure that I felt was important for that student. Not only that, but I am required to give grades.

But I found that as we work gradually through the semester, they get to the place where they're seeing their own knowledge and their own growth. When they're willing to assume that responsibility, they grow as prospective teachers. I don't find that it kills them off.

BARBARA BACKLER:

So they're involved in the evaluation.

ANABEL NEWMAN:

Oh, absolutely.

BARBARA BACKLER:

But how are they as applicates in our elementary classrooms?

BERT WISER:

Is measurement the evil or is bribery the evil?

BARBARA BACKLER:

Both.

BERT WISER:

I don't know what you're criticizing. Bribing kids to learn with a gold star? You can give out gold stars without being a measurement theorist. And then you're saying the bribery is the evil, that positive reinforcement is a bribe. They used to let the good kids sit near the windows. They used to let the really good boys open very tall windows with a pole; until I understood Freudian symbolism years later, I didn't know why it worked so well. I mean, they were giving us bribes all the time in school. Scoring and giving people a grade, you seem to see that as the giant evil.

Assessment Is a Giant Evil
BARBARA BACKLER:

I do. I guess because I see it as a sign of lack of success. And I think a child needs to be successful every day. I don't know—maybe you can give grades and make it a success thing. I had one of the VITAL students I worked with—he was my age actually—that I tutored to read.

ANABEL NEWMAN:

VITAL is "Volunteer In Teaching Adults to Learn"; it's a program at the Monroe County Library.

BARBARA BACKLER:

Just a wonderful guy! He didn't learn to read all through school. He told me quite frankly what happened in third grade. They retained him, he flunked, he got lots of F's. So he tried again. Fourth grade, they retained him again. He said, "I gave up, put my head down for eight years until I could get out, and that was it."

That kid is not an isolated incident. That happens over and over and over. I was a school social worker in the public schools for a couple of years until I just couldn't—I mean I came home crying every day. I can't stand to see all the failure that kids face every day. A kid can't face failure day after day.

BARBARA LAWRENCE:

That's not the fault of measurement.

BARBARA BACKLER:

Sure it is!

BARBARA LAWRENCE

No. No. It's the fault of the teaching methods, the lack of teaching methods that were used in helping this child.

BARBARA BACKLER:

Show me a way that getting an F is not failing!

BERT WISER:

Would short people know that we're short if you didn't have rulers? [Titters]

BARBARA BACKLER:

What's the point?

BERT WISER:

I thought the point was clear! I mean, someone who's not doing well at school, wouldn't they know it even if you didn't have rulers?

BARBARA BACKLER:

Oh, yeah!

GENE MAEROFF:

No, they don't!

BERT WISER:

That's the point! It's not the fault of measurement, that if people aren't successful in everything....they're gonna know!

BARBARA BACKLER:

Right! You have to give them successful experiences, but it's the F that assures them that they're not learning.

BARBARA LAWRENCE:

Whether or not you put a measurement, it's the issue of grouping, even—ability grouping. That's not measurement. We don't call that grading, but it is a measurement in a way because it says that this group can do this, and that group can do that, and never the twain shall meet. A child that's in the low group knows he's in the low group, whether you give him an F or not. It's not the measurement that's the issue. It's the whole philosophy toward the child.

BARBARA BACKLER:

That *is* measurement. That *is* measurement. I could never put a kid in a reading group. I just think that's absurd. And I think that's saying to the kid, "You're not as good as this other kid," and I just don't think that makes sense.

Education Is about Enriching our Children

PAMELA TERRY GOTT (Chapter 1 Technical Assistance Center; Advanced Techonology, Inc.):

This brings us back to the whole issue of what education is all about. I think we do want, as educators, to help children improve their skills in a wide variety of areas. Whether it's child-centered, so that they determine what it is they want to learn, or whether we have creative teachers who really spark some interest or not— whether they say, "You're going to learn this, and I'm going to try to make it fun for you," or "I'm going to make it terrible for you," —whatever the teaching style the teacher uses, we do have a body of knowledge that we want people to master. As teachers, we want to be able to show ourselves and the parents and other people what a child can do at the end of a year that he or she couldn't do at the beginning of the year. Has the child learned anything in school, and if so what? This is what assessment is all about.

The other day, my sixth-grade daughter had written a letter to a publisher because she had read a book by Roald Dahl, called The Swan, which was very upsetting. She had nightmares, and she said, "I never want to read a book by him again," and she wanted to get her money back. So I said, "Write a letter or something." She sat down, and she did, and I came home, and she had done this all on her own, and so I took her back to the shopping center where she had bought the book, and she was able to return the book and get her money back, and they said they would forward her letter to the publisher.

I thought that was really neat. I had no idea that she would be able to do things like this. She had learned writing skills, and she had read and was able to think about what she was doing. I want every child to be able to learn skills like that. I think the whole importance of alternative assessment is to be able to give some kind of richness to what it is children are able to do and what it is they know after being in school for five years or six years, that they didn't know when they were starting in kindergarten, and what is it that school has added that they wouldn't get just from living life.

I think in terms of alternative assessment, for instance, when you're talking about portfolio assessment, that you do have to be able to summarize that information at some level on an individual basis. You can look at every individual paper a child writes or look at the kinds of books the child is able to read, and talk to them about how they've understood what they heard on the evening news, and whether they understand what's going on in the Middle East, and these kinds of things, on a one-to-one basis. But when you're trying to summarize what a whole classroom of children has learned, our problem is—however you name it or whatever you call it—we do need to be able somehow to summarize what the changes are in the children's growth over a period of time.

Education, Like Writing, Is a Process
WILLIAM STRANGE (Director of Research, Indiana Department of Education):
Isn't the compromise, though, much like the way a piece of writing develops? I can write several drafts, I get a chance to rewrite, I get a chance to submit for review, etc. Can't we look upon these things that are going to go into the portfolio as an evolving event, a set of events, each one of which need not necessarily be assessed at that time, but maybe at the end of some period of time when somebody in a public, responsible position is going to have to come to grips with the question, "Does this thing have some worth?" and "To what extent is this person able to move on to some perhaps more lofty kinds of objectives?"

It isn't a black–and–white kind of thing. It isn't an either-or situation to me. It's like a formative/summative discussion. We needn't put a grade on everything that comes along. I think kids ought to be able to write things and do things, lots of times, without necessarily being assessed each time. There comes a time at some point when a decision is going to have to be made.

We ought to be able to settle for learning skills in high-stakes situations. Let's exempt some of these other kinds of assessments from high stakes until we learn how to do them a little better and more consistently.

What Are the States Doing?

GENE MAEROFF:

More than thirty states have mandated alternative assessment. What are the implications? I would like to know, if anybody knows, in those thirty states, how alternative assessment is either replacing, or supplementing on a large-scale basis, norm-referenced, standardized tests.

HENRY SHERICK:

I question that figure of thirty states. I am not aware of that kind of numbers. I'm aware of a lot of states who are doing writing assessment which maybe is called "alternative" assessment, "authentic," or whatever. I'm not aware of that number of places who are doing portfolio or other kinds of performance, except writing, and probably Michigan's and Illinois's reading test might be called other assessment.

JANE ARMSTRONG (Education Commission of the States):

The only state that has mandated authentic performance is the Connecticut "common core of learning" measure. New York has a legislated science hands-on assessment. Beyond that, I don't know...

[Several people speak at once, some mention Vermont, some California.]

JANE ARMSTRONG:

But not all of these are "legislated," not "mandated"—the word "mandated" is what throws us off.

GENE MAEROFF:

The whole point is, if you're just talking about individual kids, in my opinion you can get rid of all testing. I think the best thing is teacher judgment. If you're just trying to find out how kids are doing, and whether they're in need of something or progressing, if the only reason you have for assessment is for the individual child and the teacher, you don't need any kind of testing that I know of, and just let it go with the teachers. But if testing is going to have a monitoring function in a gross way—and clearly it is going to have that—then what, if anything, is happening to change the business with norm-referenced standardized tests in terms of alternatives that lend themselves to this gross use?

BARBARA LAWRENCE:

That's my understanding of what this whole symposium is about. I don't know that anybody has the answers to that at this point. I think there are some attempts, but I don't think we have the answers yet.

Alternative Assessment of Young Children
PAMELA TERRY GOTT:

I wanted to raise a whole other issue, the area of early childhood assessment in early grades. I know in Chapter 1, most states are not required to report any kind of standardized test scores below second grade. That brings up the issue, how are we assessing children at the lower grades?

The federal government is having people in Chapter-1 programs do "Desired Outcomes"—what they want children to master during the early years of their growth when they are receiving some kind of educational program. These are outcomes that people would like to see that child be able to do at the end of the set period of time. Right now, there is some flexibility as to what's going to comprise these desired outcomes.

In Chapter 1 now, it's a requirement that students be evaluated on standardized test scores in basic math and reading and also in advanced skills, higher-order thinking skills in math and reading and language arts. They are also adding, as well, alternative assessment of desired outcomes at those levels. A desired outcome can be that children will read twenty books during the year, or a whole variety of different things. You can look at other measures, like attendance measures, whether they're missing less school because they're more interested in what's going on.

Don't Blame the Tests
LINDA BOND (Policy Analyst, State of Indiana Department of Education):

I come from a medical background: I was a nurse originally and then went into measurement; now I'm a psychologist, so I understand the theory behind positive reinforcement's being better than negative. What I haven't understood with ISTEP, for example, is blaming the test for what's wrong with the kid.

There are some wonderful things happening in summer school because those kids get into a nice small group with ten children in a group and the teachers; some of these teachers are just wonderful, and they're doing exciting things with these kids. Ought we to credit the test for that? I don't. It's the teacher and what the teacher is doing with that test information to help those kids that gets the credit. It always seems that the test ends up getting blamed for treating kids badly because of the test results. In a medical model, you identify a problem and then you treat it. I mean, first you diagnose, and then you help the person. I just don't understand the notion that because you diagnose somebody as having cancer, you've done something wrong to that person.

JANE ARMSTRONG:

There's an assumption that if we get the test right then the instruction will be right, and I don't believe that. [Male voice sotto voce: "That's backward."] That if we have the best tests, then teachers would teach appropriately. I think if we had a moratorium on testing for five years, I don't think we'd suddenly have good language instruction in the classroom. The real issue becomes, How do we train teachers?—this whole notion of in-service. Let's work on tests. Tests are very important, but that's not the place to start. It's not "measurement-driven instruction"; it's "What kind of instruction should measurement be driving?" We're asking the wrong question.

Let's Have Both: Standardized Tests and Alternative Assessment
HENRY SHERICK:

If I were a teacher or a school principal in one of those situations that Bert [Wiser] describes, where someone is pointing a gun at someone's head, I think that I would want my teachers to be developing alternative measures. We can't overturn state-mandated testing in Ohio, but if I were in a school that was at risk, or if I were a teacher with a group of students that were at risk, I would want to be developing portfolios or other kinds of assessments if for no other reason than to protect my behind when the test scores came out. When the scores come out, and your district doesn't look very good, you need some other information in order to be able say, "We had kids that didn't start very strong. Look what we had to start with!"

I am a parent. I have two children in the public schools, and I like the idea that when the test scores for my children come home, I have the opportunity to get with the teacher to see if the test scores seem to confirm what the teacher believes about the way my children are doing. I don't object to seeing test scores, but I'd like to have some other information that would either corroborate what the test scores say, or have some information to refute them. I'd say let's give the schools three days a year of criterion-referenced or some kind of testing, and do the rest of the year with other kinds of assessment.

GROUP 4

WHAT ARE THE IMPLICATIONS FOR CURRICULUM PLANNING WHEN IMPLEMENTING ALTERNATIVE ASSESSMENT?

Assessment from Within or Without?

PAT BOLANOS (Key School, Indianapolis):

In our school, curriculum development and alternative assessment are developing in tandem. The teachers are expected to be a part not only of the curriculum planning process but also of the planning and development process regarding alternative assessment. The two things are not separated; they are totally integrated in the program. The mind set or culture of our school is pulled by curriculum development and how we assess it, rather than being pulled by outside forces. The forces are internal to the school.

How It Worked with Riverside in Arizona

FRED FINCH (Riverside Publishing Company):

In Arizona, the curriculum was established—the Arizona Essential Skills—and then they set out to develop performance tests based upon those skills. Riverside has been working with Arizona on that project for about 18 months. The performance assessments were very much designed to measure an intact curriculum that already existed. In that case, the assessment was developed to measure the curriculum.

The assessment was called "alternative" not in the sense of being a "replacement for," but as a true alternative. Arizona law calls for a norm-referenced test program plus a performance-test program that measures the so-called State Essential Skills.

BRUCE TONE (freelance education writer, Bloomington, Indiana):

Do they basically do multiple-choice passages and ask multiple-choice questions?

FRED FINCH:

Negative. One of the credos of the Arizona student assessment program is: "Thou shalt have no multiple-choice items." They

156

are all open-ended; they are all demonstration; a lot of writing in it; creating things—graphs, charts, and soforth.

BRUCE TONE:

Do they provide anchors or models?

FRED FINCH:

The term we're using is "scoring rubrics." The model is an essay-writing test with guidelines. Some of the items are short answers, some of them are quite complex.

How It Works at Key School in Indianapolis

VIRGINIA WOODWARD (Indiana University):

Getting back to the Key School, it's my understanding that a group of people came together with a common philosophical orientation about children as learners, and put in place a curriculum that might foster the kind of learning that includes the children, as well as the teachers, as a major part of curriculum planning. Is that true?

PAT BOLANOS:

I would say that the children influence the planning, but that the teachers are the primary generators of the ideas of the direction that the program will go. The children get their say in the assessment part.

We use a theme-based curriculum that changes every year. All of the children are expected at the end of a twelve-week theme period to develop a project, and to present this project to their classmates. These projects are videotaped, and we have individual video portfolios of all the children in our school.

The type of project that the students elect to do is completely up to them. They might decide to do a project that would involve some form of musical intelligence, or take a science focus, but it's up to the child to decide what type of project that they are to do; so it's very idiosyncratic in that way.

Because it is so open, we have been developing an assessment instrument to go along with assessing these projects and these presentations of projects, using the video as a basis for evaluation. We've been working with researchers from Harvard for the past couple of years, and we have two more years of commitment in this process. By next summer, we will be ready to report out what we've developed so far regarding assessment, but the assessment is all focused on these projects which grow out of the theme-based curriculum.

SANDY MACCARONE (Silver-Burdett-Ginn):
Are the themes that you're using the same for every grade level, or are they different?

PAT BOLANOS:
Yes, the themes are the same for every grade level.

Assessment Means Different Things to Different People
DIANE STEVENSON (University of Illinois):
I see a similarity between today's conversation and some of the results of our research. What assessment means, what instruction means, what accountability means, varies with the contexts.

In some of the districts where we went, we said we would like to know about assessment, and they told us right away about tests. In other districts when we asked about assessment, we never heard about tests. My sense is that this causes enormous confusion, sometimes because the same contextualization pertains to instruction, curriculum, accountability, and responsibility. Assessment, like everything else, is really very tied to the context in which it occurs.

In some of the districts, "assessment" meant a responsibility that the teacher had to herself, to her classroom, to the children, to provide the best possible educational environment, and to ensure that according to her sense of what really matters, that things were going well in the classroom.

In other places "assessment" meant "I push my teaching schedule up so that I cover all this material that those people tell me I must cover before the test, so that I have to cover the whole year by April 1, so that the kids get the highest possible scores." In that case, "accountability" meant covering everything, and covering it as fast as you possibly could. In one district, they eliminated recess and cut back lunch so that they could get enough things into their program [Laughter] so that they would be accountable to "the Iowa" and the new state reading test in Illinois and the new writing test that their district had and the push for Whole Language and the concern with phonics.

I think that communication might be well served if people don't assume that assessment and instruction, school accountability and responsibility, mean the same thing. They seem to be quite different.

More about Key School

VIRGINIA WOODWARD [to Pat Bolanos]:

You said that you have twelve-week modules with themes, and then each child develops their own project, and then you do an assessment of what they did. You mentioned just off-hand musical literacy. Do you assess that project in terms of musical literacy only, or do you bring in all the different literacies?

PAT BOLANOS:

All the literacies. Not every expressive area is used by each child, so it remains idiosyncratic.

Every year, each child is expected to develop and present three major projects. This is our fourth year of operation, so students who have been with us for three years have nine projects over those three years that the students have developed. We look not only at the quality of work in the projects and what areas or domains those represent but also at the skills related to oral presentation that the students need to have in order to make a good presentation of a project. These oral presentations are where we fit into the language arts.

Our results will be put together by Howard Gardner from Harvard, and they will deal partly with portfolios, but portfolios in a much broader sense than you all are looking at here. I'm not trying to muddy the water, but our scope is much broader than what you're dealing with, and I don't want to mess things up here.

BRUCE TONE:

Your evaluation depends on teacher judgment, right?

PAT BOLANOS:

Yes, it does; and that being the case then, the teachers are not being inserviced in our program. The teachers are part of the reflective process that's necessary in order to develop an understanding in the domain.

BRUCE TONE:

Gene Maeroff advised us that the public isn't going to buy that, that the press won't trust the teacher judgment. Have you had any indication about how the public reacts to Key School?

PAT BOLANOS:

The public is hungry for information about the school. We are deluged with requests for information. When these reporters keep coming and coming and coming, I stop to think, "Why don't they go someplace else?" I conclude that there must be very few schools across the country where change truly has taken place from the bottom up. Key School got started with a group of collaborative elementary school teachers who decided that they wanted to do things better and in a different way.

BRUCE TONE:

Is there any indication there of how the public will react to teacher judgment?

FRED FINCH:

The public have trusted teacher judgment for years and years and years. They continue to do so; it's a teacher judgment that designs those report-card grades. Day in and day out, they grade the papers; day in and day out, teacher judgment is part of it. The teachers trusting their own judgments is the problem with these new performance assessments. They have to be empowered to make those decisions and feel comfortable making those decisions. The teachers have always made the judgments. We're just giving them a structure within which to work. A new structure, a different structure, not a replacement.

BRUCE TONE:

The press would probably understand and eventually accept portfolios and that kind of assessment, and understand it as well as they did the SAT, which was not at all.

BETH BERGHOFF (Indiana University) [to Pat Bolanos]:

I'm curious if your children are going to be involved in the assessment of their own projects.

PAT BOLANOS:

Yes, they are. I also need to report that we have been given no waivers to do what we are doing. We are still held accountable to the state tests of educational proficiency. What we do, we do over and above everything else that is asked of us. We're gaining strength, and we've come to consensus about standardized tests.

Although we are still measured and compared to all other schools within the system, and although our standardized test scores have been more than adequate, and they are reported in the paper with everyone else's, our strategy is never to make references to them when we are talking about our students' progress. We will just let those tests and scores die of benign neglect.

Don't view me only as a principal who's bragging about her school: I'm really trying to report to you what the staff is involved in doing. But we are so intent as a group—and this is a small group; this is a school of less than two hundred students—to develop alternative assessments, the staff has gotten involved in truly collaborating as practitioners with the theorists and the researchers. It's very different from the relationship that most practitioners have with universities. It's a very different relationship. It's a truly collaborative effort, and it's going to bear fruit. We will have that for you in writing with examples by next summer.

VIRGINIA WOODWARD:

Can you say more about how the pupils reflect upon what you're doing with evaluation?

Key-School Student Involvement in Assessment
PAT BOLANOS:

In this twelve-week period, the students keep a written record of ideas and possibilities regarding what type of project they might want to do. They practice their presentation skills as they go along near the end of the project time. After their presentations, the videos, which are very important, are shown, and the students get to critique their own presentations of their projects, discuss it with their teacher, take suggestions on how they can improve. It's a constant process, and there's not a cut-and-dried step-by-step process at all. You're constantly going forward a little bit, going back and reflecting, going forward a little bit more, going back.

The stakeholders, the people who are involved in the process, more and more people are getting involved in it. For example, one of the investigations that took place this past year was regarding how you help students prepare for giving a presentation. Young students, second-graders, get just as nervous about giving a presentation as do we adults. They decided that one strategy would be to involve other students in

161

the classroom in helping them with their presentations, so they would have another second-grader introduce the person who is going to give the presentation. More people are getting involved, and it's helping the students do better work. Nothing is static yet. Everything is in the process of being critiqued, and everyone is in the process of critiquing.

DIANE STEVENSON:

I hear you saying that assessment is part of a reflective process which is part of the curriculum which is part of the learning which is part of...and so on. What other function do you expect assessment to serve? Does the information you derive serve an external function?

PAT BOLANOS:

Wasn't that Maeroff's question? How do you report the outcomes of alternative assessment at the state level? We haven't gotten that far; it's not a concern right now. Perhaps it will emerge later on.

SANDY MACCARONE:

Have your standardized test scores gone up since you started this process?

PAT BOLANOS:

We have only three years of standardized test scores. They vary from group to group, from grade level to grade level, depending on the makeup of the group that's being evaluated. There's absolutely no screening of students before they come in. They get in by luck of the draw. They are selected by lottery. Having no screening process for students, we get a wide range of students, from slow learners to gifted students. We also have cross-age grouping. We have such a complex mix in the environment that it's very difficult to critique standardized test scores that come out of that environment.

Can We Have It Both Ways? Both Standardized and Alternative?

DIANE STEVENSON:

If a portfolio is a living document, and if it is really a collaboration between the student and the teacher, and reflects what the student knows, ultimately the child can perform all the steady tasks. Then, the standardized tests could still be administered to that child, and the child would do very well because we've gotten the child to think and be involved in his own assessment.

Some people think we need some standardized instrument; I don't agree that we need it, but if it's there, it's there, and if I have done my job as a teacher and gotten the kid to think about the concepts that I'm trying to get across, then the kid is going to do OK on the test. I'm not talking about individual isolated skills, but at a concept level. The kid can do algorithms in math, get concepts in social studies, can do some kind of research stuff—all the nice things that you want to pull together in your projects at the end. Then, at the end of two years, you look to see where the growth is, but it doesn't matter what you're testing at the end or what instrument you're using because the process works, however you test it.

PAT BOLANOS:

In many ways, I agree with you except that, when teachers are being held accountable by these test scores, and they are used as the measure of their success, borderline students who ought to go into special-education classes get pushed ahead to regular classes; so that, in fact, their scores get elevated.

We haven't sent one child into special education, not one. We have LD students and emotionally handicapped students in our classes. But we have a context in which everyone is supporting the teacher for keeping those slow learners in their classes and doing a good job with them. But in situations where the teachers are going to be held publicly accountable by test scores, they're not going to want to keep the slower child in their classes.

VIRGINIA WOODWARD:

Aren't you collecting some very fascinating data on the slow learners? That will be valuable data. After a few years, you'll have data that will help other people in terms of planning curriculum, but premised on the point that the child is really the informant. The children in your school are the informants.

Can We Change Instruction for the Better by Building Better Assessments?
DIANE STEVENSON:

One idea that concerns me is that by changing assessment—and by assessment, I mean that which comes from the outside and is imposed upon—that one can somehow *improve* instruction. That was indeed David Pearson's intent as the major writer of the Illinois test: By building his (quote) "better test," his intent was to improve instruction.

The research that I did with him suggested that that hasn't happened. He and I interpret our data a little differently! [Laughter] But what we see is people doing everything that they can do to change their practice so that scores go up. An example is in the first-grade classrooms, where two of our teachers now will no longer answer "yes" or "no" to a child's question; they will say "maybe." What is the reason for that? In the third-grade reading test, "maybe" is a desirable response. The teachers feel that the children have not been well prepared for "maybe's," so they try to say "maybe" fairly often. [Laughter] If you can have "yes," "no," or "maybe," you gotta get 'em ready to say "maybe."

My concern about portfolio is the assumption that you can change instruction by the use of your means of assessment. Take writing portfolios, for example. We assume that the writing process means growth over time; so, if we do portfolio assessment, we will thereby change instruction. In fact, that has not happened. It works the other way around. The teachers teach how to do well so that students can put the right kind of documents in their portfolios. It seems highly manipulative. Instead of saying, "We would like instruction to be more processed; now let's work on that," people are saying, "What do we want? How do we get that?"

SANDY MACCARONE:

That has to come from within. Were a teacher to buy into the whole concept of listening to the kids' contributions, and having kids collect their work in portfolios, the way the teacher teaches would change. The teacher would look not just at the work only, but would ask why the work is there, why the child put the work in, how the child feels about it. The teacher would be having a dialogue with the child.

I'm not interested in portfolios as assessment so much as I am in portfolios as teaching process, as a means of really looking at a child holistically, with the idea that the student is not merely somebody sitting at a desk, but somebody who is contributing to his own education. The definition of school as a seat in a row has got to give way to the idea of an interactive school, and that's why I think that portfolios as a process is what I'm going after.

DIANE STEVENSON:

Teachers often don't have that choice. It's one thing for a teacher to have the option of saying about portfolios, "I like that idea," but it's something quite different if someone comes in and says,

"You're doing portfolios! And you've got to have this many documents! And if you don't do well, then...."

We have a number of assessment instruments that are really good, when we give people the option to make informed choices about what to use. If we could trust our teachers enough to allow them to make their own choices, I think that a number of the available instruments would work.

Assessment Skulduggery
JACK SCHMIT (Indiana College Placement and Assessment Center, Bloomington):

I hear people saying that the term "portfolio" seems new to them. They hear the concept; they like the idea of teachers and learners engaging each other. But now the problem is, how to keep from screwing up a good idea. Once the politicians start making their demands, and once the administrators start looking to see if it works—and they want to know in no more than three lines how it works—and then when we have to report the results statewide, then we'll have to take what used to be a good idea, quantify it, and mandate it, and put all these requirements on this very good idea, then it's going to get bastardized.

BRUCE TONE:

If the portfolio is as open and varied as the Key School's appears to be, it ought to persuade teachers—the way Sandy [Maccarone] says—and I can't believe that your teachers feel that concerned about the objective test. Do they still?

DIANE STEVENSON:

Some do. Oh, yes, because it's public information. You say "persuade." The information that would persuade a teacher never comes to the teacher.

BRUCE TONE:

Through the process.

DIANE STEVENSON:

But it doesn't. There's not a choice. Persuasion works in a situation in which people have information, and then they choose.

In a system in North Carolina where I worked, they went to a statewide writing assessment. At the teacher level, there was a chart from which one had to teach these kids these things every

165

day. I was in a classroom where the teacher wanted to teach reading and writing, and they told her she couldn't. She could do reading after the reading test, and writing after the writing test, and until such time, she was to teach them for the *holistically scored state assessment.* She had no choice.

There was no "persuading." There was no, "What did she buy into?" They gave her one hour a week to teach reading and writing, and the rest of the time to teach for the test. They told her they wouldn't bother to come in when she taught reading and writing. They only wanted to see, "Was she preparing them for the test?" So it didn't matter diddly-squat what she got persuaded of or what she bought into. There wasn't that choice.

In some districts, when we asked people about assessment they said, "Could you please turn off the tape recorder?" When we sit in their classrooms, they say, "Could you put down your pencil? Because I don't want people to know what I really do, I'm afraid of having people hear what I think."

It's a very difficult political issue. We're not necessarily dealing with people who have free choice to make those kinds of decisions. And it's the high-stakes part of it that causes this interference.

BRUCE TONE:

Would you be as tolerant of a teacher who was very, very rigid and conservative, and *wanted* to test with homemade or purchased objective tests? Would you want that teacher to have that choice?

DIANE STEVENSON:

I think that a good teacher is a teacher who has a very strong and well-thought-out idea about what matters, and has developed ways to assess that. The issue, I think, is not *how* the teacher does that. It's not a matter of Whole Language *versus* phonics *versus* whatever. Good teachers are reflective practitioners.

GROUP 5

HOW DO SOCIETAL CONCERNS INFLUENCE THE DEVELOPMENT OF ALTERNATIVE ASSESSMENT?

What's Wrong with Traditional Assessment?
JOHN WARREN (ERIC/RCS):

> What concerns in the society have started up these ideas about alternative assessment? What's wrong with traditional assessment?

FRED SMITH (Indiana University):

> One of the big concerns to me is, if we develop portfolio assessments, if we use lots of performance assessments, but they're not based on competencies or skills, what do we do with the results? How do you use those results to inform re-teaching or follow-up instruction? Are you specifying what the kids need after the assessment?

JOHN WARREN:

> You're asking what factor of traditional assessment these portfolios are addressing? How is the portfolio overcoming the old notion of traditional assessment?

TERRY SALINGER (CTS):

> You're using very negative terms about traditional assessment. The first thing we need to do is to expand the terminology about traditional assessment. It's not a question of "overcoming." It's a question of looking at what has been done, aligning that with instruction, seeing what is good in assessment as it now stands, supplementing perhaps, but to throw out traditional assessment immediately is what is going to get portfolios thrown out very quickly.

JOHN WARREN:

> What issues, then, are we addressing with portfolios in reference to traditional assessment?

FRED SMITH:

I think that society is seeing a number of graduates from public schools who don't read or write very well. They have become very distrustful of the schools, and they've said, "We don't think you're doing a good job." The schools come back and say, "Well, we're doing a good job. We're doing the best we can." Now society is saying, "Prove it! And give us some information that you are doing a good job with these students. Become accountable for what you're doing."

I'm not sure that the society has pushed alternative assessment so much as that it is a response coming from educators who want to do a better job. I think we all admit that we probably can do a better job than we're doing, and that the portfolios, or whatever, are an attempt to make the evaluation more meaningful to everybody. And of course that gets us in other kinds of problems.

JOHN WARREN:

The educational community is realizing that they do have a problem, and the concern about alternative assessment is a result of this? Is this what you're saying?

FRED SMITH:

I guess that would be a fair thing to say. I think we knew we had the problem before society reminded us of it. The question here is whether we can improve the job we're doing with our students and at the same time inform society fully as to how well we're accomplishing the objectives that society has in mind for the schools.

Society's Many Uses of Assessment
BRUCE SMITH (Managing Editor, *The Kappan*):

I'm not an expert at testing, except that in a sense we're all experts in testing: We've all been tested to death from the time we were little kids. I think what motivates people to want an alternative assessment is the very thing that is so attractive about traditional assessment, which is that it gives you reliable and valid measurements of something. What is driving educators to consider alternatives is that they think that's not a complete enough assessment, so "supplement" is exactly what you've got to say because of the two functions that testing really serves.

The one we heard the most about this morning was assessment for diagnostic purposes—the use of portfolios: It can be used in the classroom. It can be used by teachers to improve instruction next week, next month, to pass on to the teacher next year, but that's different from the monitoring function which tests serve in society. When they came out with standardized tests, we didn't like the kind of problem they said we had. We thought that the kind of writing we were teaching was not being assessed by the tests of standard written English. Now they come up with performance assessment of various kinds, and now we don't know what the devil to do with it.

I think that's really the problem: We don't know how to report it. My kids go to school here in town. The teacher may do a whole lot of stuff and collect lots of things that you might call a portfolio, but she sure as heck can't send that to Indianapolis in a box and say to the State legislature, "Look what a great job they do at Rogers School." Instead, they take the ISTEP tests, which are made up from various standardized tests.

As long as society and its elected representatives want us to give them a thermometer reading on what the schools are doing, what we're talking about here today as a way to promote the success is not going to be the answer. I'm not happy about the situation, but the fact is, we don't trust our schools when the doors close. We don't trust the teachers to do the job right. Society is paying for it, and we want to know we're getting our money's worth.

BRUCE GOLDBERG (The AFT Center for Restructuring):
I'm not sure about the term "society" used in this context. I think there is a schizophrenic attitude in which business interests and some policy makers are advocating a greater practice of autonomy in the schools, decentralized structures, and new forms of government. At the same time, these same people are also demanding to see the results of allowing this greater flexibility. They're somewhat conflicted internally about the degree to which they are offering with one hand what they are taking away with the other.

We just had a meeting earlier this week of fourteen large urban districts concerned with the issue of alternative assessments. The degree of skepticism was quite large among the conferees— including testing people, curriculum people, and teachers as well. They were dubious about the barriers to the implementing of alternative assessments, which seem to be very tremendous not only in terms of conflicting signals from society but also in terms of actual legal constraints that are presently in existence in some places. Federal regulations for Chapter 1 that require reporting on the basis of standardized tests interfere; another example of interference was court-ordered desegregation in Kansas City.

I see the demand for alternative assessments as not so much on the part of people who have been disillusioned with public schools, but as the demand for some way of understanding and making understandable what is in fact going on in the schools. It's about accountability. Without involving oneself in the discourse surrounding the particular forms of assessment, it remains that we must find ways to devise responsibility measures, measures of accountability, that don't necessarily and exclusively rely upon testing as the sole means, whether it be standardized testing or alternative or authentic type of assessments.

KATHERINE LAWRENCE:

I work with school districts to help them understand their test results. I think that technology has really impacted the schools; the tests have caused changes. If we're going to prepare students to live and function in today's society, they have to be able to do different types of tasks than can be measured by a multiple-choice test. We need this! The new NCTM guidelines in mathematics point to tremendous changes in mathematics in the next few years. Are we preparing the youngsters for this? How are we assessing this? We have to assess their thinking processes, the higher-order thinking skills. These demands necessitate different kinds of measurement. Yet, as was said, traditional testing is a very efficient way of getting at some baseline data about knowledge.

JOHN WARREN:

Maybe we need a bifurcation of assessment, using alternative assessments for the sake of the teacher and also to measure the students' learning, whereas traditional assessment could be used to demonstrate accountability to society. In that way they would be supplementing each other.

TERRY SALINGER (Educational Testing Service):

We look at, analyze, and criticize standardized testing, and make many comments about how bad the tests are, but what we don't look at are the mandates of the state legislatures and the local districts that have in some cases caused more than 10% of the school year to be given over to testing. Especially in elementary grades, testing becomes a moot point for students. They see the test coming, and they see preparation for the test as the bulk of their instruction; teachers see this, too.

We need to reconsider the mandates for the amount of testing that goes on. We can talk and talk and talk about alternative assessment methodologies, but we need to talk about the amount of testing that is demanded of students because that really is the issue. A good standardized test supplemented by good teacher observation, supplemented by some alternative systematic way of gathering information, can give a good picture of each student, can—with some careful work—produce aggregations of data for accountability. But in many states, children are tested and then they are tested another time, and then they are tested another time and they are also tested with the basal-reader test. So where is there room for instruction? Where is there room for interaction? Where is there room for reflection? There is no time for that. There is absolutely no time for that. The major issue seems to be the amount of testing and the amount of testing that is mandated. When legislatures and school districts want more accountability, they say, "Let's give another test!"

JOHN WARREN:

Are you saying, then, that what we want to do is work alternative assessment into the curriculum so that it isn't a separate testing process but an ongoing process?

TERRY SALINGER:

I think that's absolutely essential, but I also think that the amount of testing that is required is a very important issue. To lobby for alternative assessments without lobbying for a reduction in standardized testing is foolhardy because teachers who are not involved actively in their profession—and that tends to be a fairly large percentage of the teachers in this country—are going to view alternative assessment not as something to serve their instruction but as another testing program; so it will become collection day for the portfolio: "Everybody's going to sit down today because it's Tuesday, and Friday I have to look at your portfolios."

I have seen this happen in school districts in New Jersey: "Give me a check list so that I can go through all these papers, and I can check that Child X has reached a certain level of reflection; I can check that Child Y has done three imaginative pieces; I can check that Child W has made a selection of an excerpt from his or her literature log."

I've worked with one school district that has implemented a portfolio assessment project from preschool through grade three, and they have the nicest, *nicest* set of check lists. Their portfolio that follows children from preschool through grade three consists of reams of checklists. In arguing with those teachers about the need for real-work samples, they counter my arguments by saying, "First-grade teacher doesn't want to know what the kids do in kindergarten. Second-grade teacher doesn't need all that stuff." That's where portfolios are going to go, unless there is a real addressing of some of the very basic issues, and a part of that issue is the over-testing with standardized tests.

KATHERINE LAWRENCE:

As educators, we need to educate the legislators and help them to cut down these mandates in the amount of testing. They are destroying instruction in the classroom because, as has been said about these "high-stakes tests," they cause teachers and students to start preparing for these tests three months prior to the actual test. Let us as educators educate those legislators not to require this kind of testing, and to stop putting the pressure on the school people who are the scorers, and then ranking the scores in the newspapers.

Needed: Right Assessment of the Right Abilities
JOHN WARREN:

How can we implement alternative assessment while decreasing traditional assessment? How can we get alternative assessment worked into the curriculum?

LEO FAY (Indiana University):

You people who are involved in test development, test marketing, and so forth: At this conference so far I've heard us talking about only two alternatives—either portfolios or tests.

And the public wants to know about the kids, "Can they do something?"

We have a large center here [ICPAC] that is working with two hundred eighty thousand high-school kids helping them adjust to the idea of going to, and getting ready for, college. We get thousands of letters from high-schoolers, and I would say that at least three out of four are very poorly written, starting with the basic form, let alone the language in them. (It's rather interesting: In following up, we find that the majority of the kids who write a decent letter have taken a course in Business English in addition to the regular English curriculum!) My question becomes, "What kind of thought is going into other types of alternative assessment?" Portfolio, putting things in a folder, seems a little skimpy.

Motorola made an analysis of what was required for people applying for employment on their assembly lines. They found that arithmetic skills that typically are taught through the fifth grade, and literacy skills that come out on a test about seventh grade, would meet the requirements for job entry. They found that of the people applying for those jobs, they had to provide remedial help for sixty percent of them.

An analysis like this suggests to my mind that we need to find ways to show that people going though school actually reach a mastery level at doing certain things. Are we coming up with assessment approaches to attempt that? I don't know that a portfolio would necessarily accomplish that purpose. Does the question make any sense to you people who are developing tests?

The Results of Alternative Assessment: The Kids May Be Worse Off than We Thought
TERRY SALINGER:

ETS does not do assessments by and large for school-age populations. We have in some of our regional offices contracts with state development programs, state departments of education. We're looking very much through those efforts primarily at writing alternatives and various forms of constructive response items. We're also looking at the differences in scores of students who take items in a multiple-choice format *versus* those students who take the same items—and this is in math— as constructed-response item.

We're finding something that substantiates what you're saying—and this is not market-driven work, but within our research division—that when students are given multiple-choice items in the math tests, they tend to score at certain levels depending on their ability. Giving students of matched ability the same tests as constructed-response items, however, decreases the percentage of students who pass the test by as much as, in some cases, fifty percent.

This result interestingly substantiates criticisms of student learning. I think it also tells us something very important in terms of assessment. As we look at alternative assessment methodologies, whether portfolios (which is rather wide-open and can be far too loose to be useful) or constructed-response items (which the student constructs rather than choosing a response), we may find that we're in worse shape than we thought in education.

Required to come up with an answer, even if it is simply to do a math problem, students are not able to do this. We know from the national assessment that they can't write essays particularly well.

I don't have an answer to that. I'm a former classroom teacher, and I know the game, but I'm certainly not going to sit here and say: " If we want to get good scores, we give a certain test, but if we want to get bad scores so that we can get more funding, we give a different, a harder, test." But I do think that we really need to be prepared for the information that alternative assessment is going to give us, and about what we are going to do when we don't like the thermometer-reading that it presents us. The thermo- meter of alternative assessment methodologies has the capability of telling us that our kids are really in trouble, that they really can't think, that they really can't solve and explain math problems.

The States of California and Massachusetts have both been experimenting very thoughtfully with alternative state-level assessments, different from Michigan and Illinois in that the majority of the experimental assessments have been constructed-response. Students have been asked to solve math problems in California, and explain their solutions.

Interesting information results from that. In Massachusetts, in reading, social studies, science, and, I think, math, there has been a pilot study of constructed-response assessment at the fourth-, eighth-, and, I believe, the eleventh-grade level. Wonderful, wonderful test items! *Not* wonderful results!

Massachusetts is in trouble financially, so we can't think of an immediate infusion of money into the schools. The impetus for the Massachusetts work, and to some extent the impetus for the California work, was to get a window into students' higher-order thinking skills. The window tended to tell more than the states wanted to know. If we push for alternative assessments other than portfolios, I feel that we're going to get some information we really don't like. We need to be prepared as an educational community then to respond to that.

What's a Portfolio?
MICHAEL PRIESTLY (Macmillan-McGraw-Hill):

I think that you are asking whether we have alternatives other than portfolios, and, if so, will they tell us whether kids will achieve mastery of anything if we use them. I think portfolios are misunderstood; they can include anything you want them to include. A portfolio is just a folder, but most of the progressive programs involve including all of the alternative assessments within the portfolio. The portfolio is a reaction to a standardized test that gives you one score; a portfolio is designed to give a number of different forms of evaluation: "Here's how the kid does writing, here's how he does reading, here's my observation of his interactive skills, here's his listening ability." All those things would be combined and structured in the portfolio.

LEO FAY:

So a portfolio is just a mechanical gathering together...?

MICHAEL PRIESTLY:

...just an organizational tool, and it gives structure to the teacher and to the student for what's expected of the student and how to organize it all—all the different kinds of assessments—and a place to put all the results. I don't think anyone at this point is willing to say that it's for mastery, but it's similar.

The other key that's often left out is that the portfolio has to begin with a set of goals, and it has to begin with some kind of baseline data at the beginning of the year. Otherwise it's a meaningless instrument. So if you give some kind of an assessment, or if you have some previous year's information on the student, you know where the student is. Set some goals for the student to reach by the end of the year—maybe one goal in writing or a goal in reading to reach a seventh-grade reading level, to be able to write a business letter with no mistakes, and so on. Those might be the set of goals that go with the portfolio. Then, devise the assessments, or select a variety of different assessments, to measure whether the student reaches those goals. But even then, you don't know whether the student has made progress unless you have some baseline data to start with.

LEO FAY:

Bill, do you buy all of that?

Instruction and Assessment Are One

BILL BINTZ (Indiana University):

No. I don't buy that at all. For a fact, I think that you [Michael Priestly] underestimate what I think is the power of a portfolio. Listen to an artist talk about his or her portfolio! They don't enter into it with a set of predetermined standardized criteria at all. In fact, through the talk, much learning takes place; it's through the act of conversation—talking about their work—that a lot of insight into what is driving that piece of work, as well as how that work is connected with other work, takes place.

The problem I have with portfolios used in that traditional way is that it's nothing more than a collection of representational forms filed in a different folder, simply a collection of the same standardized criteria. Unless we're willing to change the criteria, then assessment won't change. In this country we're unwilling to make those changes as long as we continue to use "mastery" learning models, behavioral objectives, and things of that sort. As long as we are unwilling to change the criteria of assessment, assessment will continue to be based as a methodological issue.

People assert that there is a difference between assessment and instruction. I would argue that there is no such difference, that assessment and instruction are the same thing. For instance, every time you give a standardized test in reading, you're giving a piece of instruction. Within that test, because that test is theoretically based, that test has a theory of reading imbedded in it. When you give those tests to kids, I think you are, at the same time, giving those kids lots of messages about what constitutes reading.

The problem with those standardized tests is the great gap between the theory of reading that drives standardized testing and the theory of reading based on recent advances in reading

176

theory. Instead of thinking of alternative assessments in reading, my position is this: We should think about updated assessments in reading. There is a tremendous chasm between them. My indictment, quite frankly, is that the tests that you are producing, while theoretically sound, are based on outmoded, antiquated models of what we currently know about reading.

MICHAEL PRIESTLY:

You've lost the focus of your discussion here, haven't you? You started proposing a portfolio model, and now you're criticizing me for developing tests that I don't write. [Laughter]

BILL BINTZ:

What I'm trying to say is that what's driving the use of the portfolio is collection of data that represents the same old criteria. We haven't moved very far. There is very little difference between a standardized test and a portfolio in terms of reading, if the criteria about reading are the same for both.

[Everyone speaks at once.]

Letting Go of Prescribed Curricula
BILL BINTZ:

I'm trying to articulate what I think is the fundamental problem here: Our criteria have to change. By changing criteria, then we can start looking at how those criteria can guide us in changing assessment tools.

MICHAEL PRIESTLY:

I agree. What I was mentioning is the structure of the portfolio. Let's say that the goal is for a student to become a strategic reader who selects books and reads on his own. That's a goal that you can't measure with a multiple-choice test. By using that goal, you have determined that you now have to use some kind of strategy-based reading model, you have to use some kind of oral reading assessment, you have to use an alternative assessment to see what the student is selecting and whether the student enjoys it, and you have to interview to see if he liked it.

I agree with what you're saying to the extent that what you have in the assessment and in the portfolio depends on what your goals are. If your goal is to be able to use a comma correctly in a sentence, then you haven't changed any assessment. If your goal is to become a strategic reader or to enjoy reading by the end of the year, then you have changed the assessment.

BILL BINTZ:

Let me follow up on that. When you talk like that, the thing that comes to mind is that assessment is now a curricular issue. You are describing a curriculum that is socially negotiated in the classroom; it evolves from kids taking control over their own learning in those classrooms, as opposed to having it come from without.

Are we willing to let go of privileging ourselves by mandating a curriculum and then devising assessments to determine whether that curriculum is met? If that's the case, then we've got to find alternative assessments to get at the learning that actually goes on in the classroom, as opposed to learning that *we want* to go on, and that we prescribe from outside. The issue is, to what extent are we willing to let go of the predetermined curriculum.

MICHAEL PRIESTLY:

Or "supplement," as we put it before.

Thoroughly Restructuring the Schools
BILL BINTZ:

And that is a political issue.

MICHAEL PRIESTLY:

To me, the essential issue in alternative assessment is restructuring the schools. I think that none of this is going to matter very much unless, at the same time, changes are made not only in assessment but also in curriculum, instruction, and governance. All of those things have to change simultaneously; otherwise we run the risk that Terry Salinger brought up. Teachers by and large are exceedingly fearful of these portfolios or alternative assessments being another "add-on program" with the same kind of consequences-driven and high-stakes implications. And this conflicts with all the other messages that they are getting about increased autonomy and professionalization in the classroom.

We have to be willing to give up the notion of curriculum not only as an intellectual act but also politically. Curriculum is, in fact, rooted in the very political organization of school districts, how they are constructed, and the turf that the people are willing to defend and fight over; and educational politics goes all the way up through the school districts to the State Departments of Education and so forth. Unless there is some actual restructuring of the way in which all those things are operative, the whole issue of alternative assessment will die out in a period of years and become just what it was intended initially to overcome.

Curriculum as a Power Question
BILL BINTZ:

I want to ask a question. Who are "we" who are "giving it up?" And who are we giving it up *to*? Whom are we talking about?

If I used the term "giving it up," I'd like to take that back because I think that's a poor use of words. I don't think that teachers, or anybody in this room, simply throw the doors open and "give up" anything about responsibility for the curriculum. On the contrary, when I use the phrase "give it up," it means to share with kids in a classroom, and to demonstrate and to support them in asking their own meaningful questions, pursuing those questions, helping them answer those questions, but most important, getting them to continue asking better, more powerful questions than they asked before.

By "giving up" the curriculum, I'm implying that somehow we've got to negotiate what is a power issue. The curriculum is a power issue, and as long as we hold power over curricula, then schools will be nothing more than a credentialing service, will be nothing more than putting kids through institutions, reactionary institutions, at the whim of big business.

Who is dictating the agenda with the terms of business? They are playing more and more a role in what kinds of kids we produce. The same people that are trying to infiltrate schools, and to use their powers to dictate who gets what and how they get out, are the same people who are dictating my role in those classrooms. So by giving back the power to kids, I'm also at the same time giving back the power to myself to conduct myself in a professional way in classrooms.

FRED SMITH:

I'm a little concerned. I like to think of myself as being liberal, but are we saying that there shouldn't be some kind of a broad curricular structure proposed for schools in this pluralistic society of ours? Is it all decided by the teacher, or the teacher negotiates it with the child, or are we talking about some broad guidelines within which the teacher has a certain amount of autonomy, and that autonomy can then be shared with the kids?

179

Are we talking about a strictly centered curriculum, or does society have the right to expect that there be a certain kind of product produced by schools in order to participate in, and contribute to, the society in a meaningful way?

I understand that once I close my classroom door, I'm in charge of the curriculum, but over the years I've also been indoctrinated— using the word in a positive sense—through my own education, through my own living in the society, to know *something* in my discipline, *some* of the things that people are going to need to learn. Now, I can negotiate with kids, or the school corporation can negotiate with me, the teacher, in order to teach in a certain constructive way. For example, if I want to work on higher-order skills with kids, that flexibility can be negotiated. But I have a hard time thinking that a third-grade at-risk kid by himself or herself can ask fully meaningful questions. Granted, their questions may be meaningful for themselves, but they can be very, very disadvantaged by their own limits in asking those questions.

MICHAEL PRIESTLY

I think that this is perhaps the major issue upon which we'll focus in the '90s. Thinking about Chubb and Moe's book, for example, there will be one group advocating increasingly that the only way in which the kinds of responses and self-directed students and higher-order thinking skills can be developed, is with increased autonomy, given some sort of voucher plan. There will be another group, as I view it, according to which the only way that public education can survive is if there is some degree of national consensus around issues of standards, and the development of something like a national test to implement it. I think these two groups are going to be the central groups of the 1990s, and it's probably something in between that'll come out.

JOHN WARREN:

Seems like many of the problems arise because students come from different backgrounds. You [Fred Smith] mentioned the third-grader at risk. Would that third-grader be at risk if at an earlier date he or she had been taught a question-driven curriculum rather than an answer-seeking curriculum? Do evaluations of a student determine that student's willingness to ask questions about his or her own educational development?

TERRY SALINGER:

It's a socially driven question being debated quite intensively in the Baltimore Public Schools. It's an important question, but it's a question that cannot ignore the backgrounds from which these children come and the lack of structure in many children's lives—the lack of academic preparation in children's lives, and the lack of value structure that they in increasing numbers bring to school. We have children coming into schools who have been severely damaged by the first five years of their lives. They are not going to be prepared for a question-driven curriculum because these children were born of teenage mothers, were born addicted to crack, were born in abject poverty. The school's role must include providing some structure for their lives. For a five-year-old from that background, structure is answers, not more questions. I think that if we listen to the very, very powerful debate on the impact of process *versus* product instruction on inner-city children, and if we take that seriously and not sanctimoniously, then we have to evaluate what exactly our expectations are going to be, and what we're willing to do for those children.

INTRODUCTION OF DON ERNST

DONALD WARREN
(Dean of the School of Education, Indiana University):

As a historian, I have to tell you that I am finding this conference both reassuring and stretching. Reassuring, in that it's nice to know that among assessment people there is conflict. [Laughter] It's also nice to know that at least some of you on some occasions have a sense of humor, and that you have a refined sense of history. That came out this morning in some of your technical language. Historians have a very clear sense that things are "sort of new" or "sort of old" or "sort of this" or "sort of that," and I'm sure you'd be reassured to know that "sort of" is a technical term for a measure that historians apply frequently. [Laughter]

The conference is stretching because it's an important conference. It's dealing with a topic that is crucial to the improvement of American education, and we may have a chance to pull off some improvement this time because world events are driving education off the front pages of the newspaper. [Laughter]

A few weeks ago when Indiana's Governor, Evan Bayh, was appointed to the new National Governors' Association panel to assess the progress of education in the United States, newspapers around the country carried the story, and the *Washington Post*, at least, noted that one reason Governor Bayh was selected for this panel was because of the high quality of his staff. Donald Ernst, our speaker today, is probably accustomed to such mass recognition. In fact, one could argue that he personifies one of the problems that you were discussing in assessment this morning, that is, what may be termed "subterranean achievement."

Don became Governor Bayh's Executive Assistant for Elementary and Secondary Education last April. From 1982 to 1986, he had served Governor Bill Clinton in Arkansas in a similar capacity. In between, he got a fair dose of Academia as a doctoral student at the University of Washington working with John Goodlad in the Center for Educational Renewal. He has been, in short, at the center of school-reform efforts in the United States, and his knowledge of the education policy environment at both national and State levels is well documented. But I want to add that he has also been a schoolteacher, and a very effective one at that. Educational achievement and reform are achieved in discrete steps, and so it's worth noting that in 1981, Don was named "Teacher of the Year" at Southside High School in Fort Smith, Arkansas. It is my pleasure to introduce Donald Ernst.

PUBLIC ATTITUDES AND POLICY CHANGES: OBJECTIVE TESTS AREN'T ALL THEY'RE CRACKED UP TO BE

DON ERNST

I hope to raise some important policy tensions about the issues with which you are all dealing. I also hope to raise some of the important tensions that are particular to the public-policy side of the discourse on assessment—assessment in general, that is, as I make no claims to be able to bring any enlightened view to assessment specific to language arts.

In 1983, I was in Arkansas, a state that one of my former history professors once described as a place so unwilling to invest money in education, that if the people of the state were required to vote a tax increase so that the Lord, Jesus Christ, might return tomorrow, the tax-paying voters of Arkansas would vote him down.

In 1982 and 1983, Governor Bill Clinton, one of the more thoughtful leaders in this country, decided to devote almost all of his time to educational improvement. As the governor held hearings in all 75 counties, one of the things that began to take some shape was the difficulty that parents and others had in indentifying problems. Another thing that happened was the amazing number of letters and messages that came to the governor stating that teachers were not doing the kind of job that people thought they ought to be doing.

The way this concern got translated into public policy was a statewide test for teachers. Arkansas was the first state to develop a basic skills test. The governor and others began to realize that maybe one hook to satisfy the undefined yet real concern that many Arkansans had, was to respond politically to that growing concern with a basic skills test—Why not a test to help determine whether or not teachers have the basic requisite skills to walk into a classroom and stand before children?

I want you to understand how difficult that issue was for me. I was one of the first people to come directly from a classroom to a governor's staff—a very daunting, and occasionally troubling, transition to make. I was on a leave of absence; I thought, "I'm going to do this for a couple of years, and then go back to being a social-studies teacher." Once you've jumped into this policy world, I'm finding out, you can never leave.

At any rate, I came to this job as a teacher on the governor's staff. I'd historically been involved intimately in the politics of education in Arkansas and in teacher politics. So you can understand the tension I was feeling. Here I am, a policy advisor to Governor Clinton, who's proposing that we test all in-service teachers! We're not talking about a test for certification; we're talking about a test that you have to take before you get recertified—the first time anybody had ever done that. You can imagine the difficulty.

I remember one night I was flying back from south Arkansas with the governor, and he shook my knee. I was asleep, and he shook my knee, and he said, "Ernst, I never knew that the public would react as they did. I never knew that teachers would be so mean as they turned out to be." I'd warned him about that, but he'd failed to read my memo.

The truth is, that the test was fundamentally a political ploy to raise taxes. Indeed, the chairman of the State Senate Finance Committee said, "I will not allow any of the tax legislation to reach the floor of either House until and unless we have a teacher-testing bill." The governor had gone to all 75 counties, and after he floated this trial balloon, it was clear that he had struck a chord with the public. The more the teachers worried, the more the teachers complained, the more the teachers took on the governor, the more the public became convinced that a basic skills test was exactly the right thing to do to correct all the problems in education.

The result, after a 1.2 million dollar appropriation, after the test had been stolen not once but twice [Laughter], after the reports of cheating [Laughter], almost 97% of all the Arkansas teachers passed the test.

Unfortunately, the test issue proved to be a lightning rod for school improvement in Arkansas because what did happen was that for the first time in twenty-six years, and the first time in the history of that State, significant amounts of new money were put into that underfunded system largely because of the political leadership of Bill Clinton. I don't say any of this to speak ill of Governor Clinton; he's one of my most important mentors and someone for whom I have a great deal of respect and love very much.

But the truth is, that test caused a problem that, I would argue, still exists today in schools. The morale was dramatically low following the test. Lots of people were hurt. On the other side, a new sales tax was implemented and severance taxes on both timber and natural gas were raised, and 10% of that new money was devoted to the educational needs of Arkansas's children.

You get a sense then of some of the schizophrenia that I'm bringing to this discussion. On the one hand, from a policy perspective in a system that's underfunded, that's desperately in need of new resources to deal with more significant and substantive needs of children, I'm thinking if we have to test the teachers to pass tax money for schools, why not?

I feel drawn to the perspective of those who want firm, quick, immediate feedback from schools and school children. Addiction to the notion of the quick fix is the father of the modern-day notion of accountability. You all know that better than I do. Certainly, one of the drugs of choice in this quick-fix category is tests—I suspect—both norm-referenced tests (as in "Johnny learned more than Mary did") and criterion-referenced tests (as in "Johnny, Mary, or any other student learned what we've tried to teach them"). We also know that such data from tests have been used to provide the stuff that modern-day educational accountability is made of. For governors, legislators, educators, and, indeed, even the public, the use of tests have satisfied this addiction to the quick fix.

On the other hand, as a teacher, I understand that maybe it's not worth that. Maybe there are some things in a democratic society that are more valuable than selling your life for a penny sales tax and severance taxes on natural gas and timber.

Let me raise a problematic question: Have we corrected the problems of schooling by this fixation with psychometrics and tests? I answer, no. The tests remain a primary tool for policy makers to use to gauge the quality of the educational system, but, at the same time, the tests do not improve the quality of the educational system.

This question brings me to the next struggle: The makers and users of these norm-referenced tests are guilty of sorting students on the basis of the bell-shaped distribution or the normal curve—whatever the hell "normal" means. I agree with John Goodlad and Ken Sirotnik that there is nothing normal about this statistical and psychometric invention. Indeed, problems associated with children being sorted based on a very narrow view of the universe is contrary to my views and my understanding of a democratic society. Do we not believe, as Jefferson taught us, that there is a connection between human learning potential and democratic values?

But then, how do we maintain this notion of accountability and also insure that children are learning? How do we gauge both of those at the same time? We have created this notion in our society that accountability is as simplistic as giving one test at one time of the year, the results of which are reported to governors, legislators, educators and others, while neglecting the larger issue of school improvement and ongoing evaluation.

Borrowing from John Goodlad's view of the world, that one of the synonyms of accountability is responsibility—*responsibility*—then one of the many challenges to policymakers, in my view, is (to use the "P" word) to make a paradigm shift, a subtle but important shift from accountability to responsibility. Borrowing again from Goodlad and Sirotnik, let me share some heuristics for shifting from accountability to responsibility.

- Let me suggest that we go with *process* instead of *product*.

- Let me suggest that we talk about *profession* rather than *work* or *trade*.

- Let me suggest that we talk about *meanings* and *understandings* instead of *symbols* and *explanations*.

- Why don't we talk about *long term* instead of *short term*?

- Why do we have to talk about *closure* when we might be talking about how we might help students deal with ambiguity? (We live, I think, in an amazingly ambiguous world—and all we have to do is look at the Middle East to understand that.)*

- Why do we have to *confirm* things instead of *continuing to explore*?

---

*Iraq had recently invaded Kuwait.

- We talk about *uniform*. Why not talk about *contextual?*

- We are *reactive*. Why are we not *proactive?*

- We speak of *authority*. Why not talk about *leadership?*

- We talk about teacher *isolation:* Let us think about *collaboration.*

- *Power* and *manipulation*—why don't we replace that with *facilitation?*

- We talk about *external rewards*. Why not *internal motivation?*

- We talk about *legitimate right*. I think we should be talking about *trust.*

- We ask teachers to *follow,* and, indeed, part of what we do is to mandate their followership. Let me suggest that we talk about *working consensus.*

- I'm talking to you, and I hope this is more than a conversation, but I would prefer to use *discourse* or *communication.*

- From an economic perspective, we talk about *cost/benefit analysis.* I prefer *critical analysis.*

As we talk about this shift from *accountability* to *responsibility*, I acknowledge the struggle involved. Certainly, I don't believe that not using criterion-referenced testing is the way to go. However, I'd like to believe that that kind of information is simply one piece of the larger data used to guide the discourse on educational improvement. These tests *ought* to be one piece of a greater body of knowledge—not unlike the kind of knowledge and understandings of contextual realities of schooling that Sarah Lightfoot talks about so eloquently in her book *The Good High School.*

Nonetheless, I would take the position that, right now, we are overrelying on tests, and that causes the need for this kind of debate and discussion. I applaud you for joining this. As a policymaker—whatever that means—I have to be informed by this discussion. Someone earlier talked about broadening this discussion, so that we don't use an esoteric language, so that the discourse includes parents and others outside the realm of the school, so that they can also participate. It's an important and difficult question.

Benjamin Barber, a political scientist at Rutgers, talks about strong democracy, and about how this society had better start thinking about creating new institutions to engage the public in serious conversation, something to which a democracy ought closely to attend. I'm not sure that's happening in this country. Indeed, I think that what's happening is that we're reducing the participation of serious public talk in the democracy. That frightens me, particularly as we look at an issue like assessment because I don't know—let me be very candid—I don't know how it is that we begin the conversation with a larger public using the language that I'm hearing, as talked about in this room. I ask that as a question, and I'm interested in responses.

As a student of schooling and education, I know that schooling is a very complex phenomenon, and I also know that politicians and the public have a difficult time coming to grips with that. We've all been to school. We all understand what schools are like. Schools haven't changed.

One of the most important books I've ever read in my life was Seymour Saracen's book, *The Culture of the School and the Problem of Change*. Saracen has this little space person who hovers over the school, and the little space person—from Mars, I believe—could not tell the difference between the little people who came to school and their actions, and the big people on PTA night when the parents were doing the same kinds of things: raising their hands when spoken to, moving when the bell rings, grown-ups doing the kinds of things that children do. The point that Saracen was making obvious is that change doesn't come easily in schools.

I also know that no test in the world is going to guide me to answers to the questions that are enduring and imbedded in schooling. So where is the answer, if one exists, to this tension between the problems of schooling and the policymaker's desire to be able to gauge and measure what it is schools are about and how students are progressing?

Perhaps the answer rests, again in the words of Seymour Saracen, with an exploration of the use of alternatives—alternatives is the focus of your symposium today. Let me briefly explore a few alternatives. Implied in my words that schooling is a complex phenomenon is a notion of gathering additional information about schooling and student learning. But I'm not suggesting that we replace the overreliance on testing with an overreliance on the collection of a wider range of information.

As a student of both Ken Sirotnik and John Goodlad, I'm drawn to their notion of a different epistemology regarding evaluations and the roles that people and data play in the process. Information ought not be an end in itself, nor should one piece of information, one test, be the sole criterion by which all else is judged.

Ken Sirotnik talks and writes about this alternative, a constant tension among educators concerning a systemic and rigorous deliberation over any and all information relevant to improving schools, serious and ongoing critical inquiry into the renewal of the school site, where the learning and the rubber meets the road, that is, how it is that the teachers are engaging children in knowledge.

I understand that from a policy perspective this is perhaps too idealistic. I can't imagine how, before a legislative committee, I would talk about putting the responsibility of evaluation completely and solely at the site level. Think about how difficult that might be! I also understand that this would be a demanding new role for those at the school site, and to be quite frank with you, I'm not sure the policy world nor the educators are ready for such a view. It points to the fact, I think, that teacher education must deal more seriously with producing teachers, educating teachers—I don't like the term "producing"—educating teachers to be more thoughtful and responsible for changing their own world and their own school, for renewing their own school. Indeed, my sense is that pre-service teachers would be well served by being informed by the conversation that's occurring here today.

Another alternative: Perhaps we should consider more seriously Sarah Lightfoot's penetrating analysis of schools where the focus is on the quality of life in the school environment. I'd like to believe that has something to do with education and how children learn. "Goodness," in Lightfoot's definition, is the ability of those in the schools to reflect honestly on their own practice and their own conditions and their own problems. Indeed, at the core of her notion of goodness is the ability at the school site for the people most involved to be self-critical—something that's not now ingrained in the culture of most schools.

Perhaps the work of Ted Sizer and his colleagues, some of whom are working with state policymakers, would provide an alternative. I understand that Grant Wiggins is working in Connecticut to develop alternatives to multiple-choice tests—Grant Wiggins, obviously borrowing from Sizer's notion of exhibitions of mastery for his proposed "the horse as compromise." Indeed, the notion of exhibition of mastery is, I guess, the cornerstone of an essential school. The intent of the exhibition is to help schools and districts, perhaps even states and nations, create more authentic, engaging, revealing, and trustworthy measures of students' intellectual ability.

I think that Sizer's reference to "engagement," as Wiggins has also said, is important because it's a response to the drudgery and boredom found in many schools in this country. If we don't respond to the circumstances and conditions of teaching, I'm not sure I care about the assessment process.

One small example: Would not the publication of a literary magazine by a class with individual assignments, directed by a thoughtful English teacher, be a helluva lot more authentic and exciting for students than a multiple-choice-question test? I think so.

This leaves me with some important tensions and questions. I understand that John Dewey used to get up in front of crowds and give three- and four-hour lectures, and when he would end, he would say something like, "Thank you, I'm much clearer on that now." [Laughter] So, I'm not going to leave you with answers; rather I'm going to leave you with some questions that are troubling for me. What I hope is that you can help guide policy debate in this country in a way that makes sense for conditions, circumstances of learning for children. We are in a time, I think, when we are backing up from the notion of a common school. I see in *The New York Times* that Oregon is putting on the ballot the whole notion of the Chub-and-Moe theory of choice. I worry about that.

Some questions:

- How do we break the habit of testing—testing that only narrowly informs educational improvement?

- How do policymakers move beyond the current use of tests—tests that now are equated with notions of accountability?

- How do all of us make the shift from the notion of accountability to responsibility—responsibility that shifts the monitoring of schools from the State House (with its mandated testing programs) to the individual school sites and to those who inhabit those schools? This might suggest that the state role then becomes one of providing a rigorous framework of curricular values, principles, and goals, while leaving room for site-level decision-making to respond more adequately to the needs of every learner.

In conclusion, the question that I'm dealing with here—and worrying about—is that traditional tests are inadequate alone to guide fundamental improvement of schooling in a democratic society. Yet, I'm troubled that we don't seem to be making this paradigm shift very rapidly, and we seem still to be relying more and more on tests, perhaps because unreliable reliance on test scores as the exclusive indicator for schools is a helluva lot easier than confronting issues of authentic assessment coupled to issues of school organization, professional working environments, and the way children are engaged in knowledge in our schools.

I would like to solicit your assistance on behalf of governors' aides: How do we begin to prepare our governors for the National Goals Panel, whose main charge, by the way, is one of assessment. How do we think about assessment at the national level? I'm not talking about Mark Tucker's notion of a national exam, mind you. But, these governors are going to have to get up to speed quickly and think about this issue.

To be very candid with you, I'm daunted by that: I'm not quite sure how to begin preparing the governor for this discussion. Particularly, when it's clear that this is also a very political process, defining the national goals is not exclusively an educational process. I agree with Paolo Freire: If you begin to think about separating education and politics, then you're barking up the wrong tree. I'm soliciting assistance, counsel, advice for six governors, a President, and others who are going to be engaged, whether or not we want to, like it or not, in a very important process for thinking about assessment at the national level.

Questions, comments, spears, arrows?

UNIDENTIFIED SPEAKER:

Your office has a consulting firm roaming the streets....

ERNST:

No longer. They're gone.

UNIDENTIFIED SPEAKER:

[Unintelligible]

ERNST:

[Repeats question] What did the policy consultants who early in the spring and summer were roving the state find out about what the public is thinking? I'll be candid: I don't know. I have not seen the summaries of their work. I can tell you that there was some frustration with what they had done. I can also tell you that, I assume, the governor is continually polling to find that information out.

I think it's a mixed reality. I think that we know, for instance, that there was a deep concern, but how that concern gets documented, gets translated into policy is a fifty-four-dollar [sic] question. I don't know. I think there was frustration. But you know what, more importantly, I think there is unfortunate apathy. I think there are many people who feel that they don't know how to access schools. They don't know how to participate. They don't know where to get answers. They feel daunted about participation at the school level.

I think also that there are some other factors. If we believe that all children can learn, one of the important populations of students that we're worried about are the at-risk kids, and I think that what we know about them, at least a great many of them, is that the demographics of their family life is so problematic that it is unclear about how their parents feel about where policy ought to be headed.

On the other hand—this may be a very political answer, but I don't care—I'm reminded of one of my favorite politicians, Senator Dale Bumpers from Arkansas, who argues that his role as a senator is more nearly that of an educator, and that certainly he has an obligation and responsibility to be attuned to public opinion. But more importantly, he has an opportunity to inform the public in a way that is sound and moral. So, whatever the public feels, I think we ought certainly to pay attention to that, but, at the same time, I think that leadership has a responsibility to inform the discussion as best as possible.

ANABEL NEWMAN (Indiana University):
How was the information gathered by the consultants supposed to come out?

DON ERNST:
It's internal information primarily, as I understand it, and I'm not even certain, to be honest with you, that it has been compiled in any readable fashion. Those people were doing their work before I ever showed up here.

UNIDENTIFIED SPEAKER:
Going back to your first question, how do we break out of the testing cycle? For those people in the state who are devoted to breaking out of the testing cycle, what is the best way to get information to you?

DON ERNST:

Call me! There is a common feeling among many people that while there may not be a direct policy path, we now have to move beyond ISTEP, add to it. At least I hope there's an opportunity to talk about that in a way that makes sense. So I think that you jump right in; be willing to show up at State Board meetings and talk to legislators, and be a citizen. I'm very happy to listen and to learn.

BRUCE GOLDBERG (AFT):

What alternatives are being offered to the idea of a national test? What has been the response on the part of the governors or the governors' aides to Tucker's idea and to the Commission's idea? What is the range of options that you believe exists for enabling some degree of accountability to be given to the national goals?

DON ERNST:

You and Al Shanker! Mark Tucker is not alone with this national test business. Let me be clear on that; let me repeat that again. Al Shanker also supports national tests, and that's why you asked the question.

What is the response? Mixed. There's a group of us who, like Woody Allen, would blame Al Shanker for destroying New York City. In the movie *Sleeper*, when somebody asked Woody Allen how New York City was destroyed, he said, "Al Shanker got hold of a nuclear bomb."

Mark Tucker is a very charismatic and engaging fellow, as is Al Shanker; and in political worlds, that kind of personality works. I can tell you that there are a number of governors who have relied upon Mark Tucker a great deal, and I like Mark a lot. I think he's a very thoughtful fellow, and I agree with a lot of what he says. I disagree with some.

I have to tell you that I think that it's a distinct possibility that a national test is going to be part of the proposal. I can also tell you that because politicians have to be responsive to political constituencies, that it won't be without cost, and it won't be without serious listening to the variety of actors and players in that discussion.

I have very mixed feelings about...no, no, I *disagree* with the notion of a national test for reasons that are beyond my concerns about tests in general. The common worry is that the national test would then create and drive a national curriculum. I think that's enough to kill it, to be honest with you.

Options? I think that discussion is just beginning, and I guess I would say to you that certainly the notion of a national test is part of that discussion.

GENE MAEROFF (Carnegie Foundation):
On what basis have some governors concluded that the public in general wants a national test? Moreover, from your conversations with governors and your insights, what is it that you think that they think the public wants of assessment?

DON ERNST:
That's a powerful question, and one to which I'm not sure that I have a full answer. In April, during a dialogue among about 26 governors' aides, we heard a presentation from Jack Foster who invited all of the governors' aides to begin participating in the discussion that's going on now in Kentucky about looking differently at assessment. I'm encouraged by that, but I'm not sure that it's occurring fast enough for governors and others. Part of what we're dealing with here is the rate at which these things gather speed without thoughtful and important discussions such as this one today. I question whether a national test is a good idea, and I am sure that it has not been been fully debated.

In Connecticut and Kentucky there is going be some sharing, and organizations like ECS and NGA will ensure that there is broad- based discussion about a variety of alternatives in assessment. While I hesitate to pin-point any of those, I think we can look to the work of the Relearning Project, and Ted Sizer and his staff working in collaboration with ECS. There are some strategies, obviously small ones, that are trying to leverage the system to think differently about assessment.

The interesting thing about that is that those are small operations, and they are largely operated by people who, with all due respect, are not unlike you all: They are academics, and they have trouble being comfortable in a political world. I have an amazed and abiding respect for John Goodlad, but I think one of his frustrations throughout the course of his fifty years of worrying about education and democracy is the lack of attention paid to him by policy makers. I suspect that's one of the reasons that Ted Sizer, and now John Goodlad, both have thoughtfully connected with ECS as facilitators, hoping to get their ideas into the policy world.

I'm optimistic right now. Next year, I may not be because the truth is that the President and the governors have more power than do ECS and John Goodlad and Ted Sizer.

GENE MAEROFF:

How did they decide that they think the public wants a national test?

DON ERNST:

I don't know. My hunch is that the kind of stuff that Mark Tucker and others and even Al Shanker supports—this is going to be controversial—is politically sexy. (Oh, that was candid, wasn't it? I'm leaving after this!) [Laughter]

HOWARD HILL (Phi Delta Kappa):

No. Stick around. You're doing just fine. You've given ample food for thought, and I think we're going to leave here better prepared to dabble into some of the issues that are before us.

As we look at policies and how policymakers tend to come up with some of the obvious solutions, they try to be proactive and reactive at the same time, as though the two can be concomitants. But policies tend to precede professional preparation, so that unless all of these mainstream ideas can merge, coming to a point where we can say, "This is the path we should take," we will continue to be reactive and proactive at the same time. So how can we find a proactive starting point so that we can hope to come to a common end that is not reactive?

DON ERNST:

At the end of Robert Bellah's book *The Habits of the Heart,* he's talking about the notion of common good, and how it is that we achieve common good. His answer, I guess, is that we achieve the common good together and in common and in debate and discussion.

If you look at the last ten years of educational reform—Larry Kubin's piece in AERA back in the spring, "Reforming Again and Again and Again"—reform has been very top-down. I think we've corrected some of those problems. I think ECS has to be given some credit for deepening the dialogue to include thoughtful researchers who have spent a great deal of time understanding the conditions and circumstances of learning and teaching. I hope that will begin to inform the process, unlike before, so that we have good knowledge driving policy.

We have to start with governors and others who are willing to open themselves up to that wider and deeper conversation; and that's tough because historically the role of these people is to make policy, not to be guided by, or to be facilitators of, policy. My response is that we have to be more democratic about the process, which, I acknowledge, causes really serious timetable problems. We policymakers have to have things ready for the next legislative session, and indeed, I'm facing that right now. "What are we going to be doing for the next legislative session?" is the kind of question that puts *your* question back in the file drawer.

I think we need to be thinking differently about how we engage in policy discussions. Again, I'm applauding ECS's role in helping to facilitate a paradigm shift from this notion of top-down to the notion of policymakers also being part of the larger discussions so that everybody gets to play a role.

Part of the reason I enjoy my job in the political world, which lives on the quick fix, on the immediate, "we gotta get things done tomorrow!", is that if we rely on this approach—the idea that the politicians have to have the answer before the next legislative session—then we also know that at the next legislative session after that, we're going to be going through the same process again. I'm troubled by that, but I'm also fascinated by it. I guess one of the reasons I enjoy a job like this so much is that the opportunities are immense; the frustrations are also great, but the opportunities are immense.

Your question is a powerful one, and I'm not sure that I have been very responsive. I guess my answer as both an educator and a policy person is that we have to deepen and broaden the discussion, and insure that before we make those kinds of policy decisions, that we're thoughtful.

PUBLISHERS' FORUM: THE FUTURE OF ASSESSMENT

MIKE BECK (Beck Evaluation and Testing Associates):

This is the "Publishers' Symposium on the Future of Assessment," and knowing these people, I think that none of them is pretentious enough to speak on quite that global a topic. I think they are going to speak about assessment this *fall*...[Laughter]

I give a lot of speeches, but I never write my own. My eight-year-old daughter, Amanda, writes my talks for me; I get my words of wisdom from her, so as I was preparing for this one, I said, "What shall I tell them about in Indiana?"

She said, "You know what gets me? You go every week..." (It's not *that* often!) "...and give these talks to teachers, and all you talk about is testing. Why is it that you talk about testing when what we're supposed to be doing is stuff about school? That's about *teaching*, isn't it?"

I thought, that's actually the theme of this symposium, so I said, "This isn't just the regular kind of test." (She does the keys for most of the tests that we write, as those of you who have used some of them know! [Laughter] "We're not going to talk about these multiple-choice kinds of tests; we're going to talk about the other kinds of tests." Because she's written my other talks, Amanda knows about "authentic assessment" and all these other neat things—she knows just as much about them as most of the people who write the articles! [Laughter]

I said, "You know about multiple-choice tests, and authentic ones like writing essays and putting things in your folders and all that kind of stuff, and your school is a Whole Language school." (I had been told by her teacher, "We're a Whole Language school because we teach all of language." I replied, "That's good; what does that mean?" She said, "Well, we teach *all* of the skills." [Laughter])

So I asked my daughter: "You know about both of these tests— which one do you like better?"

And she said, "Well, Dad, I really like the multiple-choice kind the best."

I was very flattered by that because that's mostly the kind of stuff that I do, so I thought, "Well, she does it because she really likes her father, and has gotten used to eating two or three times a day, and really values the things that her father contributes." So I said, "Oh that's great, Amanda! Why do you like it? Because of the reliability coefficients and things like that?"

She said, "You know why I like 'em? They're a lot faster! You just get them out of the way, so we can get on with school." [Laughter]

Today you're going to hear about, in Jerry's [Harste] term—a "first-draft world," the first-draft world of assessment. What will be said will scare a lot of you as it scares some of the people on the panel, and it will depress or excite a lot of you. But we will at least hear some thought-provoking ideas from a semi-random assortment of publishers on what they are about in creating the future of assessment.

CATHY TAYLOR (CTB):

I'm the Senior Project Manager for CTB. I decided to talk about high-stakes assessment because, even though there are lots of kinds of performance assessments being used right now, the ones that motivate CTB are high-stakes assessments. Even though I have personal values concerning the uses of test scores, I'm here to represent CTB, and not my own values; so here I am.

What is "high stakes?" I want to make it real clear. I know there are a lot of confusions about definitions. By "high stakes" I mean, "the scores are in the newspaper." Teachers are evaluated. Schools are evaluated. Districts are evaluated. States are compared. That's high stakes. Decisions are made about kids based on scores on tests. Those are high stakes.

My daughter was in third grade last year, and third grade is a CAP year in California. That's the "California Assessment Program." Every week she brings home a stack of homework papers, and she has until Friday morning to finish them. I don't like them because they're discrete worksheets unrelated to one another, and every week I would get more and more annoyed.

Finally, in January, she brought home five sheets of paper related to language arts. One was a list of spelling words that included "Santa Claus," "Martin Luther King," "who," "what," "when," and "how"; her job was to write a story. [Laughter] There were also words like "body" and "leg." So I got angry. There was also a cartoon comprehension worksheet, which was a series of cartoon pictures and multiple-choice questions next to it; and there was a memory exercise—memorizing one of Shel Silverstein's poems; and then there was a following-directions exercise that included coloring and drawing pictures. And I got really angry.

So what I did was I sat down and I had a glass of wine, and then I sat down at the typewriter and wrote a long-overdue letter to the teacher about what was happening to my daughter's education. Because I care about that. What I said was, "I don't understand the homework. I don't understand why she's getting these homework assignments. I couldn't write a story out of those spelling words. No one asks me to write stories out of spelling words. I think that there are ways to integrate all of these things. One way to do it is to have her read a story and write about it, and maybe even do a book report and follow directions, and then maybe talk about the story in class. And wouldn't that involve memory and following directions and reading and writing?"

I wrote all that down, and I sent it to the teacher, and I got a letter back. He said he wanted to meet with me and the principal, and I was so scared. I was going to be called to the principal's office, and I was a parent. So I thought about it for a couple of weeks and decided that I didn't want to do this alone, so I photocopied the *English/Language Arts Framework and Model Curriculum Guide for California,* which I was working on at the time, and sent it to him, and said, "I don't want to do this alone. I really have thought a lot about how to respond to this, and my decision is to have you read this."

It turned out that no teacher in the district even had a copy of the *Model Curriculum Guide for the State of California.* So I thought that was pretty amazing, and I decided that in-service is pretty critical. If we're going to change education, we've got to work with teachers. It was the superintendent that pointed out to me that it was a CAP year, and that was why my daughter was being taught all these separate, basic skills.

There's a lot to say on behalf of performance assessment. There's a lot to say for what it will do to help kids integrate. But why do we use multiple-choice questions?

We use multiple-choice questions because it's easier to make them reliable. It's easier to measure one thing with a multiple-choice test than it is with a performance, so if we want reliable measures of some kind of trade, we use multiple choice. The goal of assessment is to know what kids know, what they can do, and what they think about. We've found ways to do that in multiple choice *sort of,* and we know that multiple-choice tests are limited in terms of what can be assessed, but we know that we have done it reliably. What we *have* measured we have measured reliably. We have put a lot of energy into models and psychometric procedures to do that.

When teachers do assessment in the classroom, they have opportunities to ask questions. When a student does something that does not reflect what the teacher already knows about that student, the teacher can ask, "Why did you do that? Why did you answer that way?" The teacher can disregard it, if it's not relevant and doesn't match what she knows about the student, or she can retest the student.

When I was a high-school teacher, I did retest kids if they didn't show me what I knew they knew. When they would come in with a score that made no sense to me at all, I'd say, "What's going on here?" and I would retest the student. I could do that because I was a teacher in the classroom. Teachers have multiple opportunities for observation, and they base grades on it. We do empower teachers; teachers give grades, and that's where GPA's come from.

With standardized tests we try to get multiple observations that are independent from one another so that they will be reliable observations. CTB considers each item as an observation of the student. If we have 20 items, we have 20 observations on that particular scale, whether reading or language. Those observations are independent observations. That means that a student doesn't get a score on one item that impacts the score on the next item. The scores are independent from one another.

Further to refine that measurement, we use something called "three-parameter item response theory" according to which we put the results through these very complicated programs and come out with the best measurement at each point on a growth scale. We try to pick items that measure across that scale.

The items are chosen to measure the breadth of what's possible. The goal of standardized assessment is measurement. We're trying to build good rulers. All of these rulers have to apply if we're going to use performance assessments for high-stakes assessment. We still have to have standardized measurement. We still have to find a way to get multiple observations that are independent from one another to build a scale. That is what CTB is in the process of doing now.

We've been working for about two years on developing and piloting different kinds of performance assessments to see what works. We started out looking at the literature and finding out what people are saying about processing meaning and reading, and about writing-process models, and giving a student multiple opportunities to interact with text.

Performance assessments let us get at synthetic thinking when students construct, when they create, when they process ideas and come up with their own ideas that are novel. So we wanted to develop performance assessments that could measure those things—those things that can't be measured by multiple-choice—but have our tests uphold all those rules about measurement. Good measurement tools. Good rulers.

Bert Wiser joked earlier that he was going to give his teachers rubber rulers. We don't want to do that. This development process is at the beginning stages. It's really amazing to me that CTB has done this, for it is kind of a one-test company. We have our best minds in the company on the process of developing computer programs and item-analysis programs for the purpose of analyzing responses that might be scored in more than one way, a writing response that might be scored in terms of rhetoric and in terms of correctness and completeness.

We are looking at models of assessment in which students get to interact with the reading multiple times, and then go back and respond to it. We're looking at open-ended responses that include diagrams and drawings and mappings and listings as well as written responses, so that writing in itself doesn't limit the performance of students.

We're doing a lot of experimentation in doing that, but at the same time our researchers are running over to the development department and saying, "It's got to be objective; it's got to be dependable; we have to be able to have reliable measures!"

The reason is because we get RFPs—"requests for proposals." The things that people are wanting right now are large-scale assessments with which they can build pools of performance tasks so that they can compare students, districts, teachers over time. That cannot be done with rubber rulers. That has to be done with good, sound measurement.

What I'm trying to say is that the challenge that we have taken on at CTB is not to do a quick-fix, not to come up with something immediate to meet the needs today for assessment that will not serve the functions I just mentioned, but to research and develop and experiment with the ideas needed to get student productions that are creative, that give them opportunities to express their own thinking, and that at the same time are good, sound measurement.

I want briefly to tell you about the prototype test that we have developed for Maryland. One of the things Roger [Farr] said was, " In Michigan you can develop a test over the weekend." Well, it has taken us a month to develop the prototype reading/language/writing task for Maryland. This is a prototype task. They will have 45 tasks altogether, 15 at a grade level.

The task looks something like this: The teacher sets a context and introduces the students to unfamiliar terms and anything that could interfere with their being able to understand the task placed before them. Then they do a primary reading task. They are assessed on the four stances of reading that are part of NAEP, the personal, critical, global, and interpretational stances. Then the context is reset for them; then they read a secondary reading passage which may be of another type. The first might be expository and the second literary, but they are thematically related. Then the students are assessed again on the four stances. Then they have a prewriting task and preparatory work towards a writing assessment. Then they do a writing assessment. They have a couple of opportunities to review it both in terms of correctness and in terms of ideas, and then they do a final draft. That is essentially the model for the Maryland assessment for reading and writing and language usage.

We're really excited about it, and it's presenting us with challenges: How do we get the independence that we need? How do we get systematic measurement? How are these tasks going to be calibrated? How do we deal with issues of bias? Discrimination? Good reliability?

The discussion group I was in today was talking about top-down decision making *versus* grass-roots. I remember that, when I was a teacher, I was always waiting in anticipation for the next change. My classroom was really not my own. My job was to wait, to find out what the administration was going to tell me to do next; and the last thing that they did before I decided I couldn't do this anymore, and had to become a professor [Laughter], they decided they would do writing assessment every month; so I had to have my students write. I had my students, who were in the inner-city high school in Kansas City, write every month, and those papers were collected. I was not allowed to give them the writing assessment a day early, so I couldn't look at it. The writing assessment was taken out of the room and graded by someone else, and I never got any feedback.

We talk about dialogue, we talk about top-down decision-making *versus* grass-roots! This is the kind of thing that has to be eliminated—the assessments that have no impact on classroom behavior, the assessments that do not arise from what is natural in the classroom. Really good classroom assessments have to come from the classroom and have to come from the teacher and from the teacher/student interactions.

FRED FINCH (The Riverside Publishing Company):

The title of my presentation is "Toward a Definition for Educational Performance Assessment," and I call your attention to the word "toward." We make no special claim to wisdom, but we do think we can make progress toward the definition.

During the last twelve months, it has been difficult to pick up an issue of *Phi Delta Kappan* or *Business Week* or *Education Week* or *The Reading Teacher* without reading a reference to the need for "new" kinds of tests. I've read the manifesto for the Campaign for Genuine Accountability. I've read the proceedings of the "Beyond the Bubble" conference. I've read *Beyond Standardized Testing* and about "authentic assessments" and "portfolio tests." All of this literature reminds me of one of my favorite verses in the *Rubaiyat of Omar Khayyam:*

> Myself when young did eagerly frequent
>
> Doctor and Saint, and heard great argument
>
> About it and about: but evermore
>
> Came out by the same door where in I went.

Each writer and speaker seems to have his or her own idea of what constitutes the so-called better "test" that we should have. I think the prize for obfuscation should be awarded to the International Reading Association person who said, "Authentic tests are obviously better than conventional tests because they are more authentic." [Laughter]

Well, I guess that calls for a transparency. [Laughter; Finch uses transparencies projected on the screen.] Before attempting to formulate a definition for educational performance testing, I'd like briefly to discuss some terms intrinsic to tests and testing.

Figure 1 shows a simplified family tree for tests. Because our primary interest is in educational achievement tests, I take the liberty of relegating everything else to a classification that, for the

A SIMPLIFIED FAMILY TREE

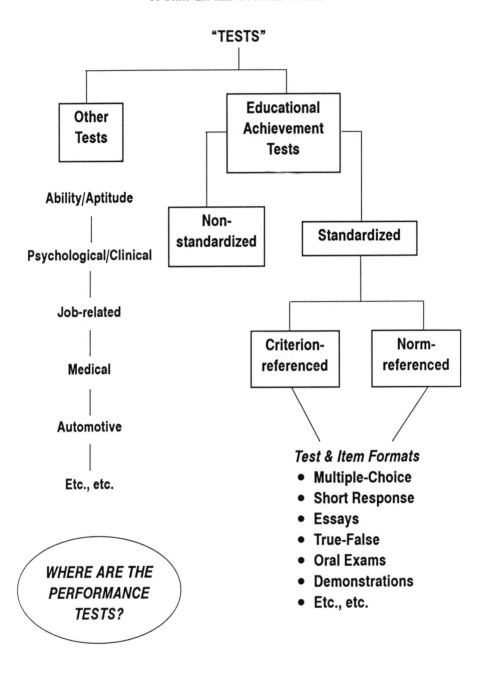

FIGURE 1

purposes of today's discussion, I call "other." For example there are ability tests and aptitude tests and medical tests and psychological tests and automotive tests and job-related tests and so on.

On the educational achievement test section of this chart, the first dichotomy illustrates that there is a difference between standardized tests and nonstandardized tests. This is particularly important because there seems to be a great deal of confusion about the term "standardized tests." Also, some have assumed that the term "standardized" and "norm-referenced" are synonymous. This is not the case, as is indicated by the second dichotomy. Norms are developed during the process of standardization, but tests without norms may also appropriately be labeled "standardized tests."

Most critics of "standardized tests" also use this term in a restrictive manner. They equate standardized tests with multiple-choice items, whereas "standardized" means that the tests are administered under standard conditions. While it's true that most standardized tests use multiple-choice items, other standardized tests do not.

According to Anastasi, a standardized test is one that uses uniform procedures when administering and scoring the test. Those who know the correct definition understand that this is not a small point. Without standard procedures for administering and scoring a test, it is not possible to compare scores earned by different persons. For this reason, nonstandardized tests have limited uses for any practical purpose.

Consider, for example, a simple medical test such as taking someone's temperature. Unless you put the thermometer in a standard place, for a standard period of time, any reading on that thermometer would be worthless. If the correct terminology is used, there is little of interest "beyond standardized testing."

Standardized tests are of two primary types: criterion-referenced and norm-referenced. Either of these two may be based on a wide variety of item and testing formats, such as these: multiple-choice items, short-response items, essays, true/false items, oral examinations, demonstations, etc., etc., etc. This list could be expanded to include an almost endless array of test and item formats, but where are the performance tests?

Riverside has spent about eighteen months working with the Arizona Department of Education on performance tests designed to measure Arizona's Essential Skills. These tests will be used in conjunction with norm-referenced tests, the "Iowa Tests of Basic Skills," and the "Tests of Achievement and Proficiency," to provide information about student performance as it relates to both national and state standards. The concepts and principles that evolved during the development of the Arizona performance tests were also applied to the development of Riverside's "Integrated Literature and Language-Arts Portfolio Program." We believe that these projects provide two examples of good educational performance assessment.

Riverside's work on the Arizona project and in developing the Portfolio Program, leads us to believe that the primary distinction between performance tests and other tests occurs at the item level. As with any other useful test, performance tests must be administered under standard conditions, and scored in a standard fashion to provide consistency of test results. Performance tests are not "beyond standardized testing"—they also should be standardized tests.

We have taken the position that performance tests can most easily be identified by exclusion. They are not multiple-choice tests; they don't contain multiple-choice items. It will be a great temptation to develop tests with multiple-choice items because they are so easy to grade, and then call them performance tests. The distinguishing characteristic of a performance test is that measurement takes place in a fairly realistic situation. I think that most educators interested in alternatives to multiple-choice tests would agree that an essay test of writing is a performance test—just as judging the skill of a quarterback in action or a bassoon player in concert or the health of a surgeon's patient or a painter's work of art would all be good performance tests. In performance testing, a student constructs or provides the response rather than selects an answer choice.

A complete discussion of performance and product evaluation is provided by Robert Fitzpatrick and Edward J. Morrison in the second edition of *Educational Measurement.* As this section was eliminated in the third edition, The Riverside Publishing Company has made arrangements with the American Council on Education to reprint this chapter in its entirety in the book *Educational Performance Assessment,* which will be published by Riverside in January 1991. This book will also include contributions by Lois Easton of the Arizona Department of Education, Morris Mueller of the Sacramento School District, Steven Osterlind of the University of Missouri, Nambury Raju of the Illinois Institute of Technology,

Sheila Valencia of the University of Washington, and Lonnie Valentine of the Air Force Human Resources Laboratory.

PERFORMANCE TESTS

- **Student-Constructed Responses**
- **Focuses on the *Process* of Problem Solving**
- **Scored by Teachers**
- **Criterion Referenced**

OBJECTIVE TESTS

- **Student-Selected Responses**
- **Attends to the *Result* of Problem Solving**
- **Scored by Computers**
- **Norm Referenced**

FIGURE 2

Figure 2 shows a simplified comparison of objective tests and performance tests. Performance tests are based on student-constructed responses. That is, the students write a response, write an essay, create something, demonstrate something, and so forth. Objective tests are based on student-selected responses. The student selects a response from a set of multiple-choice answer options. That's it.

The second contrast, performance tests focus on the *process* of problem solving. In the performance test, you can make inferences or even directly observe how the student goes about solving that problem, what he or she is actually doing. Whereas as in objective testing, all you know is whether they got *to* the right answer, whether they picked the correct choice; you know nothing about why they selected that choice, even if they got lucky.

Thirdly, performance tests are normally scored by a teacher, shall we say, or by another human being; they cannot be scored by computer, not if they're not multiple-choice kinds of tests. The classroom teacher—the person most interested in determining how the student arrived at a specific answer—must observe. A student puts something down, and the teacher has to look at that in order to make a decision. Objective, multiple-choice tests are scored by scanners; that's their strength. They're very efficient. You can zip those answer sheets through a million a minute.

Performance tests are usually criterion-referenced instruments whereas objective tests are typically norm-referenced. This distinction is not one that I'm prepared to battle to the death. The distinction itself is subject to much debate, but here's my logic. Performance tests are usually criterion-referenced instruments because the process of constructing a performance test requires that the developer have some criteria in mind which the students are expected to meet.

Finally, educational performance tests are most useful when they are designed to provide a good model for instruction. Educational performance tests properly used can *be* staff development.

Those whose primary interest is in replacing norm-referenced tests with performance tests may find that the nature, purpose, and uses of the two kinds of tests are so different that an either/or choice is not appropriate. Norm-referenced tests are so efficient, so cost-effective, and so useful that they will continue to serve as the foundation for group achievement testing America, like it or not. Performance tests, while inefficient in a variety of ways, provide an important opportunity to add an entirely new dimension to the assessment of students.

I'm not coming down on the side of norm-referenced tests; I think performance tests are nifty. We're doing them in Arizona—the Literature Portfolio Program is a good example. We have several more in the works. They can provide an important new dimension for educators, and for this reason we all need to work together—researchers, administrators, educators, the public—to make sure that we implement this new idea in a rational and professional manner. In other words, let's not take this good idea and screw it up.

References

Anne Anastasi, *Psychological Testing*, sixth edition (Macmillan, 1988).

Doug A. Archibald and Fred M. Newmann, *Beyond Standardized Testing* (National Association of Secondary School Principals, 1988).

Ronald A. Berk, *A Guide to Criterion-Referenced Test Construction* (The Johns Hopkins University Press, 1980).

Fredrick Finch, editor, *Educational Performance Assessment* (The Riverside Publishing Company, 1991).

SANDRA PAKES (The Psychological Corporation):

When Gene [Jongsma] and I knew that we were going to be on a panel after theoreticians and the practical people from school districts had spoken, it put us somewhat on the defensive. We wanted to tell you that we felt a little bit like the big bad wolf.

There are two sides to that story, and I'd like to take a moment to tell you about the true story of the big bad wolf. [She holds up an illustrated children's book,* and begins to read.] You can tell I was an elementary teacher! [Laughter]

> Everybody knows the story of the three little pigs or at least they *think* they do, but I'll let you in on a little secret. Nobody knows the real story because nobody has ever heard *my* side of the story.
>
> I'm the wolf, Alexander T. Wolf. You can all call me Al. I don't know how this whole big-bad-wolf thing got started, but it's all wrong; maybe it was because of my diet. Hey, it's not my fault that wolves eat cute little animals like bunnies and sheeps and pigs. That's just the way we are. If cheeseburgers were cute, folks would probably think you were big and bad, too.
>
> Like I was saying, the whole big-bad-wolf thing is all wrong. The real story is about a sneeze and a cup of sugar. This is the real story.
>
> Way back in once-upon-a-time time, I was making a birthday cake for my dear old granny. I had a terrible sneezing cold. I ran out of sugar. So I walked down the street to ask my neighbor for a cup of sugar.
>
> Now this neighbor was a pig, and he wasn't too bright either. He had built his whole house out of straw. Can you believe it? I mean, who in his right mind would build a house out of straw? So of course the minute I knocked on the door, it fell right in. I didn't want to just walk into somebody else's

---

The True Story of the Three Little Pigs, by A. Wolf (as told to John Scieszka) (Viking, 1989).

house, so I called, "Little Pig, Little Pig, are you in?" No answer.

I was just about to go home without the cup of sugar for my dear old granny's birthday cake. That's when my nose started to itch. I felt a sneeze coming on. Well, I huffed and I snuffed and I sneezed a great sneeze. And you know what? The whole darn straw house fell down, and right in the middle of the pile of straw was the first little pig. Dead as a door nail. He had been home the whole time.

Now it seemed a shame to leave a perfectly good ham dinner lying there in the straw, so I ate it up. Think of it as a big cheeseburger lying there.

The story goes on, the second house and the third house—let me just paraphrase a bit—but the big bad wolf gets to the house that's made out of brick, and he knocks on the brick house. No answer.

I called, "Mister Pig, Mister Pig, are you in?" And do you know what that rude little porker answered? "Get out of here, Wolf! Don't bother me again!"

Talk about impolite! He probably had a whole sack full of sugar and he wouldn't give me even one little cup for my dear sweet old granny's birthday cake. What a pig! I was just about to go home and maybe make a nice birthday card instead of a cake when I felt my cold coming on. I huffed and I snuffed and I sneezed once again.

Then the third little pig yelled out, "And your old granny can sit on a pin!" Now I'm usually a pretty calm fellow, but when somebody talks about my granny like that, I go a little crazy. When the cops drove up, of course I was trying to break down that pig's door, and the whole time I was huffing and snuffing and sneezing and making a real scene. The rest, as they say, is history.

Now the news reporters found out about the two little pigs that I had had for dinner, and they figured that a sick guy going to borrow a cup of sugar didn't sound very exciting, so they jazzed up the story with all that "huff and puff and blow your house down," and they made me out to be the big bad wolf. That's it, the real story. I was framed.

As test publishers, we feel like we have been framed. [Laughter] So we'd like to tell you *our* side of the story, and I'm going to ask Gene Jongsma to tell that true story. [Applause]

GENE JONGSMA (The Psychological Corporation):

Thanks, Sandra. I told Sandra that, with Jerry Harste here, we had to work in some children's literature somehow into this presentation to make him feel comfortable. [Laughter]

I would like to reflect on the experiences that I've had over the last year and a half. I've been in the trenches, so to speak, developing performance and portfolio assessment products for The Psychological Corporation. I've talked with a lot of people and visited a lot of State Departments [of Education] and read a lot of articles. I'd like to reflect on this new movement that seems to be taking place. I can categorize my remarks about the movement towards performance and portfolio assessment into the "good news" and the "bad news," or promises and pratfalls.

The "good news," looking at this movement as a reading educator, gives us reason to applaud because it's healthful. We've all known that reading and writing are multifaceted processes, and that we shouldn't rely on a single score as the measure of performance. You know we're struggling for consensus here today. I think that's one thing we can all agree on, that we don't want to rely on a single score as a measure of performance. The movement towards performance and portfolio assessment will broaden our concept of language-arts assessment, and we'll be forced to rethink what it is we want to assess and how we want to assess it. So the movement is healthful.

The other encouraging aspect is that the new performance and portfolio tests that you're going to be seeing, will be more closely aligned to instruction. These new tests will look more like what teachers do as part of normal instruction. We'll begin to bridge that gap between assessment and instruction. At least our new language-arts performance tests do, and from what Cathy [Taylor] describes in Maryland, and from what I've seen of other publishers, I think we're going to see the same sorts of things. Therefore these new measures will have greater face validity to teachers and to many administrators.

Another promise is that if you believe in measurement-driven instruction, the new measures hold out the promise of driving instruction in the right direction. Of course, this depends on what kinds of sanctions and rewards are opposed with their use, but still if we've learned anything from the educational reform movement of the

1980s, it's this: When the stakes are high, teachers teach for the test. So, indeed, the tests can drive instruction.

I think it's interesting that the renewed debate over testing reflects the dual role of testing in the educational reform movement, and that is that tests are recognized as instruments of change as well as instruments to measure the effects of change.

Now let me turn my attention to the "bad news," and maybe "bad news" isn't the right label for this: maybe "causes for concern" or "reasons to be wary." At the top of my list—it shouldn't come as any surprise after some of the exchanges this morning—I would put polarization. I sense a growing movement of the good guys *versus* the bad guys. The good guys being the advocates of (quote) "authentic assessment," and the bad guys, those purveyors of staid multiple-choice, standardized tests.

It reminds me of what has happened in the area of reading instruction—the polarization that exists there between the Whole Language people and phonics people, and so on, so that if you're not with us, you're against us, and the notion that there is only one right or legitimate approach to reading instruction. I see some of the same things happening in assessment, and that concerns me because, in point of fact, we need both types of assessment.

We have precious little research or hard data that shows the relationship between student performance on multiple-choice measures with their performance on authentic or performance measures. We do know that direct-writing assessment taps many of the same skills as multiple-choice tests of writing, yet they also tap some unique features. We do have some research in that area, but other than that, believe me, it's rather scarce. Much more research is needed to define and explain the differences between performance measures and multiple-choice measures so that we can logically determine which type of measurement is appropriate for which purpose.

The State of Massachusetts has done some interesting things along this line as part of their state assessment, looking at student responses on open-ended items *versus* multiple-choice items, and the relationship between the two, and so on. We need a lot more of that kind of research so that we can intelligently decide which type of measurement is appropriate for which purpose. My guess is that both types of assessment would rank and order results in the same way; however, they may yield different kinds of insights into a student's performance.

Another concern I have—and this isn't new; it has come out several times today—is satisfying a variety of test users. In many ways, performance and portfolio assessment has been a grass-roots movement growing out of the efforts of individual teachers, small pockets of teachers, and innovative districts. Nevertheless, as performance assessment becomes more wide-spread and used more for accountability functions such as state assessment, many of its appealing features will be lost. Security will become important. The openness that characterizes much of the authentic-assessment movement will be lost, or at least greatly reduced.

Another concern I have is training. Many of the districts and states that have embraced performance assessment do so with the intention of getting their teachers involved in the scoring process. We've got several state models already set up for doing this. Diane [Bloom] talked a little bit about the New Jersey situation, California, Connecticut, and several others. Local scoring has the additional benefit of providing staff development. The assumption is that what teachers learn in the scoring-training process will positively influence their teaching.

Local scoring serves, therefore, as a sort of staff development; however, such training is not without its price. Are districts willing to spend the money and to vote the resources to conduct large-scale training programs? Furthermore, are teachers willing to spend the time and energy to learn how to score performance-assessment tasks, and then use them in their classrooms? I think the answers to these kinds of questions will significantly determine whether performance assessment and portfolio assessment will continue to grow as a movement, or not.

One other concern I have involves integration. Many of the new performance measures emphasize the integration of reading and writing and other language skills. "Aha!" we say, "At last, we're developing assessment instruments that reflect the instructional program. The name of the game is integrated language-arts instruction; let's develop integrated language-arts assessment."

This approach has a lot of intuitive appeal to practitioners because it reflects the current trend in instruction; however, integration leads to messy assessment. Almost by definition, psychometricians like to isolate whatever it is they are measuring. It's cleaner. It leads to more valid assessment. It insures that you are indeed measuring what you say you are measuring—or so Bert Wiser and people like that would tell us.

Will the measurement community accept integrated measures? Will we have to use new procedures for establishing validity and reliability?

The question of integration goes beyond the language-arts area. The mathematics community, for example, is calling for authentic math tasks that involve reading and writing—"communicating about mathematics," they say. Preliminary research evidence suggests that adding a heavy verbal component to those math tasks, equalizes the gender differences that we usually find between boys and girls in mathematics tasks.

The last issue of *Journal of Ed Measurement,* for example, has two articles relating to this. One from Ireland and one from England, but we've seen some of the same things here in the States. Are we then introducing, by adding a heavy verbal component to a math performance task, a form of bias? That raises more questions than it answers.

I think that publishers have a lot to offer in this process. Firstly, they've got some able professionals and some measurement expertise that we ought not lose track of. Secondly, they've got an extensive and powerful communication network in the nation's schools, and I think that schools depend on them as a major source of information and training. Like it or not, publishers are going to be important players in this movement towards new kinds of assessment. We just hope that we can make a positive contribution in that direction.

BARB KAPINUS (Coordinator 1992 NAEP Reading Consensus Project; Maryland State Department of Education):

I have been working this past year on the National Assessment of Educational Progress in Reading for 1992. This time last year, I was a State Department of Education person in Maryland in reading. I taught graduate courses. I did inservice, and I didn't do a whole lot with reading. A year ago, I never would have dreamed that I would be standing here talking about assessment. When I started working with reading, I thought, "I think I know quite a bit about reading, and I know a little bit about reading assessment, and I know about teachers." As I neared the end of my project, I realized how much I don't know, and the symposium today has probably highlighted that for me.

This poem by Steven Crane summarizes some of my feelings about reading assessment, and I think it gives us the theme for today, too. Steven Crane knew that the truth is seldom so simple as some would have us believe.

> Truth, said a traveler, is a rock, a mighty fortress.
>
> Often have I been to it, even to its highest tower from whence the world looks black.
>
> Truth, said a traveler, is a breath, a wind, a shadow, a phantom.
>
> Long have I pursued it, but never have I touched the hem of its garment.

I believe the second traveler. Truth was to me a breath, a wind, a shadow, a phantom and never had I touched the hem of its garment. That's how I feel about reading assessment after spending a year with NAEP. There's a lot to be said about where NAEP is for 1992, so I'm going to highlight some of the differences.

The first difference is that the process for constructing NAEP has been different this time around. Traditionally, ETS pretty much has overseen the whole process, the developing, the objectives, as well as the actual assessment. For this round, because for the first time in 1992 NAEP will produce state-by-state comparison data for fourth-graders, the process of developing the objectives and the vision of the assessment had to reflect a wide consensus.

To my way of thinking, that was one of the best parts of being on NAEP. We've heard talk about process and product and assessment, and from my perspective, because I've been involved a lot in the process of developing the assessment, I've discovered that if nothing else, the process of developing a large-scale assessment can help you clarify your thinking about what you want, about your goals, about what you are about in education. I think that process is extremely valuable.

People have mentioned "the need for dialogue" several times today. I do think the process of developing the assessment for 1992 was a process of dialogue that took place among a wide range of people. People that I talked to in the course of this development ranged from Gene Schultz to Jimmy Taylor. We heard taxicab drivers who told us, "If you just found out if kids could read words, that's all we want to know." We heard people say that there should be no assessment *whatsoever.* So we heard the whole range, and we tried to keep the dialogue going.

The members of the Planning Committee that was asked to generate the framework and item specifications for the National

Assessment of Educational Progress in Reading realized the importance of addressing some important concerns in the education community regarding large-scale assessment. They endeavored to formulate a vision of this assessment that would reflect current theory, support a wide range of effective instruction, and provide useful information to the public and policy makers. Characteristics of the NAEP reading assessment planned for 1992, while based on past assessments, definitely set the 1992 assessment apart from previous NAEP reading assessments.

Scales. Because reading is a complex set of behaviors and attitudes, there will be three cognitive scales and a scale for habits and practices on the 1992 NAEP. The three cognitive scales are based on the notion that readers construct and respond to meaning in different ways depending on the type of text and the context or purpose of the reading situation. A reader has a different orientation to reading a novel than reading a chapter in a textbook. This difference is acknowledged by the three cognitive scales for the 1992 NAEP in reading: reading for literary experience, reading to be informed, and reading to perform a task.

Reading for literary experience usually involves reading novels, short stories, plays, and poetry in order to see the author's view of the human condition or to be guided through experiences by the author. Reading to be informed usually involves reading textbooks, articles, editorials, and memos in order to gain information. Reading to perform a task usually includes reading items such as schedules, directions, maps, and forms in order to accomplish a specific task. Although it is possible to read an article as a literary experience, or to read a novel and gain information, these three categories work well for the purpose of delineating different types of reading on a large scale assessment.

Interactions with text. The taxonomy used to generate questions for the 1992 NAEP in reading is a new one. Although it builds on the notion that reading involves constructing, extending, and examining meaning, it focuses more on the specific ways in which readers should be able to interact with, and respond to, text. Based largely on research done by Judith Langer, the new taxonomy includes four interactions: initial understanding, developing interpretation, personal response, and critical stance.

Initial understanding questions or tasks ask the reader to construct a global meaning or first impression of what the text is about. Global understanding questions might include the following:

- Who was the main character?

- What is the general mood of this passage?

- What is the major problem faced by the main character?

- What is the main argument that the author is making?

- What is the purpose of this text/document?

For the most part, readers should be able to answer global-understanding questions without going back into the text for further information.

Developing interpretation questions, on the other hand, usually requires that readers reinspect the text in order to extend or examine the meaning. Developing interpretation questions might include the following:

- How does the attitude of the main character change from the beginning of the story to the end?

- How does the mood change as the setting changes in the story?

- What efforts does the main character make to solve his/her problem?

- What major points does the author present to support his/her argument?

Personal response requires readers to step back and think about the meaning of the text as it relates to their own background knowledge and experiences. In asking readers to respond personally to questions on an assessment, it is important to have students anchor their personal response in the meaning constructed from the text. Personal response questions could include the following:

- Compare someone you know or have read or heard about to the main character in this story.

- Do you agree with the author's arguments? Why?

- Would this information be useful to you? Why?

- Compare your home, neighborhood, or school to the one described in this story.

Critical stance questions require readers to stand back from the text and consider how, why, and how well it was crafted. They involve reflecting on such ideas as how the author constructed the text. The focus of critical stance questions is not so much on the meaning as on how the author conveyed that meaning. Critical stance questions are often similar to what has traditionally come under the heading of literary criticism, and they include items such as the following:

- How does the author's choice of words build the mood in this story/poem?
- How did the author organize this passage?
- Could this story take place in another setting? Explain.
- Has any important information been omitted from this article/document?

These interactions are neither hierarchical nor linear. It is possible that readers will have a critical or personal response to a passage before really developing a global understanding or interpretation. These four types of response subsume other taxonomies such as Bloom's, and they promote not only a range of interactions with text but also require the use of multiple dimensions of thinking about text.

Item format. Forty percent of students' time on the 1992 NAEP in Reading will be spent answering open-ended questions. Some of these will require brief responses whereas others will require extended writing. The extended responses will be scored according to rubrics that are similar to NAEP writing rubrics in that they employ scores along a five-point scale; however, the focus of these guides will be on evidence of constructing and examining meaning from text rather than writing skill. In addition, some items ask students to make lists or complete charts. Overall, the items for the 1992 NAEP in Reading look different from traditional items, not only in format but also in the depth of text processing and range of thinking that they require.

Item characteristics. The cognitive items were generated using story maps and diagrams of textual information to provide a focus on important ideas in the text rather than trivia. In addition, three separate groups of reviewers looked at the items and considered several factors. Did the items tap the important ideas in the passages, or were critical aspects of the text overlooked? Do the questions tap important notions from the passages that proficient readers would consider, or do they focus on details or considerations that would only occur on an assessment and never in an honest literary discussion? Reviewers stood back from the passages and items, considering whether the set of tasks supported readers' substantive involvement with text and reflected the types of responses literate people would make to the passages.

Passages. The specifications for the passages for the 1992 NAEP in Reading called for text that occurs naturally. Abridgments and editing as well as excerpts were not to be used. Stories and articles were analyzed for richness of ideas and clarity of structure before being included in the assessment. At least two blocks of proposed items have tasks that require comparing and relating information from two passages.

Documents used to assess reading to perform a task also will be different. In the past, items that tapped document literacy used only a part of the document as a stimulus: a chart, a map, part of an index, or directions with no illustrations or diagrams. The documents used for reading to perform a task on the 1992 NAEP have been kept intact. For example, a whole section of the phone book, a complete train schedule, and directions with diagrams or narrative explanations are the types of text for this part of the assessment.

In addition to the developments described above, there are blocks of items at the eighth- and twelfth-grade levels that are based on students' choosing a story or several stories and answering open-ended questions on the literature that they pick to read. This provision for choice is a new and exciting characteristic of the assessment.

The Integrated Reading Performance Record. The process that developed this assessment was one of gradually coming to consensus; at the outset, however, it was clear that some members of the reading education community and some members of the community of parents and citizens were convinced that the 1992 NAEP in Reading should seek to find out if students could simply read words out loud. Another contingent in the reading community was generally opposed to large-scale reading assessment, and they supported classroom-based assessment. Among the members of this group one particularly popular notion in classroom assessment grew into what is now called the Integrated Reading Performance Record. This is part of a special study that will look at oral reading of a story and portfolio samples at the same time that it will explore some other questions related to the assessment.

In the course of individual interviews, a sample of fourth-grade students will be asked to do the following: 1) tell about a book they have recently read, 2) read a story orally, 3) answer an extended response, open-ended question orally (a question that they will have already answered in writing on the main assessment), and 4) talk about three-to-five samples of their best classroom work in reading (which will be analyzed later for evidence of the types of interaction with text tapped by the regular assessment questions).

This study will tell us about students' responses to their own self-selected reading. It will provide a comparison of oral and written responses to the same item so that the degree to which writing proficiency might limit their responses on the main assessment can be examined. It will link the assessment items to actual classroom tasks, and it will provide insights into students' attitudes that are based on interviews rather than multiple-choice questions. In summary, this study will "extend and examine" the regular assessment.

Metacognitive Study. Many members of the reading community have emphasized the importance of readers' being strategic. The Michigan and Illinois state reading assessments both attempt to tap students' knowledge of reading and reading strategies; however, the methodology for tapping strategic knowledge is still limited. Rather than trying to assess and report using a scale on reading knowledge and strategies as was originally planned, the 1992 NAEP will include a study on metacognition. The study will focus mainly on the methodology by which metacognitive knowledge and awareness can be assessed. Findings about students' strategic knowledge that provide important background for the regular assessment are to be reported with the results of the main assessment. A research team has been assembled to develop and conduct this study.

Summary. The 1992 NAEP in Reading will not look like past large-scale assessments either in its format or in the information that it reports. It will challenge our students and our teachers. While it isn't perfect, it shows that we have made some definite progress in attempting to represent reading as a complex, constructive process. It stretches assessment methodology, and it is a promise that NAEP will continue to inform, challenge, and push future assessments especially through the use of special studies.

What I've learned by working with NAEP is this: I knew what I'd wished for in assessment when I started this job; now I don't know if I want it.

The last point I'd like to make is that what "authentic" is and what authentic assessment is for, is not altogether clear. The "real-world people" want authentic artifacts, things like people will do and use in their real lives. Well, folks, the things people do in classrooms are not always what you and I do in real life. So when I say "authentic," I'm trying to think: What is authentic for a fourth-grader? Is it what a fourth-grader might be doing in the classroom or at home or what a fourth-grader ultimately is going to do as an adult? And just how "authentic" can you get? I mean, it's still education. Is education authentic? It's still an assessment. How authentic can that get? I don't know. [Laughter] Each kind of thing that seems to be an advance also raises additional issues and gives us additional problems. We don't take a single step without a little bit of a jolt to our whole system.

This is what *I* believe: I believe, along with Janet Emmick, that any literacy is not worth teaching if it doesn't provide access, if it doesn't sponsor learning, if it doesn't unleash literal power, and if it doesn't activate the greatest power of all, the imagination. I think NAEP for 1992 is *moving* in that direction. We're not there yet, but we're definitely making progress in that direction.

TERRY SALINGER (Educational Testing Service):

I work for Educational Testing Service in the more traditional aspects of ETS, including multiple-choice testing. I'm here to talk to you today about some of the things we're doing with test development, psychometrics, and in research.

Among some major questions that we're trying to answer, the first is how—how—do you go about organizing information that is multi-trait, and is derived from multi-dimensional behaviors. That's a new question for ETS. It's a really new question. That is to say, it's perceived as a new question. It's been a question at ETS for a long time because people in both research and psychometrics for a long time have known that there's more to traditional measurement than uni-dimensional scales.

Our goal now is not to come up with better instruments *per se*. We'd like to come up with some better instruments, but the goal is not to come up with better instruments but, instead, to develop more effective and more systematic ways of evaluating students and test takers.

We don't do a lot of work any more in ETS with the assessment of school-age students. We do some, but not nearly so much as we used to do. We do much more work with older individuals.

223

Interestingly, much of our research work is done with school-age students, and we do go after some of the RFPs that have been mentioned here.

We feel—and this is a test-development perspective as well as a research perspective—that many of the standardized instruments that are available now both from us and from other companies can blur the understandings that should emerge from evaluation. You get very skimpy information when you've got only one score. We also feel very strongly that more complex instruments don't necessarily provide better information. They provide *more* information that is still skimpy.

We are attentive to the thrust within the measurement community to look at alternative assessment methodologies, to look at them from a methodological perspective, and also from a psychometric perspective. This movement exists within the measurement community as well as within the educational community, if we construe education as instruction.

We are trying to respond also to school interests, to school pressures. We are aware that schools look to ETS, often with hatred and distrust, but also often as a source of the kinds of research that we've done over the years. We're looking at some of these issues from a research-and-development perspective because, while we are not a profit-making company, we are not a company that is supposed to function at a loss, either.

Our new executive vice president, Nancy Cole, formerly the Dean at Illinois before coming to ETS, has done research in the past dealing with bias. She is a fine scholar looking at assessment with these questions in mind: What makes a test biased? How can we formulate unbiased instruments? She also has been very strongly involved in the movement to align assessment and instruction. When she participates in some of our meetings—talking with school districts, talking with ourselves, and with some of our special-interest groups about assessment and instruction—she wears a professor's hat, and it's delightful to see. It's very motivating.

Much of our work with alternative assessments is funded internally. We have some external funding, but very little. This represents a commitment we've made to pursuing these issues. We're looking at the feasibility of alternative assessment. We're looking at the practicality of alternative assessment. We're looking at validity. We're looking at reliability. We're also looking very carefully at the usefulness of data that are gathered from alternative assessments. We're looking very hard at the issue of how one aggregates data collected through alternative assessments without reducing those data to a checklist. And we're looking at this in several contexts. We're trying to establish a unified, well-articulated theoretical framework for our alternative assessments before any of them hits the street.

So, while I am talking about some in-house research and some projects that are under way, I'm not talking about any specific products yet. In looking at reading comprehension tests, Winn Manning in the research department is looking at what he calls "cloze allied." This is a cloze methodology that flips the idea on its side in that the passages that individuals read contain extraneous information. The purpose of the assessment is to have students try to find what's illogical, what doesn't work, and then explain it. Moderate results so far, worth pursuing.

Brent Bridgeman, also in research, is investigating the differences between constructed-response items—those items wherein the student provides the information—and multiple-choice items. Many of his items come from math, although he does work in reading and in writing, too. He administers matched groups of exactly the same items to groups of third-grade students, some with multiple-choice items, some with constructed-response, and then looks at the differences.

What is he finding? We'd like to think that he's finding better results with the constructed response. [Pause] *Very decreased scores* when individuals must produce the responses themselves! This is distressing.

It tells us something about test wiseness. It tells us something about a student's thought process. It tells us something very, very important about constructed-response items. It may be telling us that even though we get terrible results with some standardized tests, we are, nevertheless, getting an inflated measure of students' competency. Interesting research; important research. It's the kind of research that can have a real impact on schooling because of all of the inferences that can be drawn.

Randy Kaplan, also in research, is looking at the feasibility of using computer scoring for constructed-response items. I'm not talking about essays; he hasn't gotten that far, yet, but short constructed-response items. He is using linguistics theory to develop a grammar for each of the constructed-response items in his sample tests. These grammars are strings of potential answers, the noun-verb-adjective-adverb combinations that could be used to answer short constructed- response items.

As individual students take these tests and respond to the questions, their work is run through a spell-checker for uniformity and then scored. Randy Kaplan is finding very, very high inter-rater reliability between the computer rater and human scoring. This has tremendous potential. It's still short constructed-response, but it is constructed-response. It has tremendous potential for lowering the cost of constructed-response testing, for expanding the acceptability of constructed-response testing, and for giving us a new and better way to assess some of the language arts in reading.

Some of the more outside, maybe even practical, work that's going on is being done by Ted Chittenden, a research scientist at ETS. I am privileged to work on some of this with him, and I feel very strong interests in this because of my own background in Early Childhood. Ted is funded by the Bruner Foundation and the Diamond Foundation, and every six months we try to get some MacArthur funding. We don't have it yet, but were gonna keep trying!

Ted is looking at a balanced selection of school districts, mostly in the Northeast, ranging from Mamaroneck, New York, which is very wealthy, to Camden, New Jersey, which is at the other end. He's looking primarily in Early Childhood classrooms at various components of literacy instruction—looking for the particular context in which literacy can be assessed, looking at the different ways in which teachers can, and should be, assessing children's growth.

His word is "documentation," and he is attempting to work through principals, supervisors, and teachers to develop models for documentation of children's progress as they learn to read and write. He's making video tapes through the Diamond Foundation, a project that can be used in training teachers to be better observers, to become true kid-watchers. He's working with good teachers, but teachers who do not necessarily consider themselves capable of evaluating. As he works with them and teaches them to look at their students' work qualitatively—which they probably already do—but also quantitatively, he is making important inroads into their thinking about assessment of young children.

We have been working together with school districts where there is strong, strong support for taking on the New York State bureaucracy to say: "We don't want standardized testing in the early grades!" We have strong support from supervisors for this, and from superintendents, but we don't have the support from parents, and we don't have support from some of the teachers. We are learning—in addition to methodologies for working with teachers—about some of the political barriers to bringing about the kind of assessment that I think Ted thinks is appropriate for young learners and, by extension, for older learners as well.

Ted is also working on a project that is jointly sponsored by the Fund for New York City Public Education and the New York City Office of Research Evaluation and Assessment. This is a project in response to the new New York City Chancellor's charge to the various community school districts to get their act together, to start looking at school-based management, including some changes in assessment. (New York State might have "the testing state" on its license plate as well as Ohio!) This work is only beginning. It is an extension of some work that he and I have been doing with Central Park East School and Debbie Myers School. We are serving as ETS consultants to school-based projects that are looking at assessment in a very clear, thoughtful, and practical way.

Other things we're doing: The "Arts Propel Project" has been going on for several years in Pittsburgh's public schools, funded by the Rockefeller Foundation, and administered jointly by the Pittsburgh Public Schools, Harvard's "Project Zero," and ETS. We're now producing a product—changes, very important changes in the instruction and the assessment of visual arts, music, and language arts for public schools.

We're attempting to design assessments that are closely integrated with the instruction in visual and performing arts and writing in the middle and secondary schools in Pittsburgh. The goals have been to produce a climate conducive to the use of portfolios, and they are using portfolios.

The teachers and the students have taken ownership in all of these areas, working towards a model of working with students and teachers that encourages reflection, that brings about in classes "evaluative conversations" between teachers and students. It's been centered on the use of portfolios, but it has corollary behaviors as well: teacher-training, teacher support, work within the classroom by ETS and Harvard researchers, to produce within this environment students who are encouraged to reflect on their work, who know how to reflect on their work, and who do reflect on their work. We've also been working very closely to plan and develop teacher-training programs on the use of portfolios and alternative assessments. We do a considerable amount of teacher-training on scoring essays, just as we involve many of the teachers in the essay-scoring programs.

We're working with various consortia of historically Black colleges throughout the South, with the aim of developing a replacement for the Nelson-Denny! [Laughter] If I get credit for nothing else than for working on a valid replacement of the Nelson-Denny as a placement instrument for individuals entering historically Black colleges—! The goal is not to replace the Nelson-Denny so much as to develop an instrument that will truly illuminate the reading strategies that these individuals either do or do not bring to their freshman work.

We're doing some software development in many of the programs, but I want to talk about the NTE because the NTE and other teacher-assessment programs are what I work on and also direct. I'm in charge of the pedagogy-based NTE test as part of the new generation of teacher tests that will be available in 1992 and 1993. To that end I am working, still, with multiple-choice testing, but I am also working with much more, with constructed-response. We're working toward teacher-assessments that will be from one-half to three-fifths constructed-response. We will be asking teacher-licensing candidates to write about instruction and students, to analyze student work, to perform tasks that will come as close as possible to the tasks that they will be performing as beginning teachers.

The challenge here is to engage the teachers themselves in alternative assessment. We can talk about alternative assessment with students forever, but if teachers don't have an inclination to alternative assessment, and if they don't have the confidence to look at a student's paper and do more than correct the commas, then we'll still be talking twenty years from now about the same sorts of things.

At NTE, within our mandate about minimum competency—and that's real scary!—we're trying to come up with assessments that will be "authentic"—(No, they're not going to be authentic! Because the only authentic assessment of a teacher is "out there," getting the kids out of the bathroom on time or reading a story or whatever)— but some measure that will give us and the states a better sense of these individuals' potentials to become the kinds of teachers who will tackle the hard issues that have been raised today.

SETTING THE FUTURE AGENDA

CARL SMITH (ERIC/RCS, Indiana University):

Looking to the future and asking ourselves what we want to do, from here, it's important not to be bound by the statements that have been made all day, but to think of other things that we haven't discussed. We haven't resolved a lot today, but certainly we have laid out a number of ideas that can keep us thinking. Perhaps that's the best we can say as we leave a symposium like this, that we have a lot to think about.

Gene Maeroff pointed out to me that when Terry [Salinger] talked about the computerized scoring techniques that ETS is using, that was the first time during this whole day that anyone had mentioned computers as an alternative means of assessment. Gene thought that it was unusual that computers had not come up earlier, considering that this is supposed to be a futuristic-thinking group.

Some points have become fairly generalizable during our discussion today. "Assessment" is a term that is used with many purposes in mind. Some of those purposes are political, some are reflective and self-reflective, some are instructional, and some of those purposes are for giving grades—maybe that's political, too—but at least it's a way of monitoring for the benefit of students and parents.

Another result of today's discussion is the recognition that definitions are extremely important, and that they are quite sloppy at the present time. We used the words "test" and "assessment" and "evaluation," but I'm not sure that we ever consistently made any kind of distinction among them. We are familiar with the word "test," we are familiar with the notion that a test often produces a score, but thanks to Fred [Finch], we also were made aware that there are all kinds of standardized tests, and not just a single notion of a normed test.

229

The term "assessment" was used in a variety of ways. This is a very sloppy term at the present time. It's used by test people, curriculum people, theorists, Whole Language people, and all in different manners. "Assessment" to test people may in fact be a synonym for "test," that is, a test that produces a score. "Assessment" for Whole Language people means a kind of on-going, interactive conversation between a student and him/herself, or between student and teacher—and that's a different use of the word "assessment" from the way we have typically used it in the past. It seems to me, then, that whenever we use that term in this group among these people, we have to start with some kind of definition. We have to say: "Here's what *my* definition of 'assessment' is."

In the discussion group I was in, I mentioned that this morning I had breakfast with a group of folks with whom I meet once a month —and it was not my family [Laughter]—and I told them what I was doing today.

One of the gentlemen defined two things that he wanted from schools as far as assessment is concerned: He wanted to know how the school is doing compared to other schools, and that includes the Japanese. Bert [Wiser] alluded to this interest in assessment. The other thing was, he wanted to know how his kid was doing related to some indicator of success in life.

I said that educators now were trying to implement portfolios. He asked what a portfolio is. And I said, "Well, we put all this stuff in a folder." "Oh," he said, "You mean a work folder; teachers have been showing me work folders for years." (Two of his kids are now in high school.) "And every time I see those folders, and they pull out a piece, and say: 'Look at this!' I applaud, and I say: 'Gee, my kid's great!' and I applaud again; then they pull out another piece, but I never know what it means in terms of my kid's success in getting to college or my kid's success at getting a job." And he said: "That's what I want to know." That kind of reality check is part of what we're doing in addition to the checks we give ourselves when we talk about "reliability" and "validity."

Another generalization: I do believe that different paradigms are operating in the schools; I don't know which paradigm dominates the school systems and the teachers today, but I do think that different ones are operating. These paradigms, logically, cause differences in the ways we approach this thing called "assessment," and we ought to recognize that. We also need, therefore, to identify the assumptions under which we are operating when we start. We have to say: "My assumption is that schools/education/learning is based on a continuous growth in inquiry," or "My assumption is that there are community and personal values that are operating." Those are two different approaches to the notion of assessment. That's part of the definitions that have to be developed as we go ahead to analyze what assessment is to do.

Gene Jongsma said that this movement is towards matching assessment with the multi-faceted process of language learning, and that we have to respond to it. If it is multi-faceted, what are those many facets? We must define what the facets are so that we can provide authentic demonstrations of those processes. We have to have some sense of the appropriate match of facet with demonstration.

Another important issue mentioned by a number of people: Training of educators becomes a major factor for all of us in this movement towards performance assessment. But that's not going to happen with any speed or regularity unless we find some way of dealing with our learners.

Were we to have a second assessment symposium, what are matters that you think we ought to put at the forefront? How can we make the next symposium valuable to you? What topics, ideas, issues do you think ought to be on that agenda?

[Unidentified voices of the symposium make proposals for the future agenda:]

- We need to devise ways of achieving a better balance between the psychometric goals and the subject or content goals in any kind of assessment, be it performance, multiple-choice, standardized, or non-standardized.

- We've talked a lot about what teachers know or don't know, can and can't do. Teacher education, then, is a very important part of this. We need some discussion on the what and how of educating teachers to use alternative forms of assessment, and also teachers need to be educated about dealing with the politics of assessment. Teachers need to know enough about the various issues in assessment to be able to get involved in the debate.

- One of the biggest complaints about the newspapers is that all they report is test scores. People from the media need to be involved next time so that they can do a better job of informing the public about the silliness of single-test scores and some of the absurdities of comparisons. We ought to talk about the standards of the Education Writers Association, the group that reports the test scores.

- We need to hear more from the legislators, the people who are passing all the laws that we have to live with. The legislators need to take part in this dialogue so that they can hear why, perhaps, they are doing damage to education.

- Two other groups we need to hear from are parents and students. We've been making assumptions about what parents want to know. We've been making assumptions about what students want to know that they can do. A third group that we ought to tap into is teachers—we've been talking about the role that teachers ought to have in assessment, but no one here has been speaking for the teachers. Maybe some teachers ought to speak for themselves.

- We should hear from some teachers who have tried portfolio assessment. Some have tried it and found that it works, and we need to hear them talk about it.

- We could coincide the next symposium with the release of the international test data on literacy. If we could really get at the issues, talk to particular instances, we might clear up some of the theoretical problems.

- NCTE, IRA, and NCRE have put out a little book on case studies in literacy; they deal with different issues, from functional literacy to multi-cultural literacy. A series of little conferences on topics like that would be good. ERIC could open up the forum by generating a document something like that in which various stakeholders would come together to talk about the issues and keep this conversation going.

- Larry Barber of PDK has just returned from a trip to Russia. An overview of what's taking place there would be very useful.

- There's an awful lot of diversity in schools and other educational settings. Some things that might work in one educational setting would not work in another. We need to examine the diversity of needs in our public schools, and invite representation from the various settings so that we can come up with not a single solution but a set of solutions that fit all the needs that are out there.

CARL SMITH:

When you talk about diversity of needs, are you talking about at-risk schools, rural schools, bilingual schools, and others? [Agreement]

[More voices speak out:]

- We ought to think together about "impact studies." For example, in New York State, there was an impact study when they instituted statewide assessment in writing, and the amount of writing went up—whether it was good writing, or not, it went up. In other states that are skills-driven and behavioral-objectives driven, we need impact studies in the area of portfolios as well. What happens? What is the impact of portfolio use? What is the impact of the assessment in the public mind, in the school-teacher mind, to education broadly defined, when we institute new kinds of assessment?

- We need some discussion of various ways of disseminating assessment results to various audiences. Who wants to hear what, and in what form?

- We need to narrow the range of topics to be discussed, and agree on what we're going to talk about. No one who comes to a conference like this objects to authentic assessment or performance assessment, but some people are cynical because they think that the stuff that's been developed has been developed for the wrong purposes. The people who are forcing performance assessment to occur are not the language educators; they're state directors of testing. They may not have made it up, but they're being told to do it. The people who are afraid that we're going to mess up a good idea don't object to the philosophy of authentic assessment, but they do object because we're doing this too fast or for the wrong purposes or because somebody's gonna cheat or whatever.

- We need to keep the focus of the next symposium sharp—is it high-stakes performance assessment or classroom performance assessment? There's no such thing as performance assessment in general. We got a lot of cloudy stuff today by saying "It's good." It's *not* good: It's good if it's for a certain purpose; it's bad if it's for a certain purpose. For the kinds of stuff that are going to occur in 30 states in a couple of years—if that's true, God help us—it's going to be awful!

- I'm in favor of performance assessment, but not at the speed and the cost and within the time limits and the constraints

233

that are going to be imposed. Let's say which session is going to be about classroom assessment, and make it different from the session in which we talk about the state tests. Let's narrow the discussions in order to be able to follow them better.

- Educational performance tests should be used by the classroom teachers. They should be developed for the classroom and used in the classroom. If we start using them as means of statewide assessment, we're going to have problems with unreliability.

CARL SMITH:

In the name of all of my colleagues from "PDK" and ERIC and those of us in the IU Language Education Department, I want to thank each of you for being here. We think that today has been a major contribution on your part to helping us all comprehend better what's going on in performance assessment. We truly thank you for your participation.

APRÈS SYMPOSIUM:
THOUGHTS ON WHAT HAPPENED AND NEXT STEPS

MARILYN R. BINKLEY

THE NEED FOR A COMMON LANGUAGE ABOUT ASSESSMENT

The purpose of this symposium, as one looks back upon the meeting, was to explore three important dimensions of the current curriculum reform effort that is sweeping the nation as they relate to the language arts. As Steven Osterlind so succinctly noted, "What we would like to build towards is the integration of curriculum, instruction, and assessment. The integration of these three requires a common understanding of the purpose of each, a common understanding of the definition of each, and a common language."

What is abundantly clear is that there must be a great deal of effort before we can develop the necessary common understandings that will allow for the integration of the three. This is particularly true because each of the three dimensions is currently in flux. Innovation and evolution are rapidly changing how we view curriculum, instruction, and assessment in isolation, and each as it has an impact on the others. Given the theme of the conference, "Alternative Assessment in the Language Arts," the emphasis was on looking at assessment.

Alternative assessments raise any number of important questions, including issues of what assessments ought to look like, how they function, what—and whom—they measure, and the many purposes they serve. Assessments also raise some fundamental theoretical issues which were at the crux of this meeting. These include such things as how alternative assessments relate to curriculum, how they represent the curriculum, and how the reporting of assessment results affects what happens to the people involved. Both sets of issues can be discussed at multiple levels.

As I reflected on the conference, it seemed to me that participants talked passed one another because, although they were addressing the same issues, their vantage points were significantly different. For example, consider the difference in perspectives with regard to curriculum and assessment definitions. Barbara Backler exemplified one perspective when she tied the differences in assessment purpose to differences in curriculum definition. She noted, "There is a real, basic difference between the person who believes in a sacred curriculum, a canonical body of knowledge that must be imparted, and the person interested in what students want to know and how they want to learn it. Not believing in the sacred curriculum, I look at assessment as part of instruction. Someone else hears assessment as asking 'How am I doing? Am I accountable? Am I teaching what I am supposed to be teaching?'"

Backler was emphasizing instruction rather than assessment or curriculum. She would place assessment in the context of interaction between student and teacher, and it would not necessarily be formal.

For contrast, consider Jerry Harste's four explicit criteria for good assessment:

1. Assessment must be grounded both in theory and practice.

2. Assessment must focus on engaging participants in literacy events.

3. Assessment must implicate and hold all stakeholders responsible.

4. Assessment must further inquiry.

These criteria represent a researcher's theoretical stance with regard to curriculum, and it focuses on continuous inquiry which is likely to generate ongoing discussion and debate and more theory-building, equally exemplary of the researcher's stance.

Irrespective of whether I agree with the particular proposed curriculum implicit in Harste's criteria, I raise this question: If the assessment is so tightly aligned with a particular theory, how will I be able to demonstrate the relative advantages and disadvantages of one or another program related to particular theoretical stances?

By asking the question, I am demonstrating yet another perspective: No longer interested in a specific child, no longer wedded to a particular view of curriculum, and no longer interested in theory-building, I am, rather, looking for evidence that would support one or the other program. These shifts in perspective raise new sets of questions, and they add to the need for establishing a common language.

236

One of the most interesting things that happened at the symposium was the crossover between perspectives. Seated in the room were researchers, test publishers, teachers, state and district administrators, curriculum specialists, and policy makers. Very few of these people wore only one hat. Consequently, they could see and understand several perspectives at any time. Nevertheless, we each seemed to be stuck in particular roles, and roles determined whether we saw the forest or the tress. This or that role also determined how big a forest or how small a tree we were able to see. So, as we explored the issues of defining alternative assessments, there was a constant pull between differing needs and goals.

Extended dialogues must take place if we are to develop the needed common language. Participants in the dialogues must consciously try on other perspectives. As I look across the presentations and discussion groups, I see a great deal of evidence suggesting that the conference was a major step in that direction.

DEVELOPING A DEFINITION OF ALTERNATIVE ASSESSMENT

What is "alternative assessment?" The meeting was peppered with highly ambiguous references to this newly emerging assessment form. Almost all participants agreed that alternative assessment could not be a multiple-choice question test. Alternative assessments depend on a product or response being constructed. The tasks had to have characteristics that closely resembled what people actually do in a given environment. So, alternative assessments take the forms of constructed responses, open-ended essays with no single correct answer, portfolios that are collections of students' work over time, and project work that involves collaboration with peers.

Alternative assessments, when they take the form of tests, become performance tests. These might focus on the processes of problem-solving such that the examiner could make inferences about, or directly observe, how a student goes about completing a task.

As long as these forms of assessment exist within the context of interaction between student and teacher, there is little need for the rigors of psychometrics. Teachers' judgement and feedback—as they always have done—can continue to serve as an important piece of instruction. With this type of assessment, teachers come to be viewed as professional. Feedback to parents can also be provided in the form of rich examples.

However, once we move out of the particular instructional interaction and into questions of comparisons between students, classrooms, programs, schools, districts, and states; and when we ask the questions that serve a gatekeeping function, the richness of these assessments must be counterbalanced by the psychometric rigor of reliability and validity, and ease in scoring and reporting.

OVERCOMING THE PSYCHOMETRIC LIMITATIONS OF ALTERNATIVE ASSESSMENTS

The essential characteristics of standardized tests were clearly specified by Fred Finch as "...tests that are administered under standard conditions....A standardized test is one that uses uniform procedures when administering and scoring the test. Without standardized procedures,...it is not possible to compare scores earned by different persons." These characteristics do not necessarily lead only to a multiple-choice format; however, the strength or advantage of standardized multiple-choice tests rests in their psychometric properties that provide reliable estimates of students' knowledge or ability in regard to what is being measured. Reliable estimates achieved by using a "common ruler" make it possible for comparisons to be made.

As Cathy Taylor pointed out, "We use multiple-choice questions because it is easier to make them reliable....With standardized tests, we try to get multiple observations that are independent of one another so that they will be reliable observations. If we have 20 items, we have 20 observations on that particular scale, whether reading or language. These observations are independent observations: That means that a student doesn't get a score on one item that impacts the score on the next item."

Performance tests and classroom tasks are comparatively more labor intensive, both on the part of the test taker and of the administrator and scorer. Consequently, one is likely to have fewer test items and fewer independent observations. This, then, cuts down on the reliability of the estimate. The challenge to test designers and psychometricians is to overcome the limitations of fewer items while maximizing the richness of the available data.

A number of research and development initiatives are already well underway. Each of the test publishers represented at the meeting discussed test products that move strongly in this direction. Not only were there commercial tests available for local and state education agencies but also a number of states were launching tailored initiatives that incorporated the major available types of alternative test formats. At the national level, NAEP incorporates these item formats in both the reading and writing assessments for 1992.

Given the evolving state of psychometrics relative to these types of assessment items, one may wonder why districts, states, and federal data-collection agencies are willing to take the risk. The answer lies in the potentially rich data that could result, and the more explicit connections to classroom assessment and instruction.

The virtues of standardizing performance tests in terms of tasks, administration, and scoring may still seem to be inconsistent with the instructional characteristics of alternative assessment. Alternative assessment in an instructional sense would be diagnostic, and would be tailored to the needs and interests of each child. Given this tension, one wonders whether an alternative assessment in the form of a performance test could serve the two purposes of diagnosis and comparative or normative measure.

Roger Farr pointed out that it is the use of the test or resulting information that best determines the test's design. So, as we move away from instruction within the classroom to, say, a selection function, it may become more important to maintain the high reliability of the estimate, to distribute student performance or knowledge accurately across a well defined range, and then make the least biased (or most objective) decisions.

On the other hand, there are many other uses of assessment data that do not require individual student estimates. Consequently, having fewer observations of each student's performance capabilities in those cases is less important. For example, to fulfill the requirements of the NAEP monitoring function, sufficient advances in psychometric design have made it possible to produce national and state estimates of performance, even though individual students take only a subset of items on the test.

FINDING WAYS TO REPORT THE RICHNESS OF ALTERNATIVE ASSESSMENT DATA

Two important dimensions in alternative assessments argue in favor of their use. First, they provide rich explanatory information about student capabilities to perform tasks that are valued. Unlike the multiple-choice tests, they are more than mere indicators of an underlying ability, they are actual artifacts of the desired goal. As such, they bring about a close integration of instruction and assessment. Second, when alternative assessments take the form of standardized performance tests administered and scored by classroom teachers, they provide a strong vehicle for staff development. Too often, this richness is lost in the reporting of data.

For the purpose of district or state-level decision making, where the decision may affect the allocation of resources, policy makers are most interested in the aggregation of information. Curriculum people, however, resist this political-economic rise of testing. As Sharon Dorsey pointed out, "I don't want to reduce it [the portfolio] to one score or one digit....I don't think one can do that, and I think that's where the education of parents has to come in. I think we have to draw them in and have them work with us as we're working on the portfolio."

Similarly, she noted the need to educate legislators to look for more than just one score. What continues to be missing from the discussion, however, is an analog to something like a behaviorally anchored scale that succinctly and system- atically describes global behaviors.

The challenge, then, is to represent the information in appropriate ways. It is more than the normative or criterion-referenced score, it is descriptive information that can also be conveyed. These descriptions would more strongly reflect the desired goals of instruction. Here is an area needing major work by test devel- opers and curriculum people alike.

CLOSING THOUGHTS

Alternative assessment, school restructuring, curriculum change are all efforts at improving the outcomes of schooling for all children. What is at issue is how best to make them happen. While alternative assessments offer possibilities, they are not the panacea. They are not risk-free, and they are not yet well developed. The challenge before us all is in coming to the integration between solid curriculum, student-friendly instruction, and multiple-use assessment so that this integration of essential elements can strengthen our ability to improve education. This Symposium on Alternative Assessment in the Language Arts clarified the discussion and furthered the debate.

RESEARCH APPENDICES

What's a portfolio?

PORTFOLIO ASSESSMENT:
A SURVEY AMONG PROFESSIONALS

JERRY L. JOHNS, Northern Illinois University
PEGGY VAN LEIRSBURG, Elgin Public Schools

A portfolio approach to classroom literacy assessment has been described in recent literature (Jongsma, 1989; Mathews, 1990; Valencia, 1990). Disenchantment with traditional modes of assessment and changes in reading curricula have probably contributed to this approach for evaluation. Portfolios offer an alternate means of documenting and evaluating growth in literacy. Some classroom teachers have begun to institute portfolio assessment as a valid means to measure literacy growth in the classroom. In addition, some school systems (Mathews, 1990) are beginning to develop the portfolio as an assessment tool to be used within their districts. How widespread is knowledge and use of portfolio assessment? Do professionals value this type of individual student measurement?

RATIONALE FOR PORTFOLIOS

Valencia (1990) cited these four guiding principles to serve as the rationale for the portfolio assessment of literacy development:

1. Sound assessment is based on authenticity.

2. Assessment must be a continuous, ongoing process that chronicles literacy development.

3. Assessment must be a multifaceted, multidimensional process to reflect accurately the complexity of the literacy process.

4. Assessment must provide opportunities for collaborative reflection by both teachers and students.

These naturalistic evaluations focus on real literacy activities occurring over a period of time. Evaluation is linked to instruction and values the interaction of teachers and students in the development and maintenance of the portfolio.

Professionals can already read about the theoretical basis, suggested contents, and even potential problems related to portfolio assessment. But how do classroom teachers, specialists, and principals perceive this evaluative process? It is our purpose to offer the views of educational professionals toward four aspects of portfolio assessment: general knowledge, theoretical bases, contents, and practical problems.

PROFESSIONALS RESPOND TO SURVEY

We administered a written survey in June, 1990, to 128 educators attending a reading workshop. Approximately two-thirds of the educators were elementary teachers; the remaining one-third were secondary teachers, reading specialists, or administrators. Half of the total group had six or more years' teaching experience. More than half of our sample had attained a master's degree or beyond. In addition, more than half had taken twelve or more hours of coursework specifically in reading. Workshop participants came from many different school systems in the northern part of Illinois.

FINDINGS

Knowledge of Portfolios

Educators were asked to rate their familiarity with the "portfolio" concept using a five-point scale that ranged from "extremely familiar" to "I'm not." Nearly 71% rated their knowledge "very little" to "none." No one felt that he or she was extremely knowledgeable. Only 8% viewed their familiarity with portfolio assessment as "quite a bit."

Portfolio Contents

Our sample was then requested to rate a list of possible contents of a portfolio. They were requested to use a five-point scale ranging from "I'd definitely include it" to "I definitely wouldn't include it" to rate each possible source for portfolios. Items were listed for possible inclusion in a literacy portfolio, and our survey results are shown in Figure 1. Total percentages for each item may vary between 99 and 101 due to rounding.

FIGURE 1

OPINIONS OF PROFESSIONALS TOWARD INCLUDING SELECTED ITEMS IN A PORTFOLIO

Percent						Portfolio Items
DI	PI	U	PW	DW	N	
13	27	41	13	2	4	audio tapes
13	30	34	15	4	5	videotapes of classroom reading activities
8	27	36	17	8	4	photographs of reading activities
46	33	11	5	1	5	a listing of materials read
54	25	16	1	0	4	writing samples related to reading
55	30	20	2	0	5	a checklist of relevant reading behaviors
38	40	14	2	1	5	student self-evaluations
45	36	13	2	0	5	a thoughtful selection of student work on important reading skills or strategies
41	36	16	2	1	5	teacher evaluations and insights
34	29	28	2	2	5	collaboratively (student and teacher) produced progress notes
32	27	27	8	1	5	classroom notes

DI	= I'd definitely include	PW	= I probably wouldn't include
PI	= I'd probably include	DW	= I definitely wouldn't include
U	= I'm uncertain	N	= No response

Only 35-to-43 percent of the educators surveyed would definitely or probably include audio tapes, video tapes, or photographs in a portfolio. Classroom tests would definitely or probably be included by 59% of the sample. The remaining content items, with the exception of collaboratively produced progress notes, would be included by at least 74% of the sample. The item most selected (81%) to include in a portfolio of literacy assessment was "a thoughtful selection of student work on important reading skills or strategies."

Theoretical Basis for Portfolio Assessment

Our survey requested that the educators respond to Valencia's (1990) four statements of rationale for portfolios on a five-point scale ranging from "strongly agree" to "strongly disagree." Approximately 60% agreed that authenticity should anchor reading assessment. Nearly 80% also agreed that assessment should be ongoing, multidimensional, and collaborative. Importantly, nearly 90% of the professionals agreed that assessment should be a continuous, ongoing process. Fewer than 2% of the respondents disagreed with any of these underlying principles of portfolio assessment.

Practical Problems with Portfolios

The fourth area we surveyed was that of possible practical problems inherent in portfolio assessment. Our questionnaire asked educators to rate a list of possible problems on a five-point scale ranging from "a very serious concern" to "no concern." The potential problems that may confront users of portfolios are shown in Figure 2 (page 184).

Importantly, about 11% of the educators surveyed did not respond to this list of potential problems with the use of portfolios. Of those educators who responded, over 50% expressed very serious, serious, or some concern with all of the items except using portfolios in parent-teacher conferences. Nearly half of the educators had very serious or serious concerns with planning, organizing, and managing issues related to portfolio assessment. At least 72% expressed at least some concern with the issue of "having portfolios replace standardized reading tests or achievement tests."

DISCUSSION AND CONCLUSIONS

In our sample of 128 elementary teachers, secondary teachers, special reading teachers, and administrators, little general familiarity with the concept of portfolio assessment is evident. Most of the sample, nevertheless, agreed with these theoretical bases of assessment: authentic, continuous, multidimensional, and collaborative. These four guiding principles serve as the rationale for literacy assessment (Valencia, 1990). It appears that although most educators agree with its theoretical bases as an assessment device, portfolios were not widely understood at the time of this survey in June, 1990.

FIGURE 2

OPINIONS OF PROFESSIONALS TOWARDS POSSIBLE PRACTICAL PROBLEMS WITH PORTFOLIOS

Percent						Possible Practical Problems
VS	SC	S	VL	NC	N	
17	31	37	2	3	9	planning portfolios
17	28	39	5	2	3	organizing portfolios
20	31	37	2	1	10	managing the contents of portfolios
13	30	42	3	2	10	developing checklists for the portfolios
5	14	40	23	7	11	where to keep portfolios
3	29	38	16	3	11	providing access to students
12	26	30	13	9	11	talking to students about contents
9	32	38	9	2	11	preparing notes; completing checklists
18	19	28	15	9	12	all teachers in my school using a portfolio
20	13	30	15	12	11	all my school system embracing the use of portfolios
9	19	31	21	9	11	using portfolios in parent-teacher conferences
17	20	32	12	8	11	using portfolios as sole means of evaluating student progress
6	22	27	21	13	11	using portfolios as one means of evaluating student progress
23	22	27	11	6	11	having portfolios replace standardized reading tests or achievement tests

VS	= Very serious concern		VL	= Very little concern
SC	= Serious concern		NC	= No concern
S	= Some concern		N	= No reponse

Perhaps this lack of familiarity explains, to some extent, why approximately 11% of those surveyed did not respond to practical concerns related to portfolio assessment.

Those educators who did respond, however, expressed numerous concerns with such an assessment mode. They want to know how to plan, organize, and manage portfolios. They indicate concern about whether or not portfolio assessment will replace or add to already existing standardized testing programs.

The contents of a literacy portfolio are also at issue. Most of those surveyed would not include audio tapes, video tapes, or photographs. We infer that most teachers view these items as time-consuming, costly, and bulky. Paper-and-pencil tasks, as well as dialogue with students, were chosen more often for inclusion.

Portfolio assessment requires teachers and school systems to make decisions about which data are important to include. These choices can only be made when the objectives for learning are clearly defined. Teaching to these objectives is interwoven with continuous, ongoing assessment. What product will measure which process? Once this question is answered, the contents of a portfolio can then be designed to include those sources that measure important objectives.

Practical concerns, not conceptual issues, may keep portfolios from achieving their full potential. Assuming that portfolios gain a level of general acceptance, the heavy demand on a teacher's time may prohibit their widespread use. Some teachers may willingly devote the necessary time and energy to build and maintain portfolios, but it is not realistic to expect that all staff members of a school or district will embrace the process. Veteran teachers may reject the "pain" of change as not worthy of the "gain."

There are things that all students *can* do. These things are documentable. A review of anecdotes, checklists, and work samples will help demonstrate a pattern of student progress. A literacy portfolio, with multiple types of data, exhibits a broader base of information about the abilities of a specific learner than does either a letter grade or a test score alone. Portfolio documentation offers the teacher information to extend and "encourage significant growth far beyond the measurements reflected in formal, standardized testing" (Goodman, Goodman, & Hood, 1989, p. 260).

We feel that steps need to be taken to inform educators—teachers *and* administrators--that portfolio assessment affords the classroom teacher information for decision-making that is valid and specific. Initiating and monitoring portfolios present genuine challenges that must be met and answered in order for portfolios to have a chance to succeed as an innovative form of literacy assessment.

REFERENCES

Goodman, K.S., Goodman, Y.M., & Hood, W.J. (1989). *The Whole Language Evaluation Book.* Portsmouth, New Hampshire: Heinemann.

Jongsma, K. (1989). "Portfolio Assessment," *The Reading Teacher, 43,* 264-265.

Mathews, J.K. (1990). "From Computer Management to Portfolio Assessment," *The Reading Teacher, 43,* 420-421.

Valencia, S. (1990). "A Portfolio Approach to Classroom Reading Assessment," *The Reading Teacher, 43,* 338-340.

LITERACY PORTFOLIOS: A PRIMER

JERRY L. JOHNS

In recent years, a portfolio approach to classroom literacy assessment has been described in the literature (Mathews, 1990; Valencia, 1990). This approach has been stimulated, at least in part, by changes in reading curricula and by disenchantment with traditional modes of assessment. Portfolios offer a different way to evaluate and document growth and progress in literacy. They include a wide range of items that enable students to document their skills, achievements, and progress in literacy. Valencia (1990) noted that a portfolio may be a large, expandable file folder that holds: 1) samples of the student's work (selected by both the teacher and the student), 2) observational notes made by the teacher, 3) self-evaluations by the student, and 4) progress notes collaboratively prepared by the teacher and student. In this article, my focus is reading; however, the portfolio concept can also be used to include writing. Other sources (Jongsma, 1989; Krest, 1990; Simmons, 1990) offer some very helpful ideas for using writing samples in literacy portfolios.

BASES FOR PORTFOLIO ASSESSMENT

According to Valencia (1990), there are four guiding principles that serve as the rationale for portfolios in literacy assessment:

1. Sound assessment is based on authenticity.

2. Assessment must be a continuous, ongoing process that chronicles literacy development.

3. Assessment must be a multifaceted, multidimensional process to reflect accurately the complexity of the literacy process.

4. Assessment must provide opportunities for collaborative reflection by both teachers and students.

In essence, portfolios place a high premium on using a variety of *real* literacy activities over a period of time that involves the interaction of teachers and students in the development and maintenance of the portfolio.

SOURCES OF DATA FOR PORTFOLIOS

Many possible sources exist for portfolio data. The following are items that the classroom teacher can hope to see in a student's portfolio:

- audiotapes of a student's reading
- video tapes of classroom reading activities (e.g., plays, discussions, partner reading)
- photographs of reading activities
- a list of materials read (e.g., books, magazines)
- writing samples related to literacy experiences (e.g., pages from reading logs)
- a checklist of relevant reading behaviors
- student self-evaluations
- a thoughtful selection of student work on important reading skills or strategies (e.g., story map, comprehension)
- other teachers' observations and insights (e.g., attitudes toward reading, growth in discussion about stories and books, use of various word identification strategies)
- collaboratively-produced (by student and teacher) progress notes and checklists
- classroom tests

The large number of sources available for providing portfolio data make the selection process particularly important. One of the real dangers of portfolios is that they can become an unfocused grab bag of too many pieces of information. An unorganized accumulation of bits and pieces of information lacks in usefulness. To avoid this problem, you will need to think carefully about the purposes of a portfolio as it applies to your curricular and instructional priorities.

DESIGNING PORTFOLIOS: SOME PRACTICAL CONSIDERATIONS

Since portfolios are a means to an end, you must first decide why you are using them. Consequently, you will need to establish the broad goals of your reading program that are consistent with the goals or objectives of your classroom, school, district, or state.

Suggested Objectives. Many goals or objectives are possible; nevertheless, I believe that teachers and specialists in reading would support at least these two broad objectives:

The first objective has been expressed by the Illinois State "Goal for Learning": Students will be able to read, comprehend, interpret, evaluate, and use written material. The focus of this goal is, in a single word, comprehension.

The second objective is directed toward developing students who are motivated to read and who have positive attitudes toward reading. This objective focuses our efforts on helping students read to satisfy personal needs. This objective is reached when: students develop positive attitudes toward reading and become motivated to read to satisfy their needs. The focus of this goal is to help students develop an appreciation of reading so that it becomes something they do on a regular basis in the classroom, at home, and throughout their lives.

These two broad goals contain subgoals. You must be careful, however, not to have too many overly narrow objectives. Specificity could tend to fragment the reading process. For the first broad goal (comprehension), I recommend that you review the seven general knowledges and skills related to comprehension. (Illinois State Board of Education, 1986). For the second goal (positive attitudes and personal reading), the following items may be possible subgoals:

to acquire a positive attitude toward reading.

to enjoy reading as a leisure-time activity.

to satisfy interests and needs through reading.

to achieve personal development through reading.

Suggested Format for Portfolios. Once you select your objectives, you will need to decide upon the actual portfolio. "Physically, it is larger and more elaborate than a report card. Practically, it must be smaller and more focused than a steamer trunk filled with accumulated artifacts." (Valencia, 1990, p. 339) What might you use? Boxes are probably too big to be practical. File folders may be too small to hold work samples and audio tapes in a reasonably secure manner. Valencia suggested using a large expandable file folder. Folders are a good possibility, but they could be difficult to store unless you have a file cabinet in your room. Perhaps cardboard magazine holders would be a compromise. They are sturdy, have a place for the student's name, and can be easily stored on a shelf or window counter. Another choice might be tough, plastic file crates that hold hanging file folders. Regardless of your choice of portfolio, the collection should be readily accessible both to you and your students.

Managing Portfolios. Once you have determined the goals of the portfolio and selected something to hold the evidence, you may want to organize the collection into two layers of information. The first is the actual data (e.g., reading logs, representative daily work, progress notes). The second is a summary sheet or some other means to help you synthesize the information. (Valencia, 1990) This second component is vital for the effective use of portfolios. For example, if one of your goals is to promote positive attitudes and personal reading, the checklist shown in Figure 1 might be adapted for use to record your observations and to evaluate the student's reading records in the portfolio.

Teachers in Orange County, Florida began modestly by including four core elements in their portfolios: 1) a reading development checklist, 2) writing samples, 3) a list of books read by the student, and 4) a test of reading comprehension. The checklist was used by teachers to record observations three times throughout the school year. These same teachers recognized the need to revise the components of the portfolio and to add additional pieces of information. Portfolios are a dynamic means of monitoring progress in literacy. If you remember this basic principle, the necessity to reevaluate portfolio contents on a regular basis is seen as an integral and essential part of the whole process. (Mathews, 1990)

USING PORTFOLIOS FOR CLASSROOM LITERACY ASSESSMENT

Portfolios are useful for all partners in the literacy program: students, teachers, parents, and school officials. Portfolios can also be used in conjunction with other sources of information (e.g., standardized tests, local assessments, class grades, teacher observations). Collaborative examination of portfolio contents with other students and the teacher can be the occasion for a student to discuss progress and important learnings as well as to add written notes relating to these examinations. Students should be taught how to maintain and manage their portfolios so that excessive amounts of time are not required of the teacher. Plans can be made for the inclusion of other pieces of data that may be especially relevant. Toward the end of the school year, you could spend some time with each student to decide what stays at school and what goes home. The portfolio could then be "passed along as a continuing document from year to year" (Wolf, 1989, p. 37). Farr suggests a minimum of four student-teacher discussions on portfolios throughout the school year. (see Jongsma, 1989)

FIGURE 1

CHECKLIST FOR STUDENT'S ATTITUDES AND PERSONAL READING

Student   **Grade**   **Teacher**

Seldom			Sometimes			Often			
Oct	Feb	May	Oct	Feb	May	Oct	Feb	May	
									1. Possesses books or printed materials not assigned
									2. Uses classroom library
									3. Checks out books from school library
									4. Voluntarily shares outside reading
									5. Talks with other students about reading
									6. Seems to have a favorite author
									7. Requests more reading about topics
									8. Uses reading to satisfy personal interests
									9. Reads for recreation
									10. Chooses reading when given choices
									11. Reading reflects interests
									12. Applies ideas from reading to his/her life
									13. Seems to enjoy reading
									14. Participates in classroom book club
									15. Participates in book exchange club
									16. Parents report reading at home

Most schools have parent-teacher conferences. Data from the portfolio could be used to show progress toward the objectives that formed the design of the portfolio. I know teachers who used "modified portfolios" during parent-teacher conferences long before the label "portfolio" appeared in professional journals. For example, one teacher used tape recordings of each student's reading early in the fall and just before conferences to supplement the written work the student kept in a folder. Viewed from this perspective, portfolios are not a new concept. Current portfolios are different from these informal beginnings in that they are the intentional effort of professionals to legitimize the important role that naturalistic, ongoing evaluation plays in literacy assessment. Data like this yields authentic validity and integrity. Another new emphasis is the role that students play in helping to evaluate their own progress in achieving the important outcomes of the literacy program. Viewed from this perspective, students have a *personal* responsibility and involvement in their progress as readers and writers.

LIMITATIONS OF PORTFOLIOS

The potential of portfolios for monitoring literacy growth is great; nevertheless, as with other assessment instruments, limitations do exist. Most of the limitations have very little to do with the *concept* of portfolios. Practical concerns will likely limit portfolios from achieving their full potential. One concern involves the general level of acceptance among school officials and the public. The current trend for accountability is likely to raise questions about innovative means of monitoring and evaluating student progress. Assuming that portfolios are readily accepted (and this is a big assumption), the heavy demands upon a teacher's time to use this type of assessment severely limit portfolios from reaching their potential. Even if teachers were willing to devote the necessary time and energy to building and maintaining portfolios, I doubt whether all staff members would readily embrace the process. Some veteran teachers may voice concerns that the practical problems and pain of change aren't worth the benefits. I disagree; however, initiating and monitoring portfolios do present genuine challenges. Steps need to be taken to help teachers implement portfolios.

The need for the perhaps most fundamental step is revealed in a research study reported by Johns and VanLeirsberg (1990). In surveying 128 educators, nearly 71% of the educators rated their knowledge of portfolios as "very little" to "none." Not a single educator felt that he or she was "extremely knowledgeable"; moreover, only 8% of the educators rated their familiarity with portfolio assessment as "quite a bit."

Although educators seem to lack knowledge of portfolios, the four statements of rationale listed earlier were supported strongly in the Johns and VanLeirsberg survey. Approximately 60% of the educators agreed that authenticity should anchor reading assessment. Nearly 80% agreed that assessment should be ongoing, multidimensional,and collaborative. Importantly, nearly 90% of the professionals agreed that assessment should be a continuous, ongoing process. Fewer than 2% of the respondents disagreed with any of these principles of portfolio assessment. Based on survey data, professionals accept the bases of portfolio assessment. Workshops, inservice programs, and similar programs will help expand professionals' knowledge so that portfolios ought to have a good chance to succeed as an innovative form of literacy assessment.

REFERENCES

Illinois State Board of Education. (1986). *State Goals for Learning and Sample Learning Objectives: Language Arts.* Springfield, Illinois: Author.

Johns, J. L., & VanLeirsberg, P. (1990). "Portfolio Assessment: A Survey among Professionals." DeKalb, Illinois: Northern Illinois University. [pp. 242-248 in this volume]

Jongsma, K. S. (1989). "Portfolio Assessment" (*Questions & Answers* column), *The Reading Teacher, 43,* 264-265.

Krest, M. (1990). "Adapting the Portfolio to Meet Student Needs," *English Journal, 79* (2), 29-34.

Mathews, J. K. (1990). "From Computer Management to Portfolio Assessment," *The Reading Teacher, 43,* 420-421.

Simmons, J. (1990). "Portfolios as Large-scale Assessment," *Language Arts, 67,* 262-268.

Valencia, S. (1990). "A Portfolio Approach to Classroom Reading Assessment," *The Reading Teacher, 43,* 338-340.

Wolf, D. P. (1989). "Portfolio Assessment: Sampling Student Work," *Educational Leadership, 46,* 35-39.

HOW PROFESSIONALS VIEW PORTFOLIO ASSESSMENT

JERRY L. JOHNS, Northern Illinois University
PEGGY VANLEIRSBURG, Elgin Public Schools

Portfolios offer an innovative framework for assessment. However, they are newer to literacy instruction than in other fields of study. Tierney, Carter, and Desai (1991) described the origins of portfolios as applied to collections of work by commercial artists, models, photographers, artists, and people in other fields of endeavor who want to showcase their achievements. "The portfolio is tangible evidence of accomplishments and skills that must be updated as a person changes and grows" (Tierney, Carter, & Desai, 1991, p. 43). It is from this collection of works that each person is evaluated in a variety of contexts.

The concept of the literacy portfolio as a framework for assessment is quite different from traditional, standardized methods of assessment. Achievement tests offer quantified units that can be counted and accounted (Paulson, Paulson, & Meyer, 1991). The literacy portfolio, however, offers a broader view of student progress that is complex and includes collaborative, authentic, multidimensional evaluative tasks which measure growth over time. The portfolio is a vehicle that helps students to become independent learners and encourages teachers to facilitate these individual processes.

Literacy professionals are looking beyond norm-referenced, standardized tests for ways of sampling students' language-arts performance that are more closely linked to instruction (Jongsma, 1989). Portfolios offer one such means of performance-based assessment anchored in authenticity. The integrity and validity to be gained by the use of portfolios may outweigh inherent practical issues such as the time burden of regular discussions with students and certain basic management considerations (Wolf, 1989).

Johns and VanLeirsburg (1990) surveyed a group of 128 professional educators to determine the extent of their knowledge and use of the literacy portfolio as an assessment tool. Most of the subjects surveyed agreed with four basic principles of literacy assessment: authentic, continuous, multidimensional, and collaborative (Valencia, 1990). The subjects, however, rated themselves as having little general familiarity with the concept of portfolio assessment. They further indicated concerns with practical problems in the use of portfolios such as planning, organization, and management. The contents for inclusion in literacy portfolios were also at issue.

PURPOSE

This study was an extension of a study by Johns and VanLeirsburg (1990). The purpose of the present study was to compare results with the 1990 survey of educators to determine growth in knowledge and use of portfolio assessment. There is much written about the theoretical bases, possible contents, and practical problems of portfolios, but little research has been reported on the reactions and feelings of educators who use or may plan to use portfolios.

RATIONALE FOR PORTFOLIOS

There are theoretical and pragmatic reasons for a portfolio approach to literacy assessment. Valencia (1990) offered four such guiding principles drawn from both research and instructional practices.

1. Sound assessment is anchored in authenticity—of tasks, texts, and contexts.

2. Assessment must be a continuous, on-going process that chronicles development.

3. Because reading is a complex and multifaceted process, valid reading assessment must be multidimensional and committed to sampling a wide range of cognitive processes, affective responses, and literacy activities.

4. Assessment must provide for active, collaborative reflection by both teacher and student.

The portfolio offers a natural means of assessing reading and writing within the ongoing instructional program over a period of time.

METHOD

Subjects

A total of 173 subjects, who had enrolled in a literacy workshop sponsored by a Midwestern reading association, participated in this study: 130 had not used portfolios, and 43 had previous experience with portfolio use. Workshop participants came from many different school systems in northern Illinois. No information about portfolios was shared prior to the administration of the questionnaire.

Of the group of 43 professionals who had used portfolios, 47% were primary teachers, 21% were intermediate teachers, 7% were secondary teachers (grades 7-12), 16% were reading teachers in a special reading or Chapter 1 capacity, and the remaining 9% of the teachers taught in other capacities including ESL and continuing education programs. Slightly more than 10% of this group had from 2-to-5 years of teaching experience, more than one-third had 6-to-10 years experience, and over half had 11 or more years of teaching experience. Approximately 70% of those using portfolios had earned a master's degree or additional hours, 24% had earned a bachelor's degree, and 5% were K-12 reading specialists. About one-third of this group had taken from 4-to-12 hours of coursework in reading, 42% had taken from 13-to-21 such hours, and nearly 30% had taken 22 or more hours of reading courses. Overall, this group represented experienced teachers with more than four reading courses.

The 130 professionals who had not used portfolios included 38% primary teachers, 18% intermediate teachers, 15% secondary teachers, 14% reading teachers, and 15% teaching in other capacities. Nearly 5% of this group had less than 1 year of teaching experience, 17% had 2-to-5 years experience, 18% had 6-to-10 years experience, and more than 60% had 11 or more years of teaching experience. About 35% of the subjects who had not used portfolios had earned a bachelor's degree, nearly 60% had earned a master's degree or higher, and 8% had earned a K-12 reading specialist certificate. Of the non-portfolio group, about 50% had 12 or less hours of reading coursework, 24% had taken from 13 to 21 hours of reading courses, and nearly 24% had taken 22 or more hours in reading. Overall, this group was composed of experienced teachers who had taken fewer reading courses than the group currently using portfolios.

Survey

The original survey of 34 items was modified slightly for the 1991 study. The possible contents section excluded videotapes of classroom reading activities and included standardized tests, informal reading inventories, and writing samples of different genres in which ideas are modified from first draft to final product. Further, the practical-problems section of the survey was modified to include costs associated with folders, boxes, files, tapes, etc.

The revised survey contained 42 items, and it was administered in June 1991 to 173 educators attending a literacy workshop. The findings, reported separately for "portfolio" and "non-portfolio" users, are presented in four areas: knowledge, content, theoretical bases, and practical problems related to using portfolios. In addition, space was provided for current users of portfolios to list the items that they included in portfolios. In the final section of this study, some relevant and important comparisons to the results of the 1990 survey are included.

FINDINGS

Knowledge of Portfolios

Subjects were asked to rank their familiarity with portfolios on a five-point scale ranging from "extremely," to "quite a bit," "some," "very little," and "I'm not." Nearly half of the non-portfolio group rated themselves as having "very little" or no knowledge of portfolios whereas only 10% of the group using portfolios responded in the same manner. About one-third of both groups rated themselves as having "some" knowledge of portfolios. Approximately 14% of the non-portfolio group felt that they were "extremely" or "quite a bit" familiar with portfolios, while nearly 60% of those already using portfolios shared those same ratings.

About one-fourth of the total group reported that they were involved in actually using portfolios. The decision to use them was reported by about 60% of the group to be theirs alone; over 40% reported that portfolio use was required by someone else (e.g., their school or a school district). Over 40% of those using portfolios did so only in their classrooms, 25% within their school or district, and about 35% reported portfolio use within their classroom, school, and district. Most portfolios, nearly 75%, were teacher-made. However, 5% were commercial portfolios, and 21% used a combination of teacher-made and commercial portfolios.

Contents

The 173 subjects were asked to rate a list of contents for possible inclusion in a portfolio. Items listed for possible inclusion in a literacy portfolio along with survey results are shown in Table 1. Total percentages for each item vary between 99 and 101 due to rounding.

More than 80% of the group that had used portfolios chose a listing of materials read, writing samples related to literacy experiences, student self-evaluations, a thoughtful selection of student work on important reading skills or strategies, and writing samples of different genres in which ideas are modified from first draft to final product as most important for inclusion in a student portfolio. At least 80% of the group that had not used portfolios before chose the same contents for inclusion with the addition of teacher observations and insights. Between 28% and 42% of both groups felt that photographs of reading activities or standardized tests should be included in a literacy portfolio; however, they were the least chosen options in this survey.

TABLE 1

OPTIONS OF PROFESSIONALS:
INCLUSION OF SELECTED ITEMS IN A PORTFOLIO

Portfolio Items	Percent of Responses					
	DI	PI	U	PW	DW	O
audio tapes						
portfolio (N=130)	19	26	16	28	12	0
non-portfolio (N=43)	23	31	24	17	5	0
photographs of reading activities						
portfolio	16	12	28	40	5	0
non-portfolio	8	28	32	25	6	1
a listing of materials read						
portfolio	53	35	2	9	0	0
non-portfolio	52	36	12	1	0	0

Portfolio Items	Percent of Responses					
	DI	PI	U	PW	DW	O
writing samples related to literacy experiences						
portfolio	88	9	0	2	0	0
non-portfolio	55	29	13	2	0	1
a checklist of relevant reading behaviors						
portfolio	44	35	12	9	0	0
non-portfolio	35	34	23	5	2	1
student self-evaluation						
portfolio	35	47	12	5	2	0
non-portfolio	35	41	22	2	0	0
a thoughtful selection of student work on important reading skills or strategies						
portfolio	49	35	9	7	0	0
non-portfolio	45	39	13	3	0	0
teacher observations and insights						
portfolio	58	19	14	9	0	0
non-portfolio	41	40	18	2	0	0
collaboratively produced progress notes						
portfolio	40	26	26	7	2	0
non-portfolio	25	43	27	5	0	0
classroom tests						
portfolio	28	30	17	19	7	0
non-portfolio	32	31	22	10	5	0
standardized tests						
portfolio	14	21	21	33	9	2
non-portfolio	24	18	25	23	10	1

Portfolio Items	Percent of Responses					
	DI	PI	U	PW	DW	O
informal reading inventories						
portfolio	30	40	14	14	2	0
non-portfolio	29	36	24	10	1	0
writing samples of different genres in which ideas are modified from first draft to final product						
portfolio	67	26	2	5	0	0
non-portfolio	45	38	12	5	0	0

DI = I'd definitely include   PW = I probably wouldn't include
PI = I'd probably include   DW = I definitely wouldn't include
U = I'm uncertain   O = Omitted response

The 43 educators using portfolios were asked to list the items that they actually included in their portfolios. The major items, in descending frequency, included writing samples, reading logs, teacher observations, informal reading inventories, and work samples. Other items mentioned by a few of the educators included standardized test scores, classroom tests, journals, audio tapes, and the student's evaluation of his or her own progress.

Theoretical Bases

The educators were asked to respond to Valencia's (1990) four statements of rationale for portfolios which are characterized by the following key words: authentic, continuous, multidimensional, and collaborative. The five-point scale offered these choices: "strongly agree," "agree," "uncertain," "disagree," or "strongly disagree." About 70% of both groups, those who had used portfolios and those who had not, agreed that authenticity should anchor reading assessment. However, the strongest agreement was in response to assessment being a continuous, on-going process; more than 96% of both groups agreed or strongly agreed with this concept.

About 90% of both groups also agreed that assessment should be multidimensional to reflect the complexity of the reading task. More than 84% of both groups agreed that assessment should provide for active, collaborative reflection by both teacher and student. Fewer than 5% of the respondents disagreed with any of the four underlying principles of portfolio assessment.

Practical Problems

The fourth major area surveyed related to possible practical problems with the use of portfolios for assessment. Educators were asked to rate a list of possible practical problems on a five-point scale ranging from "a very serious concern" to "no concern." The responses of both groups are shown in Table 2.

The greatest concerns by those already using portfolios included planning, managing contents, talking with students about contents, and preparing notes and completing checklists. At least 40% of this group responded to these issues and expressed either serious or very serious concerns. At least 50% of the group that had not used portfolios had serious or very serious concerns relative to planning, organizing, managing contents, preparing notes and completing checklists, and using portfolios as the sole means of evaluating student progress. Both groups felt that managing portfolios would be the biggest practical concern.

Of lesser concern to the group who had used portfolios were using portfolios in parent-teacher conferences, using portfolios as one means of evaluating student progress, and costs associated with folders, files, and tapes. No more than 22% of the group was seriously or very seriously concerned with these concerns. The issues of least concern to the group that had not used portfolios were where to keep portfolios, providing access to students, and using portfolios as one means of evaluating student progress. Not more than 26% of this group responded with serious or very serious concerns to these concerns. It is noteworthy that 25-to-43 percent of the group which had not used portfolios indicated some concern for each of the possible problems.

TABLE 2

POSSIBLE PRACTICAL PROBLEMS WITH PORTFOLIOS

Possible Practical Problems	Percent of Responses					
	VS	SC	S	VL	NC	O
planning portfolios						
portfolio (N=130)	14	30	37	12	7	0
non-portfolio (N=43)	19	37	35	8	1	0
organizing portfolios						
portfolio	14	23	37	21	5	0
non-portfolio	18	37	38	10	1	0
managing the contents of a portfolio						
portfolio	26	23	37	9	5	0
non-portfolio	28	37	26	7	2	1
developing checklists for the portfolio						
portfolio	12	30	47	7	5	0
non-portfolio	14	32	35	16	3	0
where to keep portfolios						
portfolio	14	16	28	28	14	0
non-portfolio	5	13	29	40	12	0
providing access to students						
portfolio	9	23	37	21	9	0
non-portfolio	7	18	43	25	7	0
talking with students about contents						
portfolio	21	19	26	23	12	2
non-portfolio	18	22	29	23	7	0
preparing notes/completing checklists						
portfolio	14	33	40	7	7	0
non-portfolio	22	22	38	7	2	0
all teachers in my school using a portfolio						
portfolio	16	26	30	16	9	2
non-portfolio	18	18	31	25	7	0

Possible Practical Problems	Percent of Responses					
	VS	SC	S	VL	NC	O
all my school system embracing the use of portfolios						
portfolio	19	10	42	16	12	2
non-portfolio	17	16	33	25	8	0
using portfolios in parent-teacher conferences						
portfolio	5	17	28	26	23	0
non-portfolio	6	22	33	28	10	0
using portfolios as the sole means of evaluating student progress						
portfolio	19	14	42	14	12	0
non-portfolio	31	31	25	12	2	0
using portfolios as one means of evaluating student progress						
portfolio	7	14	9	28	42	0
non-portfolio	8	18	27	31	15	1
having portfolios replace standard-ized tests or achievement tests						
portfolio	14	19	40	14	14	0
non-portfolio	25	18	37	15	5	0
costs associated with folders, boxes, files, tapes, etc.						
portfolio	7	14	30	38	9	2
non-portfolio	11	21	29	27	12	0

VS = very serious concern   VL = very little concern
SC = serious concern   NC = no concern
S = some concern   O = omitted response

DISCUSSION AND CONCLUSIONS

Based on our survey, there appears to be growing familiarity among professionals with the concept of portfolio assessment. In our 1991 sample of 173 elementary, secondary, reading, and other educators, about one-fourth were using portfolios as a tool of reading and writing assessment. More than half of those who had used portfolios rated themselves as "extremely" or "quite a bit" familiar with the portfolio concept, and only 10% felt they had "very little knowledge" or "no knowledge." About three-fourths of our sample were not using portfolios. Of this group, about 14% felt that they were "extremely" or "quite a bit" familiar with the portfolio concept. Nearly 40% felt that they were somewhat familiar with portfolios, and around half of this group rated their familiarity with portfolios as "very little" or "none." In the 1990 survey, however, more than 70% of the subjects rated their knowledge "very little" or "I'm not"; only 8% felt they had "quite a bit" of knowledge about portfolios. One year later, more educators are familiar with the concept of portfolios than was the case a year before.

The respondents to both surveys, 1990 and 1991 (portfolio and non-portfolio), agreed overwhelmingly with Valencia's (1990) four guiding principles of assessment: authentic, continuous, multidimensional, and collaborative. The greatest agreement (90%) among the 1990 respondents was that assessment should be a continuous and on-going process; 98% of the 1991 portfolio group and 96% of the 1991 non-portfolio group also agreed with that concept of assessment. The principle least chosen by the 1990 subjects was that sound assessment is based on authenticity. However, 60% did agree with that concept. From the 1991 group that used portfolios, 70% agreed that assessment should be authentic; 69% of the 1991 group that did not use portfolios also agreed. Fewer than 2% of the 1990 subjects, and 5% of the 1991 groups, disagreed with any of the four guiding principles for portfolio assessment.

The contents of a literacy portfolio are less at issue than was apparent in our 1990 survey results. An average of approximately 20% of these respondents would not include audio tapes, video tapes, or photographs. We inferred that most educators would find these costly and time-consuming. In the 1991 survey, however, both the portfolio and non-portfolio groups ranked photographs of reading activities a low choice for inclusion. Approximately half of each group would include audio tapes, although 40% of the portfolio group probably or definitely would not include this item. The second lowest

266

choice of the 1991 groups was standardized tests, a choice which did not exist in the 1990 survey. Written tasks, such as writing samples, a list of materials read, and student self-evaluations ranked high for inclusion with respondents in both the 1990 and 1991 surveys. With the exception of photographs, standardized tests, and audio tapes, more than half of the 1991 groups chose all other survey items for possible inclusion in a literacy portfolio.

The respondents who had used portfolios were requested to list those items they actually included in their portfolios. The item mentioned most often by this group was writing samples, which was one of the most chosen items for inclusion by both surveyed groups. The second item listed by portfolio users was a student reading log or list of books read by each student. This item was not included in the survey. However, the third-most-often-included item by users of portfolios was teacher observations. This item was included in the survey, and about 80% of both groups also chose teacher observations for inclusion.

Practical problems related to the systematic collection of reading and writing artifacts continue to be real issues for the educators we surveyed. Planning, managing, and organizing portfolios, as well as preparing notes and completing checklists are the major practical concerns of those responding to the 1991 survey. Both groups agreed that these were serious or very serious concerns. However, it is of interest that the percentage of concern is slightly higher in all areas for the group that did not use portfolios. For example, 44% of the group who had used portfolios responded that they were concerned about planning portfolios, whereas 56% of the non-portfolio group reported "serious" or "very serious" concern for that issue.

In our 1990 survey, the same practical issues were examined, but 11% of those surveyed omitted these questions. Less than 3% of either group in the 1991 survey omitted any item related to the practical issues of portfolio use. As familiarity and use of literacy portfolios increases, the practical concerns appear to decline. Nevertheless, initiating and monitoring portfolios continues to present genuine challenges (Johns, 1991). While these areas continue to be at issue, some of these problems appear to be have relatively simple solutions. Perhaps as educators become better acquainted with portfolios, and modify their views, they will view portfolios not as messy objects, but as vehicles that represent what students are actively doing (Tierney, Carter, & Desai, 1991).

We conclude that familiarity with portfolios has grown from 1990 to 1991. Educators from both the 1990 and 1991 groups overwhelmingly agreed with Valencia's four guiding principles of assessment: authentic, continuous, multidimensional, and collaborative. The portfolio and non-portfolio groups of the 1991 survey, as well as the 1990 sample, chose a list of materials read and writing samples related to literacy experiences most often for inclusion in the portfolio. The percentage of concern about practical problems with portfolio usage declined, while planning, managing, and organizing continued to rank as the most serious concerns in both the 1990 and 1991 surveys.

Used as an assessment framework, portfolios are systematic collections by students and teachers that serve as the basis to examine "effort, improvement, processes, and achievement as well as to meet the accountability demands usually achieved by more formal testing procedures" (Tierney, Carter, & Desai, 1991, p. 41). It is apparent that educators at all levels in our survey have become more aware of the literacy portfolio as an assessment tool. The issues of practicality continue to present challenges to the effective and widespread use of portfolios.

Knowledge of literacy portfolios is becoming more widespread. Educators agree with the theoretical bases for portfolio assessment. Although the practical problems of initiating and monitoring portfolios continue be of concern, their challenges are beginning to be met and answered. Portfolios have gained acceptance as an assessment form applied to student reading and writing. Perhaps with even greater knowledge and more widespread use, the literacy portfolio will replace standardized tests as classrooms reflect assessment grounded in instruction.

REFERENCES

Johns, J. L. (1991). "Literacy Portfolios: A Primer." *Illinois Reading Council Journal, 19,* 4-10. [Included in this volume, pp. 249-255.]

Johns, J. L., & VanLeirsburg, P. (1990). "Portfolio Assessment: A Survey among Professionals." DeKalb: Northern Illinois University. [Included in this volume, pp. 242-248.]

Jongsma, K. S. (1989). "Portfolio Assessment (Questions & Answers Column)." *The Reading Teacher, 43,* 264-265.

Paulson, F. L., Paulson, P. R., & Meyer, C. A. (1991). "What Makes a Portfolio a Portfolio?" *Educational Leadership, 48,* 60-63.

Tierney, R. J., Carter, M. A., & Desai, L. E. (1991). *Portfolio Assessment in the Reading-Writing Classroom.* Norwood, Massachusetts: Christopher-Gordon Publishers.

Valencia, S. (1990). "A Portfolio Approach to Classroom Reading Assessment." *The Reading Teacher, 43,* 338-340.

Wolf, D. P. (1989). "Portfolio Assessment: Sampling Student Work." *Educational Leadership, 46,* 35-39.

RESEARCH AND PROGRESS IN INFORMAL READING INVENTORIES (An Annotated Bibliography)

JERRY L. JOHNS

PREFACE

The intent of this annotated bibliography is to provide a readily available resource related to informal reading inventories (IRIs). The materials cited in this volume, for the most part, were published since 1977, the year the first lengthy annotated bibliography on IRIs was made available (Johns, Garton, Schoenfelder, and Skriba, 1977). The current bibliography should be fairly inclusive from about 1977, although it is not exhaustive. Some of the annotations were adapted from the ERIC database.

Because the growth in IRIs has spanned nearly half a century, I also decided to include especially useful items written prior to 1977. In most cases, these items deal with history or research areas. This annotated bibliography is designed to be useful to a diverse group of educators: teachers, researchers, and especially those involved in reading assessment or the preparation of prospective teachers.

I want to express my appreciation to Karen Mack and Elaine Kohlin for assisting with the annotations. Margaret Jacob and Tanya MaKarrall deserve thanks for typing the manuscript and for making numerous revisions. Their patience (tolerance?) with my desire for accuracy and consistency deserves very special recognition.

JLJ

BASIC INFORMATION

ANNOTATED BIBLIOGRAPHIES

Johns, Jerry L., Sharon Garton, Paula Schoenfelder, and Patricia Skriba (compilers). *Assessing Reading Behavior: Informal Reading Inventories.* Newark, Delaware: International Reading Association, 1977.

Presents annotations of approximately one hundred publications relating to IRIs. The listing is fairly inclusive from 1970 through 1976. Selected publications written prior to 1970 were also included. Entries were placed in one of the following categories: (1) history and critique; (2) overview; (3) guidelines for construction and use; (4) descriptive and research reports; (5) comparisons with standardized tests; (6) psycholinguistic insights; and (7) related factors (motivation, stress). A listing of doctoral dissertations and master's theses is also included.

OVERVIEW

Betts, Emmett Albert. *Foundations of Reading Instruction.* New York: American Book, 1957.

Deals with specific reading needs and includes very specific and detailed information on IRIs in Chapter 21. The IRI is discussed in terms of uses, basic assumptions, reading levels, inventory construction, general administration procedures, limitations, advantages, and use of group inventories. The chapter includes examples of separate checklists that can be used by experienced and inexperienced examiners to record observations made during IRI administrations. It includes a summary form used in the author's reading clinic.

Johnson, Marjorie Seddon, Roy A. Kress, and John J. Pikulski. *Informal Reading Inventories* (2nd ed.). Newark, Delaware: International Reading Association, 1987.

Presents a comprehensive description of the use of IRIs. This book is designed to provide teachers and reading specialists with practical strategies for forming diagnostic impressions that are useful for planning reading instruction. Respectively, chapters discuss (1) the purpose and nature of IRIs; (2) estimating reading levels from IRIs; (3) administering, recording, and scoring individual IRIs; (4) diagnostically interpreting the results of IRIs; (5) individual word recognition tests; (6) constructing informal reading inventories and word recognition tests; (7) group informal reading inventories; and (8) conclusions. It is argued that the best IRIs evaluate reading through procedures that are as close as possible to natural reading activities and that they attempt to achieve a close fit between assessment and instructional materials.

Further, it is emphasized that teachers must have a sound understanding of both the reading process and the flexible, diagnostic uses of IRIs before using them either to determine a student's reading level or to answer specific instructional questions. The appendix, which comprises almost half of the book, presents comprehensive reports and interpretations of the results of the administration of IRIs to three children. The discussion of these cases illustrates how numerical criteria and qualitative considerations are combined to estimate reading and listening levels.

HISTORY

Beldin, H.O. "Informal Reading Testing: Historical Review and Review of the Research," in William K. Durr (Ed.), *Reading Difficulties: Diagnosis, Correction, and Remediation*. Newark, Delaware: International Reading Association, 1970, 67-84.

Presents a historical overview of the thinking, experience, and literature of the analysis of reading performance. The author reviews the years from 1900 to 1969 for specific contributions to the present development of the IRI. Reading authorities are cited along with their research and conclusions on criteria, sources of test materials, and evaluations of word perception errors. Included is a list of references that have had significant input into the IRI.

Johns, Jerry L. and Mary K. Lunn. "The Origin and Development of the Informal Reading Inventory," in Jerry L. Johns, *Basic Reading Inventory* (4th ed.). Dubuque, Iowa: Kendall/Hunt Publishing Company, 1988, 70-80.

Traces the development of the IRI from the 1920s through the 1980s. The authors discuss the future of the IRI as a diagnostic tool and conclude that it is a valuable way to assess reading performance.

Walter, Richard B. "History and Development of the Informal Reading Inventory," 1974. Microfiche ED 098 539.

Presents the history of the IRI and the problems of validity, reliability, and the selection of performance criteria. Discusses the value of IRIs for determining the instructional level of students. The paper concludes with selected literature which supports the contention that most teachers cannot be successful in using the IRI without training in construction, administration, and interpretation of such an instrument.

GENERAL CRITIQUES

Caldwell, JoAnne. "A New Look at the Old Informal Reading Inventory," *The Reading Teacher*, 39 (November, 1985), 168-173.

Indicates that the format and the use of the IRI need to be modified in order to address recent research findings of schema theory (prior knowledge), text analysis (narrative and expository), cohesion, and metacognition. The author urges that IRIs be controlled for the effect of prior knowledge and topic familiarity while assessing comprehension through recall or retellings.

McKenna, Michael C. "Informal Reading Inventories: A Review of the Issues," *The Reading Teacher*, 36 (March, 1983), 670-679.

Reviews the literature concerning IRIs and discusses a number of issues related to them: readability, question choice, passage dependency, scoring criteria, and allowable miscues. Guidelines for constructing and using IRIs are offered. Two specific problems are noted for IRIs at the secondary level: passage readability and scoring criteria.

Pikulski, John. "A Critical Review: Informal Reading Inventories," *The Reading Teacher*, 28 (November, 1974), 141-151.

Discusses the early history of informal diagnostic procedures, points out the continued existence of several perplexing problems regarding the use of IRIs, and reviews problem areas with the idea of approaching some possible solutions. The IRI is discussed with regard to establishment of levels, evaluation of validity and reliability, use of quantitative or qualitative criteria, and question types which should be included. Admits that some imprecision and uncertainty exist with regard to informal procedures, but concludes that IRIs based upon instructional materials provide the closest possible match between teaching and testing. Suggests methodological questions concerning IRIs which deserve closer scrutiny by researchers.

Pikulski, John J. and Timothy Shanahan. "Informal Reading Inventories: A Critical Analysis," in John J. Pikulski and Timothy Shanahan (Eds.), *Approaches to the Informal Evaluation of Reading*. Newark, Delaware: International Reading Association, 1982, 94-116.

Updates a 1974 review by assessing progress in IRIs and considering new issues. This analysis considers reliability (interrater, alternate form), validity, criteria for reading levels, the impact of miscue theory, and comprehension questions. A study comparing teacher-constructed and commercially-prepared IRIs with 33 students found the same instructional level 67% of the time. Eight conclusions are presented at the end of the review.

GENERAL REVIEWS OF PUBLISHED INVENTORIES

Anderson, William W. "Commercial Informal Reading Inventories: A Comparative Review," *Reading World*, 17 (December, 1977), 99-104.

Offers some important ways commercial IRIs differ from one another and reviews three IRIs. A brief narrative description of each is given regarding validity, reliability, content validity, and passage dependent questions. Areas of commonality are listed. The author concludes that none of the three IRIs can be categorically endorsed or dismissed as having little value. Despite similarities in purposes and design, each IRI seems appropriate for different circumstances which the author depicts. Included is a chart outlining the variable characteristics of the three IRIs considered.

Cramer, Eugene H. "Informal Reading Inventories Go Commercial," *Curriculum Review*, 19 (November, 1980), 424-429.

Presents some background information on IRIs and analyzes seven commercial IRIs. Major areas for the analysis include: (1) word lists, passages, readability; (2) questions and passage dependency; (3) objectives and field testing; and (4) special features and teachers' comments. The format for presenting each IRI is the same so comparisons can be made quite easily.

Galen, Nancy. "Informal Reading Inventories for Adults: An Analysis," *Lifelong Learning: The Adult Years*, 3 (March, 1980), 10-14.

Analyzes four IRIs developed specifically for adults. Four tables summarize the results of the analysis in these areas: (1) word lists and passages; (2) comprehension questions; (3) readability; and (4) scoring and evaluation guidelines. None of the IRIs is regarded as clearly superior to the others.

Harris, Larry, A. and Jerome A. Niles. "An Analysis of Published Informal Reading Inventories," *Reading Horizons*, 22 (Spring, 1982), 159-174.

Offers advantages and disadvantages of commercial IRIs and analyzes 12 IRIs in four areas: (1) purposes; (2) format; (3) scoring procedures and criteria; and (4) instructions for interpretation and use. Results of the analysis are presented in eight tables. The authors conclude that considerable variation exists among IRIs.

Jongsma, Kathleen S. and Eugene A. Jongsma. "Test Review: Commercial Informal Reading Inventories," *The Reading Teacher*, 34, (March, 1981), 697-705.

Reviews 11 commercial IRIs in three major areas: (1) contents (features of the passages and questions); (2) procedures for administering and scoring; and (3) suggestions for interpreting results. A summary of results is presented in a lengthy, helpful table. A list of nine recommendations is also presented for those interested in purchasing and using commercial IRIs.

RESEARCH

VALIDITY AND RELIABILITY

Bowden, Nancy B. and Wilson H. Lane. "A Study of Fourth Grade Students' Reading Comprehension Measures in Short and Long Passages of an Informal Reading Inventory," November, 1979. Microfiche ED 186 855.

Compares the reliability of short versus long passages in IRIs. After 132 fourth-grade students were tested with the Standard Reading Inventory, Form B, they read longer passages in either the oral or silent modes. Students with higher silent reading scores read long passages orally, while students with higher oral reading scores or comparable oral/silent reading scores read long passages in the silent mode. The results suggested that the 70% criterion normally used with short passages inadequately predicted reading levels for the longer selections. The increased difficulty of long passages was evident by the marked decreases in comprehension scores. Students with better comprehension scores in either the short-silent or short-oral modes appeared to be frustrated by the longer-reading materials. The students with comparable oral/ silent reading levels in the short passages showed significantly different scores on the long passages, suggesting that the increased difficulty of long passages inhibited their comprehension considerably. Since the long passages appear to be more difficult than short passages at the same levels, it was suggested that the trend toward using more lenient interpretation criteria in informal reading inventories might be based on false assumptions.

Christine, Charles T., Lawrence A. Anderson, Edythe Bleznak, Jane B. Levine, and Phyllis Lewy. "The Between Teacher Reliability of the Ekwall Reading Inventory and the Classroom Reading Inventory," October, 1982. Microfiche ED 232 145.

Uses a test-retest research design to study the reliability of the Classroom Reading Inventory (CRI) and the Ekwall Reading Inventory (ERI). Independent variables of test administrator to subject, test administrator to test, subject to test, and test order were randomized. Subjects include 31 children aged 7 through 12 years. The four teachers who served as examiners were all graduates of master's degree programs in developmental and remedial reading instruction. The test was a "live" administration of one of the reading inventories by one teacher; the testing session was tape recorded. The retest was a second teacher scoring the audio tape recording of the test. The dependent variable was the agreement (or lack of agreement) in identifying a single reading instructional level between test and retest. Results showed that in 14 of 16 trials (85%) there was agreement between teachers using the ERI. In 5 of the 16 trials there was perfect agreement between teachers on an instructional reading level. None of the test-retest trails showed a teacher-teacher instructional level difference of more than one grade level. Trials of the CRI showed teacher agreement on instructional level in 10 of 16 trials (67%). Only one test-retest instance showed a between-teacher instructional level disagreement of more than one grade level. These results provide a strong indication that the CRI and ERI produce reliable estimates of a student's instructional reading level.

Fuchs, Lynn, S., Douglas Fuchs, and Stanley L. Deno. "Reliability and Validity of Curriculum-Based Informal Reading Inventories," *Reading Research Quarterly*, 18 (Fall, 1982), 6-26.

Investigates reliability and validity of standard and salient IRI procedures. Employing 91 elementary-age students, this study examined the technical adequacy of (1) choosing a criterion of 95% accuracy for word recognition to determine an instructional level, (2) arbitrarily selecting a passage to represent the difficulty level of a basal reader, and (3) employing one-level floors and ceilings to demarcate levels beyond which behavior is not sampled. Correlational and congruency analyses supported the external validity of the 95% standard but questioned the reliability and validity of passage sampling procedures and one-level floors and ceilings. Sampling over occasions and test forms is discussed as a more valid IRI procedure.

Fuchs, Lynn S., Douglas Fuchs, and Linn Maxwell. "The Validity of Informal Reading Comprehension Measures," *Remedial and Special Education*, 9 (March/April, 1988), 20-28.

Assesses the criterion, construct, and concurrent validity of four informal reading comprehension measures: question answering tests, recall measures, oral passage reading tests, and cloze techniques. Mildly and moderately handicapped middle and junior high school boys (N = 70) were administered the informal measures in one sitting, with four passages equally represented across the four measures and with the administration order of measures counterbalanced. Criterion tests, the Reading Comprehension and Word Study Skills subtests of the Stanford Achievement Test, also were administered in a separate sitting. Results indicated that the oral reading rate score demonstrated the strongest criterion validity, with adequate construct and concurrent validity. A second acceptable index was the written recall measure. Implications for designing reading comprehension monitoring procedures are discussed.

Helgren-Lempesis, Valerie, A., and Charles T. Mangrum II. "An Analysis of Alternate-form Reliability of Three

Commercially-prepared Informal Reading Inventories," *Reading Research Quarterly*, 21 (Spring, 1986), 209-215.

Studies 75 fourth-grade students from two elementary schools randomly assigned to one of three commercially-prepared IRIs. Forms A and B of the Analytical, Basic, and Ekwall reading inventories were administered to these three groups. Pearson and generalizability coefficients ranged between .60 and .78. According to estimated variance components from the generalizability analysis, little error could be directly attributed to the forms, as the subjects were the source of the greatest variance. Although the results of the study did not reveal perfect reliability, they were by no means as unreliable as some critics have suggested. Future research is needed to address the question of what an acceptable level of reliability would be for IRIs.

Klesius, Janell P. and Susan P. Homan. "A Validity and Reliability Update on the Informal Reading Inventory with Suggestions for Improvement," *Journal of Learning Disabilities*, 18 (February, 1985), 71-76.

Provides a review of research on the validity and reliability of IRIs. The areas first examined were content and concurrent validity. The research concerning the validity revealed that one cannot be assured that a passage taken from a basal text is comparable to the remaining material. The other area researched focused on reliability of IRIs. Specifically, the authors focused on interscorer reliability and effect of passage length on student performance. The authors provided ten suggestions for teachers. Also provided are suggestions for evaluating IRIs. The authors suggest a need for careful evaluation of these instruments. Teachers increase the validity and reliability of the IRI once they become aware of the need for careful evaluation.

PLACEMENT, CRITERIA, AND READING LEVELS

Anderson, Betty and Rosie Webb Joels. "Informal Reading Inventories," *Reading Improvement*, 23 (Winter, 1986), 299-302.

Reports a study composed of 136 students in grades two through five to establish the oral reading accuracy level and to determine whether repetitions should be counted as oral reading errors. Results indicated that oral accuracy levels of 90% for first-grade passages and 94% for passages two through five were appropriate. Inconsistencies and inconclusive findings on scoring of repetitions led the authors to support the recommendation of others to exclude repetitions until further evidence becomes available.

Brecht, Richard D. "Testing Format and Instructional Level with the Informal Reading Inventory," *The Reading Teacher*, 31 (October, 1977), 57-59.

Results from previous research suggest that achievement levels based upon errors made during oral reading from sight will not be representative of actual reading ability. Results differ depending on whether the test passage is read silently or orally first. A study in a rural school in Southern Illinois was conducted using 28 third graders, 26 fourth graders, and 16 fifth graders to examine the effects of oral rereading on estimates of instructional level. Two independently developed, non-published IRIs were administered to each subject. Results indicate that to get the best measure of a child's instructional reading level, the student should be allowed to read the selection silently first.

Cardarelli, Aldo F. "The Influence of Reinspection on Students' IRI Results," *The Reading Teacher*, 41 (March, 1988), 664-667.

Reports a study with 47 fourth-grade students who silently read passages from the Analytical Reading Inventory. Once the student's frustration level was reached with no passage reinspection, the same level was given on another form with reinspection allowed. Over half of the students made gains sufficient to change from the frustration level to the instructional level. The author notes the different cognitive demands in the recall and reinspection approaches to assessing comprehension and believes reinspection provides the most useful results.

Eldredge, J. Lloyd and Dennie Butterfield. "Sacred Cows Make Good Hamburger: A Report on a Reading Research Project Titled 'Testing the Sacred Cows in Reading'," 1984. Microfiche ED 255 861.

Investigates the following "sacred cows" in reading: (1) the use of IRIs for grouping students in reading instruction, (2) the homogeneous grouping practices currently used in most classrooms in the United States, (3) the use of readability formulas to identify "appropriate" reading materials for students to read, (4) the idea that students can be taught to read effectively only via basal readers, and (5) the analytical phonics strategies used to teach students phonics skills. The five experimental programs involved in the study were assigned to second-grade classrooms in four Utah school districts. Students in both experimental and control classrooms were administered pre- and post-tests in reading, vocabulary, reading comprehension, phonics, self-image, and interest in reading. Reading vocabulary and reading comprehension were tested using the Gates-MacGinitie Reading Test, Level B, Form 1. The findings suggest involving students in a lot of noninstructional reading and using: (1) an analytical/ synthetic decoding approach; (2) phonics to identify words not recognizable on sight; (3) heterogeneous grouping; and (4) children's literature rather than basal readers. Numerous tables of findings and seven appendices contain material relevant to the study.

Forell, Elizabeth R. "The Case for Conservative Reader Placement," *The Reading Teacher*, 38 (May, 1985), 857-862.

Reports a study of all students (91) who entered the third grade of a midwestern school for a five-year period. Students were placed in basal materials that were comfortable (not more than 5% meaning-changing errors and at least 75% comprehension). Using this criteria for placement, half of the students were placed in grade-level materials; the others needed readers one to three years below grade level. Reading achievement on the Iowa Tests of Basic Skills showed substantial improvement for the low group: from the 23rd percentile in beginning third grade to the 48th percentile in beginning seventh grade. The author argues for placing students in books that are not too hard.

Homan, Susan P. and Janell P. Klesius. "A Re-examination of the IRI: Word Recognition Criteria," *Reading Horizons*, 26 (Fall, 1985), 54-61.

Investigates which word recognition criterion is most appropriate for determining the instructional reading level for elementary students. One hundred and fifty students in Hillsborough County, Florida were participants in this study. The researchers used a modified version of Powell's (1970) method. Initial results confirmed previous research findings by Killgallon (cited in Beldin, 1970) strongly indicating that the word recognition criterion for the instructional level should be set at about 95% for students reading at grade levels one through six. However, a more in-depth analysis of the data revealed that word recognition criteria may be variable depending on a number of factors which are listed in this study. The investigators contend that IRIs need to be standardized so criteria can be set to coincide with each particular passage, thereby attempting to control the many variables affecting student performance.

Johns, Jerry L. and Anne Marie Magliari. "Informal Reading Inventories," *Reading Improvement*, 26 (Summer, 1989), 124-132.

Examines word-recognition criteria from an investigation that involved 83 students (43 students in grades 1-3 and 40 students in grades 4-6). Finds that the traditional Betts criterion of 95% for word recognition was generally not supported. Students in grades four through six achieved word-recognition scores of 93% or 94% when miscues such as omissions, substitutions, repetitions, insertions, and deletions were counted. Students in the primary grades achieved average word-recognition scores about 4 percent below Bett's criterion. When only significant miscues were considered (those that affected meaning), students in the primary grades achieved average word-recognition scores one or two percent above 95%. Students in the intermediate grades achieved an average of 98% word recognition. Two avenues for future research are also suggested.

Lombardo, Marie. "The Effectiveness of an Informal Reading Inventory in Identifying the Functional Reading Levels of Bilingual Students." Bilingual Education Paper Series, Vol. 2, No. 10, 1979. Microfiche ED 258 448.

Reports a study undertaken to (1) examine the development and construction of a Group Informal Reading Inventory to predict the reading comprehension levels (independent, instructional, and frustration) of junior high school bilingual students for the purpose of reading instruction and (2) validate the inventory through a three-way correlational study comparing the comprehension results with those of a cloze test, a standardized test, and a questionnaire by which teachers estimate students' reading levels. The study involved 50 bilingual students of predominantly English-and Spanish-speaking, low- and middle-income backgrounds in an urban school. All had been instructed in Spanish until they gained English language proficiency; then they were mainstreamed into the English curriculum. It was discovered that the students were all functioning far below their developmental grade levels and their assigned present grade levels, and native language grades were lower than those in English. It is recommended that (1) a decision be made for each individual student as to whether he/she should be taught in two languages or, if his/her native language skills are insufficient to transfer to English as a second language, whether he/she should be taught in English; (2) testing for reading and content areas be administered regularly to monitor progress; and (3) there be careful regulation of the timing, techniques, content, materials, and evaluation of bilingual instruction.

Newcomer, Phyllis L. "A Comparison of Two Published Reading Inventories," Remedial and Special Education, 6 (January-February, 1985), 31-36.

Examines the extent to which two commercial IRIs identify the same instructional level when administered to 50 children in grades one through seven. The results demonstrate a significant lack of congruence between the instruments, particularly in the intermediate grades. In more than 50% of the cases, the IRIs identified different instructional levels. The application of the Fry Readability Formula to paragraphs from both inventories also shows little agreement in grade level designations. Recommendations that pertain to the possible improvement of IRIs include standardization strategies and reliability data.

Nolen, Patricia A. and Tony C. M. Lam. "A Comparison of IRI and Durrell Analysis of Reading Difficulty Reading Levels in Clinical Assessment," 1981. Microfiche ED 253 843.

Compares the Durrell Analysis of Reading Difficulty and IRI independent and instructional level designations for 15 children, ages 9 to 11 years, who had been referred to a diagnostic clinic for reading assessment. The children's reading performance was first scored according to procedures outlined in the Durrell Analysis manual. A second scoring was made according to recommendations for administering informal reading inventories given by Johnson and Kress. Results suggested that the procedures yield significantly different overall grade level designations. Further analysis revealed that (1) the average independent level established by the Durrell Analysis procedure was significantly higher than that obtained by the IRI procedure, and (2) the instructional level mean was significantly higher than the independent level mean only when the IRI procedure was used.

Shipman, Dorothy A. and Edna W. Warncke. "Informal Assessment in Reading: Group vs. Individual," September, 1984. Microfiche ED 249 482.

Reports a study conducted to determine whether informal group assessment instruments could be used effectively to provide the same type of reading achievement information as that secured from informal individual instruments. The researchers developed group instruments comparable to individual instruments, including a group reading inventory for grades 1 through 12, cloze inventory for the same grades, specific comprehension skills assessments, and specific study skills assessments. The Group Reading Inventory (GRI) and a published IRI were administered to 312 students who were expected to have reading levels ranging from the preprimer level to grade 12. The results of the two inventories were then analyzed to determine the amount of correlation between the functional reading levels of each. There was a statistically significant correlation between the scores on the GRI and on the IRI. Findings suggest that since both kinds of inventories tend to diagnose comparable functional reading levels, the GRI is a valid alternative to the IRI for assessing reading levels, and at a considerable saving of class time.

Smith, Lynn C., Lawrence L. Smith, Gay Gruetzemacher, and Jane Anderson. "Locating the Recreational Level of Elementary Grade Students," November, 1982. Microfiche ED 225 106.

Compares students' recreational reading levels to their independent, instructional, and frustrational levels determined with an IRI. Subjects, 20 second-grade and 20 fifth-grade students, were administered the Basic Reading Inventory. In addition, the school's librarian recorded titles of four books chosen by each student within a 2-month period.

These books were freely selected and the children did not know that their choices were being monitored. After the books had been returned to the library, researchers estimated the books' difficulty level with the Fry Readability Graph. Results showed that second-grade students selected books for recreational reading within their independent reading level 42% of the time, within their instructional level 25% of the time, and at their frustration level 33% of the time. Fifth-grade students, on the other hand, selected books for recreational reading within their independent reading level 42% of the time, within their instructional level 32% of the time, and at their frustration level 26% of the time. When they selected books to read for pleasure, both second- and fifth-grade students chose books above their independent level 58% of the time. These results indicate that it is inappropriate for educators to prescribe the level of books read for pleasure based on an IRI.

COMPREHENSION QUESTIONS

Davis, Carol. "The Effectiveness of Informal Assessment Questions Constructed by Secondary Teachers," in P. David Pearson and Jane Hansen (Eds.), *Reading: Disciplined Inquiry in Process and Practice*. Clemson, South Carolina: National Reading Conference, 1978, 13-15.

Examines the effectiveness of informal assessment questions constructed by secondary teachers. The teacher-constructed questions seemed to be at the appropriate level of difficulty, but they often did not discriminate between high- and low-scoring subjects. The author contends that secondary teachers are frequently encouraged to develop their own informal assessment instruments despite the fact that they may not be adequately prepared for this task. The results of this study seem to suggest a need to reconsider the unqualified encouragement of teacher-constructed secondary inventories.

Duffelmeyer, Frederick A. and Barbara Blakely Duffelmeyer. "Main Idea Questions on Informal Reading Inventories," *The Reading Teacher*, 41 (November, 1987), 162-166.

Studies one of the subskill categories included in the IRI, the main idea. After analyzing three commercial IRIs, the investigators concluded that the label is frequently a misnomer. Many main idea questions do not measure what they purport to measure. Rather, they relate to topic. The investigators stress the differences between topic and main idea. They fear this may spill over into later reading with students having great difficulties in understanding and assessing main ideas. Therefore, it is imperative that teachers analyze main idea questions on IRIs to determine the skills actually being measured.

Duffelmeyer, Frederick A., Jennifer Long, and Anne Kruse. "The Passage Independence of IRI Comprehension Question

Categories: Evidence of Non-Uniformity," *Reading Improvement*, 24 (Summer, 1987), 101-106.

Investigates the passage independence of comprehension questions across subskill categories on two IRIs: the Basic Reading Inventory (Form A) and the Informal Reading Inventory (Form B). Sixty elementary school students from a rural midwestern school district, ten each from grades one through six, were administered the questions from the Basic Reading Inventory at their respective grade levels under a passage-absent condition. A second group of sixty elementary school students from a separate midwestern school district was administered the questions from the IRI under the same conditions. Percent correct scores were calculated for each subskill category on the two inventories. A lack of uniformity across subskill categories was revealed for both inventories. These results were interpreted as providing sufficient support for Schell and Hanna's caveat relative to the practice of analyzing a student's strengths and weaknesses in comprehension subskills.

Fowler, Elaine D. and Walter J. Lamberg. "Effect of Pre-Questions on Oral Reading by Elementary Students," *Reading Improvement*, 16 (Spring, 1979), 71-74.

Seeks to determine if questions asked prior to reading or questions asked before and after reading would improve performance on word recognition and comprehension. Subjects were elementary school students ranging from first to fifth grade. One group of students tested in the Fall, 1977 and the other in the Spring, 1978, on IRIs. Results from the IRI on the lowest instructional level and the frustrational level were used as the measure of subjects' performance on the post-question task. For the pre-question task, additional passages at the students' instructional and frustrational levels were selected. No significant differences were found in favor of the pre-question task on word recognition or comprehension.

Joels, Rosie Webb and Betty Anderson. "Informal Reading Inventory Comprehension Questions: Are Classification Schemes Valid?" *Reading Horizons*, 28 (Spring, 1988), 178-183.

Presents a study which examines 136 elementary school students' performance on the JAT (Joels, Anderson, and Thompson) Reading Inventory, noting variable student performance on the different question types. Reports that the discriminant validity of the JAT as a diagnostic instrument appears to be established.

Kender, Joseph P. and Herbert Rubenstein. "Recall Versus Reinspection in IRI Comprehension Tests," *The Reading Teacher*, 30 (April, 1977), 776-779.

Maintains that recall-type questions may merely test an individual's ability to remember what has been read rather than to understand it.

Describes a study of 32 fourth graders, 16 of high reading ability and 16 of low reading ability, which attempted to compare an IRI comprehension check by means of recall questions to a check by means of reinspection. The study was designed to determine: (1) the difference, if any, between recall scores and reinspection scores; and (2) whether memory for sentence content is an intrinsic part of reading comprehension. To test the hypotheses, subjects read two IRI passages at each level of difficulty; comprehension was checked by means of recall for one passage and by reinspection for the other. Findings include that: (1) reinspection scores were significantly higher than recall scores for both groups; and (2) the effect of reinspection was substantially the same for both ability groups. Concludes that readers should be allowed to reinspect IRI passages before answering comprehension questions.

Marr, Mary Beth and Kathleen R. Lyon. "Passage Independency and Question Characteristics: An Analysis of Three Informal Reading Inventories," *Reading Psychology*, 2 (Spring, 1981), 97-102.

Examines three IRIs to identify passage-independent test questions, questions which could be answered correctly without reading the corresponding passages. Fourth-grade students of good and poor reading ability were administered the test questions orally without access to the passage. The percentage of questions answered correctly was calculated for each test. An analysis of variance procedure revealed that the Classroom Reading Inventory was the most passage-independent followed by the Analytical Reading Inventory and Ginn 720 inventory, respectively. However, the two reader groups did not differ significantly in their performance across the three tests. An analysis of students' responses to the questions revealed that three question categories in particular tended to be passage-independent in nature. These categories were: (a) general information, (b) vocabulary meaning, and (c) affective. The investigation also examined the literal and inferential characteristics of the test questions. Suggestions were made for evaluating the validity of reading comprehension questions.

Peterson, Joe, M. Jean Greenlaw and Robert J. Tierney. "Assessing Instructional Placement with the I.R.I.: The Effectiveness of Comprehension Questions," *The Journal of Educational Research*, 71 (May, June, 1978), 247-250.

Investigates whether different sets of questions generated for an IRI would yield different instructional placement of students. Using identical passages, trained educators following published criteria wrote questions for an IRI. Three question sets were selected and all were administered to 57 elementary students in grades two through five. The order of administration of the three sets was rotated to counter a learning effect. Correlations between the instructional placements indicated by the question sets did not approach the reliability coefficient necessary for interpretation of individual results. Lack of agreement across the three sets of questions raised the question of dependability of placement of students on the basis of their ability to respond to questions derived from the question-generating guidelines under consideration.

COMPARISONS WITH STANDARDIZED TESTS

Amoriell, William J. "Use of Standardized Reading Tests as Measures of Reading Achievement," 1981. Microfiche ED 265 508.

Reports a study that provides insight into the consistency of reading achievement scores from four standardized tests. Several sets of data were compared to assess the accuracy of grade equivalents or instructional reading levels obtained on standardized tests. Each test was randomly assigned for administration to 23 third graders in a group setting during one of four consecutive mornings. The four tests were: (1) the Iowa Tests of Basic Skills (Form 4); (2) Stanford Achievement Test (Primary Level III—Form A); (3) Gates-MacGinitie Reading Test (Level C—Form 2); and (4) Metropolian Achievement Test (Elementary—Form F—Metro). The resulting grade levels revealed significant discrepancies across the different tests. Seventy percent of the children received grade scores ranging over more than one year. A comparison of the instructional reading levels obtained from the Metro with those obtained from a subsequently administered IRI indicated that more than 50% of instructional reading levels from the Metro varied as much as two to five reader levels from those of the IRI. The results did not support the use of standardized test scores as adequate measures of reading achievement or as a substitute for individually administered IRIs.

Blanchard, Jay S., Paul Borthwick, Jr., and Ann Hall. "Determining Instructional Reading Level: Standardized Multiple Choice Versus IRI Probed Recall Questions," *Journal of Reading*, 26 (May, 1983), 684-689.

Compares results of standardized reading tests with IRIs to determine whether teachers should favor one score over another as an indicator of instructional reading level. Subjects were 60 students each from third and fifth grade and 45 students from seventh grade from four suburban/rural racially-mixed schools. This study did not support the assumption that standardized scores run too high or that reading instruction should begin at a lower level.

Bristow, Page Simpson, John J. Pikulski, and Peter L. Pelosi. "A Comparison of Five Estimates of Reading Instructional Level," *The Reading Teacher*, 37 (December, 1983), 273-279.

Reports that reading instructional level scores of a teacher-constructed IRI, the commercially-prepared Basic Reading Inventory, the Metropolitan Achievement Test, and the students' actual level of placement in books are roughly comparable, but that the Wide Range Achievement Test reading subtest places students much higher. The sample used for this study was 72 students, 24 each from grades two, four, and six. This study indicated that each of the four tests may be useful for different purposes. A table presents the range of agreement among the various measures for instructional level placement.

Coleman, Margaret and William R. Harmer. "A Comparison of Standardized Reading Tests and Informal Placement Procedures," *Journal of Learning Disabilities*, 15 (August/ September, 1982), 396-398.

Compares selected subtests of commonly used standardized reading tests and informal placement procedures with 32 primary (grades 1-3) students in a summer reading program. Tests chosen for comparison were the Wide Range Achievement Test (WRAT), Diagnostic Reading Scales (Spache), and the Woodcock Reading Mastery Tests, Form A. The informal placement was the tutor-placed instructional level. Results indicate that the selected reading measures yield significantly different results. The independent level of the Spache was the highest, followed by the WRAT, the Spache instructional level, both subtests of the Woodcock, and tutor placement.

Manning, Gary, Maryann Manning, and Roberta Long. "First Grade Reading Assessment: Teacher Opinions, Standardized Reading Tests, and Informal Reading Inventories," November, 1985. Microfiche ED 265 204.

Investigates the relationship between and among the results of three types of reading assessment in the first grade: a standardized reading test (the Stanford Achievement Tests); an IRI (the Classroom Reading Inventory); and teacher judgment of student rank in reading achievement. The study included 165 first-grade students with a mean age of 84.6 months. The Pearson product-moment correlation was used to assess the relationship between the scores of the IRI word recognition and comprehension tests and the reading portions of the standardized achievement tests. The Spearman-Rho correlation coefficient was used to assess the relationship between teacher judgment and the students' performance on the IRI and the standardized reading test. A statistically significant positive correlation was indicated between the IRI and standardized test scores. There were also positive correlations between achievement variables and the word recognition and also the comprehension scores of the Classroom Reading Inventory. Teacher opinion correlated with all subtests of the standardized test and the word recognition portion of the IRI. The achievement of all combined classrooms and most individual classrooms was average or above, based on national norms.

Manning, Maryann, Gary Manning, and Caroline B. Cody. "A Comparison among Measures of Reading Achievement with Low-Income Black Third-Grade Students," March/April, 1985. Microfiche ED 261 074.

Compares different types of reading achievement measures for 58 low-income, urban black third graders. Two formal tests were administered: the norm-referenced California Achievement Tests (CAT), and the criterion-referenced Alabama Basic Competency Test (ABCT). Informal measures included the Houghton-Mifflin Informal Reading Inventory (HMIRI), the Classroom Reading Inventory (CRI), a cloze procedure, and teacher judgment (as indicated by the basal reader assignment for each student). Results indicate that correlations among all of the measures were moderate to high. The formal tests, particularly the CAT, tended to produce lower scores than the informal measures. In spite of high correlations, the CAT and ABCT results revealed very different distributions of student ability. With the ABCT, more students showed average and above average performance. Examination of teachers' judgments regarding reading book placement, as compared to test results, indicated that teachers underestimated students' reading ability and placements did not reflect test results. HMIRI results also suggested that a number of students could have been assigned to a higher-level reading book. It was suggested that informal measures be used for book placement and that multiple measures of reading achievement be used in decision making.

Oliver, Jo Ellen and Richard D. Arnold. "Comparing a Standardized Test, an Informal Inventory and Teacher Judgment on Third Grade Reading," Reading Improvement, 15 (Spring, 1978), 56-59.

Compares results of a standardized test, teacher judgments, and an IRI, using third-grade subjects. Fifteen boys and fifteen girls were given the Iowa Test of Basic Skills and the Goudy Informal Reading Inventory. Without knowledge of scores, teachers estimated instructional reading levels. Pearson Product Moment Correlation, Analysis of Variance, and Paired t-tests were used. Means of teacher judgment (2.9) and standardized test scores (2.9) were not significantly different. Means of IRI placements (2.4) were significantly different from teacher judgment means and standardized test scores means (p .01). The highest correlations were between teacher judgment and the IRI placements.

Smith, William Earl and Michael D. Beck. "Determining Instructional Reading Level with 1978 Metropolitan Achievement Tests," *The Reading Teacher*, 34 (December, 1980), 313-319.

Compares the reading comprehension test of the Metropolitan Achievement Tests (MAT), one of three placement tests for a basal series, cloze tests, and two standardized IRIs to determine instructional reading level (IRL). The subjects were 700 elementary school students; eleven first-grade classes and seven classes each for second, third, fourth, and sixth grades. The data indicated a strong relationship among the results of the four procedures used to estimate IRL. The MAT results compared most closely with the other techniques and appear to provide an accurate estimate of a student's IRL.

USE, READABILITY, AND OTHER FACTORS

Bradley, John M. and Wilbur S. Ames. "The Influence of Intrabook Readability Variation on Oral Reading Performance," *The Journal of Educational Research*, 70 (November/December, 1976), 101-105.

Describes a study which explored the effect of intrabook readability variation on the oral reading performance of 51 intermediate-grade students. The results suggest that the instructional level yielded by a typical IRI predicts a student's level of functioning for only a portion of a basal reader. Because of intrabook readability variation, it is difficult, if not impossible, to determine which portion of a book relates to IRI results.

Brittain, Mary M., Shirley B. Merlin, Patricia Terrell, and Sue F. Rogers. "Informal Reading Assessment: Perceptions of In-service and Pre-service Teachers," *Journal of the Virginia College Reading Educators*, 5 (Fall, 1984), 4-12.

Compares the results of a similar study (Merlin, 1983) with in-service teachers to a study involving 157 pre-service students enrolled in undergraduate reading courses. Among the results, presented in three tables, are: (1) both experienced and prospective teachers expressed a preference for individual inventories; (2) about half of each group used or expected to use published IRIs often or very often; and (3) comprehension problems were identified as the most common diagnostic use of IRIs.

Gerke, Ray. "Critique of Informal Reading Inventories: Can a Valid Instructional Level be Obtained?" *Journal of Reading Behavior*, 12 (Summer, 1980), 155-158.

Determines readability estimates of IRIs and one standardized test containing graded reading passages. Most of the IRIs examined included extractions from publisher's basal readers. Readability estimates revealed that the levels reported for some IRI passages may be erroneous, although they generally progress in difficulty.

Gillis, M.K. and Mary W. Olson. "Informal Reading Inventories and Text Type/Structure," January/February, 1986. Microfiche ED 276 971.

Studies seven IRIs, three at the elementary level and four at the secondary level, to (1) discover what text types (narrative or expository) they used at each level to measure student comprehension skills and determine instructional levels and (2) identify the rhetorical structures used in expository passages. The 18 teachers who rated the elementary passages and the 20 who rated the secondary ones had all previously administered IRIs and had studied the literature on text type and structure and reading comprehension. Each teacher examined at least four IRIs, classified each passage used in them as narrative or expository, judged each narrative passage as well- or poorly-formed, and judged each expository passage according to rhetorical structures adapted from B.J.F. Meyer (1975). The teachers found that all of the preprimer and primer passages used on the IRIs were narrative, while most of the other elementary passages and most of the secondary passages were expository. In addition, they found that many of the narrative passages on the IRIs were not well-formed, and that approximately one-eighth of the elementary and one-fourth of the secondary expository passages had no clear rhetorical structure. The findings suggest that the passages used in IRIs might produce erratic comprehension scores. In light of these findings, five practical suggestions are offered for teachers and diagnosticians who use the currently available commercial IRIs.

Gonzales, Phillip C. and David Elijah. "Stability of Error Patterns on the Informal Reading Inventory," *Reading Improvement*, 15 (Winter, 1978), 279-288.

Investigates twenty-six, third-grade developmental readers as they read and reread extended oral passages at instructional and frustration performance levels. Errors on the four readings were analyzed using the B-S-R Error Analysis system which classifies errors into 23 categories. The data were analyzed to determine type of error change resulting from rereading, consistency of pattern of repeated error, and utilization of context clues in reading. The profile of reading behavior on the two instructional and two frustration level readings revealed a consistent pattern of error production and context utilization although words on which errors were made varied. The results suggest the employment of consistent word recognition strategies by third grade developmental readers.

Harris, Larry A. and Rosary H. Lalik. "Teacher's Use of Informal Reading Inventories: An Example of School Constraints," *The Reading Teacher*, 40 (March, 1987), 624-630.

Investigates circumstances affecting the success of both IRIs and diagnostic teaching. Two conclusions were reached. First, many reading authorities view the classroom teacher's use of IRIs as a good practice. Second, in order to promote effective use of IRIs, teachers need to be better trained in the use and application of IRIs. A survey conducted with 500 Virginia elementary teachers yielded a 50% return rate. Results of the survey revealed that classroom constraints and administrative procedures for student placement affect diagnostic teaching. Also, as expected, teacher training and knowledge of IRIs affect diagnostic teaching. The survey results and teacher comments are included. The authors concluded that education is necessary for teachers to effectively use IRIs. The investigators recommend that university faculty need to collaborate with teachers and administrators in the use and application of IRIs so that they can be used most effectively.

Leibert, Robert E. "Performance Profiles of ABE Students and Children on an Informal Reading Inventory," *Reading Psychology*, 4 (April-June, 1983), 141-150.

Compares reading performance abilities for school-age children and adults attending ABE classes. Scores obtained for both groups on the Adult Informal Reading Test were formed into distribution profiles for each tested variable. Differences between the two populations for oral reading accuracy, comprehension, and rate of reading were identified for the two populations. The profile notion was concluded to be a useful means for displaying the performance trends of published IRIs.

Lipson, Marjorie Youmans, Carla H. Cox, Suzette Iwankowski, and Marianne Simon. "Exploration of the Interactive Nature of Reading: Using Commercial IRIs to Gain Insights," *Reading Psychology*, 5 (1984), 209-218.

Uses case-study data from three young readers to investigate variability across IRIs. Results are discussed in terms of the varying demands of text and task as well as the idiosyncratic contributions of each individual to the reading act. The case studies reflect that reading ability is not static, but rather encompasses a range of abilities and behaviors. Use of any one commercial IRI for placement purposes is seriously questioned; however, IRIs can be used to gain insights into reading behavior.

Marzano, Robert J., Jean Larson, Geri Tish, and Sue Vodehnal. "The Graded Word List Is Not a Shortcut to an IRI," *The Reading Teacher*, 31 (March, 1978), 647-651.

Contends that the Graded Word List: Quick Gauge of Reading Ability (GWL), developed by La Pray and Ross, is not a valid substitute for an IRI. The authors attempt to illustrate numerically the invalidity of using shortcut techniques like the GWL to determine independent, instructional, and frustration reading levels. The authors suggest that the increased administration time for administering an IRI is justified.

Masztal, Nancy B. and Lawrence L. Smith. "Do Teachers Really Administer IRIs?" *Reading World,* 24 (October, 1984), 80-83.

Reports a study on the use of IRIs. A questionnaire was developed and sent to teachers in Florida, Illinois, Mississippi, and Tennessee to determine if teachers administer IRIs in their classrooms. A total of 125 teachers from five elementary schools responded. Results indicated that 54% of the teachers actually administered IRIs in the classrooms. The authors recommended that teacher-education courses continue to include the value of an IRI with emphasis on the interpretation and use of information gleaned from the administration of the IRI.

Searls, Evelyn F. "What's the Value of an IRI? Is It Being Used?" *Reading Horizons,* 28 (Winter, 1988), 92-101.

Reports a summary of 343 professionals which indicated that 62% identified IRIs as the most frequent data source for placement compared to basal placement tests, former basal book placements, and achievement tests. When responses were analyzed by classroom teachers and reading specialists, 61% of the teachers indicated low use (never or less than once a semester) of IRIs. Among specialists, over 50% indicated moderate or high use of IRIs. Four tables contain the results of the study.

Walker, Susan M., Ronald G. Noland, and Charles M. Greenshields. "The Effect of High and Low Interest Content on Instructional Levels in Informal Reading Inventories," *Reading Improvement,* 16 (Winter, 1979), 297-300.

Studies whether there was a significant difference in the word recognition and comprehension instructional levels of male and female students in the below-average, average, and above-average reading ability groups within the fifth and sixth year when presented with low- and high-interest content contained in IRIs. The fifth grade analysis of variance which examined the main effect and the interactions between the four factors of sex, ability group, interest, and type of skill, found a significant difference in ability groups and type of skill at the .001 level of significance. The analysis of variance for the four factors in sixth grade yielded significant differences in instructional levels of ability groups at the types of skill at the .01 level. The interaction of sex and skill was significant at the .05 level. Other conclusions: high-interest content had greater effect on increasing comprehension than on word recognition at both grade levels; high-interest content increased instructional levels of males more than of females at both levels; high-interest content, while having a negligible effect on above-average readers, had a greater effect on average and below-average readers.

DESCRIPTIVE REPORTS

GENERAL USES

Bader, Lois A. and Katherine D. Wiesendanger. "Realizing the Potential of Informal Reading Inventories," *Journal of Reading*, 32 (February, 1989), 402-408.

Argues that more emphasis needs to be given to using IRIs for in-depth evaluation of reading behavior to gain insights into the reading process. The authors stress the importance of teacher judgment and believe traditional reliability data may not be one of the most appropriate ways to judge IRIs. The word "estimate" is critical when determining reading levels and making judgments.

Blanchard, Jay and Jerry Johns. "Informal Reading Inventories—A Broader View," *Reading Psychology*, 7 (1986), iii-vii.

Argues that IRIs can do much to strengthen classroom assessment and instruction if teachers are willing to adopt a broader, flexible view. In the past, some teachers have tied IRIs to rigid procedures and the measurement of a few traits. This narrow perspective diminishes the potential of IRIs to meet classroom assessment and instruction needs. A wider perspective suggests that IRIs can be considered assessment strategies that provide teachers with almost complete freedom to explore reading behaviors. Uses include: (1) assessing new students; (2) supporting intuitions; (3) practicing reading; and (4) evaluating special programs.

Carnine, Linda. "Teaching Basic Reading Skills in Secondary Schools," 1980. Microfiche ED 265 630.

Presents diagnostic and prescriptive techniques that will enable teachers to enhance secondary school students' learning through reading in content areas. Section II reviews diagnostic procedures that allow teachers to match appropriate materials with students' entry vocabulary and comprehension. The Cloze procedure and the use of IRIs are covered.

Johns, Jerry L. "Fifteen Important Sources for Users of Informal Reading Inventories," *Reading World*, 16 (March, 1977), 172-177.

Presents a brief annotated bibliography dealing with IRIs. The fifteen annotations contained in the bibliography were selected from over one hundred pertinent articles and represent a good overview of articles on the development, use, current dilemmas, and future directions of IRIs.

Johns, Jerry L. "Reading Is Easy When Students Are Placed Properly in Books: Using Informal Reading Inventories," *The Reading Instruction Journal*, 30 (Spring, 1987), 11-16.

Addresses the importance of proper placement of students in books to ensure effective reading instruction. The use of IRIs are one tool in the process to achieving the desired result. However, studies conducted by Mastzal and Smith (1984) and Harris and Lalik (1983) conclude that although most teachers have sufficient knowledge to use IRIs, only 54 percent do so. One possible explanation is that the administering of IRIs requires teachers to spend individual time with each of their students. The author stresses that this time spent is invaluable to both teacher and student; therefore, teachers should make the commitment to use IRIs. Further, although IRIs have been criticized in some respects, they remain a useful tool for assessing reading. IRIs should be viewed as a means toward an end: helping teachers place students in appropriate reading materials to help promote success in reading.

Leibert, Robert E. "The IRI: Relating Test Performance to Instruction—A Concept," *Reading Horizons*, 22 (Winter, 1981), 110-115.

Describes a procedure that allows teachers to identify and order the instructional needs of children through the use of an IRI. Test data are analyzed to show that levels are determined by observing the balance between accuracy and comprehension. Test analysis proceeds from identifying instructional needs to the implementation of trial lessons to verify procedures and strategies which assist the reader in overcoming the problems observed.

ISSUES AND CRITERIA

Ackerson, Gary E., John M. Bradley, and John Luiten. "A Procedure to Estimate the Probability of Error When Using Reading Placement Tests," *Reading World*, 18 (December, 1978), 186-193.

Delineates a procedure which may be employed to predict the amount and type of placement error present in a criterion-referenced reading placement test of a multiple choice format. The two factors that were found to relate to placement errors of this type of test were test length and the performance level of mastery. The authors conclude that test construction and selection must be improved in order to facilitate the reduction of total test error probability.

Anderson, William W. "Informal Reading Inventories: Commercial or Conventional?" *Reading World*, 17 (October, 1977), 64-68.

Discuss two types of IRIs. Commercial IRIs are those which are professionally prepared and packaged. Conventional IRIs are those locally prepared and based on potential reading materials. The four purposes of IRIs seem to be achieved in both types of inventories.

Contrary to popular notion, the author contends that a wisely-selected commercial IRI is preferable. Anderson notes that conventional IRIs are not practical in their construction and are not advantageous when more than one basal is used. The conventional weaknesses of IRIs lie in a lack of precision at primary levels, reliability, validity. These weaknesses, the author indicates, are also existent in conventional IRIs. The commercial IRI is advantageous in that it is well-organized, neatly packaged, and easy to use. Comprehension questions have been conveniently organized to aid diagnosis. Some field testing has been done. Previous exposure to the passages is less likely. Other practical advantages are listed. Although the author suggests that commercial IRIs are more appropriate than the conventional type, he would not vitiate the value of IRI construction for teacher-education students. Analyzing commercial IRIs and developing expertise in administration is recommended.

Cadenhead, Kenneth. "Reading Level: A Metaphor That Shapes Practice," *Phi Delta Kappan,* 68 (February, 1987), 436-441.

Questions the appropriateness of using reading levels. The lack of validity of grade-level scores and the bases on which various measurements were built are examples of two areas in which criticism is directed at the claims of precise measurement. Suggestions are offered for change in the way one approaches the use of the concept of reading level. For example, using children's literature in conjunction with the basal program should encourage children to read materials at various levels of difficulty.

Cavett, Dorcas C. "Use Ratio for Computing Informal Reading Tests," March, 1982. Microfiche ED 216 340.

Notes that ratios can be used to great advantage in scoring informal reading tests, such as the cloze procedure and the IRI. The paper explains the procedures for calculating cross-ratio and percentages when computing scores for informal reading assessment. Examples are provided for using ratios to determine scores for Powell's Scale for Word Recognition and Comprehension, Betts' Scale for Word Recognition and Comprehension, and cloze testing.

Lunn, Mary K. and Jerry L. Johns. "Informal Reading Inventories: Reappraising the Criteria for the Instructional Reading Level," *Reading Psychology,* 4 (January-March, 1983), 57-64.

Summarizes a study (Killgallon, 1942) that helped to establish the word-recognition criteria for the instructional reading level and examines Powell's (1970) critique of this study and subsequent research. Three concerns are raised about Powell's 1970 study: comprehension criteria, behavioral characteristics, and miscues counted.

Powell, William R. "The Emergent Reading Level: A New Concept," November, 1982. Microfiche ED 233 334.

Argues that traditional reading placement tests, determining the level at which students can read without teacher mediation, frequently lead to student underplacement. Diagnostic teaching practices, however, can be used to determine students' emergent reading level, the reading level that can be achieved through instruction. After preteaching part of a lesson—providing motivation, background, vocabulary assistance, and purposes—the teacher has students read first silently and then orally. During the oral reading, the teacher records the number and kinds of reading miscues made and notes student affect. By leading students through progressively more difficult lessons, the teacher can determine (1) at what levels the students can read comfortably without help, (2) when reading becomes so difficult that the experience is more harmful than helpful, and (3) what range of materials the students can handle effectively in a teacher-guided situation. Diagnostic testing, reflecting the original intent of diagnostic teaching, gives students the assistance and motivation needed to master increasingly complex conceptual structures.

Powell, William R. "Measuring Reading Performance Informally," May, 1978. Microfiche ED 155 589.

Proposes a differential set of IRI criteria for both word recognition and comprehension scores for different levels and reading conditions. In initial evaluation, word recognition scores should reflect only errors of insertions, omissions, mispronunciations, substitutions, unknown words, and transpositions; symptomatic behavior should not be considered. After the student has read, comprehension questions should be asked on a literal level, on implicit understanding, on vocabulary, and on evaluative skills; all should be wholly context-dependent. Baseline criteria for determining unsatisfactory reading should be established in comprehension, word recognition, and symptomatic behavior; comprehension is the most significant factor in determining placement. The initial task of the IRI is to place the student at his/her reading level. This decision is first made on the basis of quantitative data. Then an error analysis gives qualitative information. Placement precedes analysis, but both are necessary for effective reading diagnosis and placement.

Powell, William R. "Monitoring Reading Behavior: Criteria for Performance," May, 1976. Microfiche ED 120 675.

Contends that the effective use of IRIs depends upon the criteria used in determining the functional reading levels and more specifically the word recognition criteria employed in describing acceptable limits of oral reading behavior. The author of this paper looks at the diverse sets of criteria commonly used, the problems associated with these standard approaches, and the two different sets of criteria for word recognition error ratios for each condition under which the data were obtained. A rationale for each of these sets of criteria is presented for each assessment condition as they are developed within a partial theoretical framework. Emphasis is placed on clarifying the criteria problems connected with the IRI and the teaching and clinical practice which are affected by the evidence offered.

Schell, Leo M. "The Validity of the Potential Level via Listening Comprehension: A Cautionary Note," *Reading Psychology*, 3 (July-September, 1982), 271-276.

Examines historical background and relevant research to determine whether the commonly recommended procedure of determining the reading potential level via listening comprehension is valid in the primary grades. No support was found for the unstated assumptions necessary for this procedure's validity. Three major studies conclusively revealed that use of this procedure to identify children for remedial instruction would drastically over-refer and would include vast numbers of primary grade children progressing normally in learning to read. Based on this evidence, it was concluded that listening comprehension definitely not be used to determine the reading potential level in grades one through three.

Schell, Leo, M. and Gerald S. Hanna. "Can Informal Reading Inventories Reveal Strengths and Weaknesses in Comprehension Subskills?" *The Reading Teacher*, 35 (December, 1981), 263-268.

Argues that commercial IRIs fail to provide accurate, reliable, comparable scores on subskills of reading and can not properly be used to assess students' specific strengths and weaknesses in comprehension. IRIs fail to: (1) demonstrate objective classifications of questions; (2) provide and demonstrate comparable scores across subskill categories; (3) provide evidence of uniform passage dependence and passage independence of questions across categories of comprehension; and (4) provide reliable subskill scales and evidence thereof.

Vaughan, Joseph L., Jr. and Paula J. Gaus. "Secondary Reading Inventory: A Modest Proposal," *Journal of Reading*, 21 (May, 1978), 716-720.

Proposes a viable alternative to the traditional IRI format designed specifically to yield information about adolescent readers. A general framework for a secondary reading inventory (SRI) is provided which incorporates an assessment of seven aspects of the adolescent reader's behavior. Areas of assessment include comprehension of varying types of material, knowledge of vocabulary and content area concepts, and critical analysis skills. The significance of interest level as a factor in the adolescent's reading performance is emphasized and reflected in the construction of the SRI. The authors provide the reading specialist with specific suggestions to aid in the construction and administration of an SRI.

Warren, Thomas S. "Informal Reading Inventories—A New Format," November, 1985. Microfiche ED 269 740.

Identifies two significant weaknesses in IRIs developed by the teacher: (1) passages selected randomly from the graded basal readers that may or may not be on the level suggested by a publisher, and (2) the types of questions written for them, usually at the memory level of cognition. Published inventories also have their weaknesses, such as the discrepancy between the grade levels assigned to the reading selections by the publishers and actual readability levels. Another questionable feature of published inventories is the procedure used for their administration, with students directed to read one selection silently and a different one orally. Because the task of developing a good informal inventory is so complicated, teachers, if they must construct their own, should select several random passages, identify four selections for each grade level from one through ten, and use a modified version of the Fry Readability Graph—extended to determine the difficulty levels of the paragraphs chosen. Introducing teachers to a new format for published inventories is also helpful. Among its new features would be (1) a complete step-by-step procedure for administration, (2) four forms at each grade level, and (3) a readability level for each of the four selections for every grade that is close to the beginning of the grade level for which it is written.

MISCUE ANALYSIS

Hoffman, James V. "Weighting Miscues in Informal Inventories: A Precautionary Note," *Reading Horizons*, 20 (Winter, 1980), 135-139.

Cautions that weighting errors on an oral reading test with miscue analysis procedures can lead to inappropriate independent reading-level placement. Contends that qualitative techniques of assessment such as miscue analysis are a far richer source of information for the discerning teacher than simple error counts, thus revealing ways in which instruction might be adapted to meet specific student needs.

Leu, Donald J., Jr. "Oral Reading Error Analyses: A Critical Review of Research and Application," *Reading Research Quarterly*, 17 (Spring, 1982), 420-437.

Argues that oral reading error analysis contains the potential for generating important clues to understanding the reading process. In a historical overview of this investigative approach, three problems that plagued early oral reading error studies are evident: (1) the lack of a clearly articulated theoretical framework, (2) an inadequate sensitivity to important methodological issues, and (3) a failure to adequately test the major assumptions involved in this approach. The overview suggests that current oral reading error studies have overcome the first problem but not the second and third. Furthermore, methodological problems contribute significantly to the inconsistent results typically found among oral reading error studies. Finally, there are several critical assumptions that have been ignored by reading error researchers. Until the methodological problems are overcome and until the assumptions are validated, the results from oral reading error analysis cannot be used confidently in order to make strong claims about either the nature of the reading process or the most appropriate instructional procedures for students.

Pflaum, Susanna W. "Diagnosis of Oral Reading," *The Reading Teacher*, 33 (December, 1979), 278-284.

Proposes a new IRI scoring system for achieving reliability. The first step involves the recording and scoring of errors; the second involves coding the errors. Details of the system that achieve 83 to 100% coder reliability are given in the article.

Scales, Alice M. "The Informal Reading Assessment Inventory," 1980. Microfiche ED 273 922.

Proposes a strategy for merging the IRI and RMI. IRIs test comprehension through questions only, while the Reading Miscue Inventory (RMI) is too cumbersome for the average classroom instructor to administer. Since both measures offer instructors ways of collecting data, they may effectively be merged into an Informal Reading Assessment Inventory (IRAI), bringing together processes from both inventories. The oral reading component of the IRAI may be used to check learners' reading behaviors, such as recall of material via retelling, language usage, and recoding. The silent reading component allows learners the private opportunity to interact with written material during an uninterrupted period of time and to present understanding of the material through predetermined criteria in a predetermined manner. The following guidelines are suggested for preparing and administering the IRAI: (1) select several types of materials for oral reading, long enough to elicit at least 25 oral miscues; (2) compute the readability of the selections using at least two formulas; (3) devise criteria for evaluation; (4) prepare a script for miscue coding; (5) have a cassette tape player available; (6) establish rapport with the learner; (7) have the learner read an entire selection aloud, while the examiner codes miscues; (8) have the learner respond to comprehension criteria; and (9) administer the silent reading comprehension measure using selections of 450 to 500 words.

Smith, Laura and Constance Weaver. "A Psycholinguistic Look at the Informal Reading Inventory Part I: Looking at the Quality of

Readers' Miscues: A Rationale and an Easy Method," *Reading Horizons*, 19 (Fall, 1978), 12-22.

Encourages IRI users to conduct a qualitative rather than a quantitative analysis of readers' miscues. Reading for meaning is emphasized as is the effectiveness of teaching word analysis skills through the use of context. The article includes a simplified version of Goodman and Burke's procedure for analyzing a reader's miscues. Guidelines for obtaining and analyzing a reading sample are offered.

Wangberg, Elaine G. "Using Machine Theory to Analyze Oral Reading Inventory Results," *The Michigan Reading Journal*, 12 (Fall, 1978), 73-75.

Adapts miscue theory as outlined by Goodman and Burke to the simpler format of the oral reading inventory. Guidelines for using miscue analysis and a retelling method with an oral reading inventory are offered.

Weaver, Constance and Laura Smith. "A Psycholinguistic Look at the Informal Reading Inventory Part II: Inappropriate Inferences from an Informal Reading Inventory," *Reading Horizons*, 19 (Winter, 1979), 103-111.

Advises teachers to regard tests that measure a reader's recognition of words in isolation with caution since such tests commonly underestimate the reader's ability to process contextual material. The authors suggest that the use of a simplified version of Goodman and Burke's miscue analysis may be preferable to the use of most available IRIs. An advantage of the miscue analysis procedure lies in its applicability to instructional planning. The importance of evaluating the reader's strengths as well as weaknesses is emphasized.

SPECIAL POPULATIONS

Armstrong, Audrey A. and Sally P. Hunt. "VITAL Guidelines: Tutor Training for an Adult Literacy Program," 1982. Microfiche ED 244 104.

Offers a guide designed as a training tool for volunteers participating in the Volunteers in Tutoring Adult Learners (VITAL) program. VITAL is an adult literacy program that is based on active cooperation between program trainers and volunteer tutors. Various instructional resources are provided in the guide. Appended to the guide are an informal reading inventory, a general educational development (GED) fact sheet, a confidential report and learner profile report form, a workshop agenda, and a VITAL tutor job designation.

Helfeldt, John P. and William A. Henk. "Administering A Group Reading Inventory: An Initiative In Improving Reading

Instruction," *Journal of Correctional Education*, 34 (September, 1983), 76-79.

Presents background information for using group IRIs in correctional facilities and offers guidelines for construction, administration, and interpretation. A sample passage, questions, and scheme for administering the IRI in three testing sessions are included.

Lane, Martha A. "Handbook for Volunteer Reading Aides," 1984. Microfiche ED 256 900.

Presents a guide designed to assist volunteer tutors participating in an adult literacy program. Appendixes to the handbook contain an informal reading inventory, a reading placement test, job descriptions for a reading center coordinator and a volunteer reading aide, sample instructional materials, a list of study techniques, and a selected bibliography.

LaSasso, Carol and Nancy Swaiko. "Considerations in Selecting and Using Commercially Prepared Informal Reading Inventories with Deaf Students," *American Annals of the Deaf*, 128 (August, 1983), 449-452.

Offers guidelines for the selection and use of commercially prepared IRIs with deaf students. Modifications for deaf students pertain to: selection of the passage to begin testing, the criteria for oral and silent reading levels, and procedures for estimating students' reading potential levels.